# DIAGHILEV'S
# EMPIRE

# DIAGHILEV'S EMPIRE

---

## How the Ballets Russes
## Enthralled the World

---

### RUPERT
### CHRISTIANSEN

faber

First published in 2022
by Faber & Faber Limited
Bloomsbury House
74–77 Great Russell Street
London WC1B 3DA

Typeset by Sam Matthews
Printed and bound by CPI Group (UK) Ltd, Croydon, CR0 4YY

A CIP record for this book
is available from the British Library

ISBN 978–0–571–34801–5

2 4 6 8 10 9 7 5 3 1

For Ellis Woodman

# CONTENTS

# PLATES

---

# PREFACE

---

This book has been written by someone in the grip of an addiction.

I confess to being an incurable balletomane – a morbid affliction of which the chief symptom is the daily expense of an unconscionable amount of time watching, thinking or dreaming about classical dance and dancers. I don't merely like, appreciate or enjoy ballet; I deeply and secretly need it, as irrationally infatuated with my home team (the Royal Ballet, to which I have been wedded for over half a century) as others are to Spurs or the Red Sox. I study form, follow the relevant social media, review the annual accounts. Oh dear.*

Sports fanatics will recognise that this relationship is not steady: as standards slip or personnel changes, I have often despaired; there have been bitter quarrels, even periods of estrangement and disenchantment, but I am always drawn inexorably back. This isn't a matter of choice; there's nothing I can do about it. I can't renounce

---

* I cannot, though, claim to match the dedication of the American writer-illustrator Edward Gorey, so devoted to George Balanchine's New York City Ballet that 'he ended up attending nearly every performance of every ballet staged by the company for . . . twenty-three years [from 1956] – eight performances a week, five months out of the year, including as many as thirty-nine performances of *The Nutcracker* annually until 1979' (Mark Dery, *Born to be Posthumous: The Eccentric Life and Mysterious Genius of Edward Gorey*, p. 154). 'Generally, I don't care what the casting for any ballet is going to be,' he told Anna Kisselgoff for the *New York Times*. 'I'm going to be there anyway. If it's going to be terrible, I'd rather not know in advance.' (*New York Times*, 13 November 1973.)

or transfer allegiance – this is family, this is in my blood. My life, my sense of myself, would not be complete without it. And people like me will crop up repeatedly throughout what follows.

Why do I feel like this? I can only say, naively perhaps, that to me ballet communicates a compelling idea of beauty, a form of dramatic poetry that can be expressive beyond words, and an endlessly fascinating struggle with the possibilities and limitations of the human body. A dream of perfection is within its reach; a frisson of erotic attraction enters the mix too. Read on to discover more.

Although I very much hope that this book will please all those who suffer in a similar way, you, my brothers and sisters, are not its primary target. Nor have I set out to thrill scholars and experts with a substantially original contribution to academic research. I aim simply to chart the course of a long story, making connections that can explain the allure of ballet to those uninfected with my mania but curious to know what the fuss is all about. More specifically, I want to trace the historical moment when, thanks to a unique enterprise and the individual who drove it, ballet became a crucial piece in the jigsaw of Western culture.

Conceived in 1909 by its mastermind, the impresario Sergei Pavlovich Diaghilev, as a Russian export designed to appeal to Western tastes, the Ballets Russes came to an official end after many vicissitudes with Diaghilev's abrupt death in 1929. But the achievements of its heroic prime had established a paradigm that would continue to define the terms and set the standards for the next generation – a period during which ballet for most people meant 'the Russian ballet'. How that phenomenon grew and flourished is the theme of chapters 2–6; how it was absorbed and arguably declined will be the theme of chapters 7–9.

# 1
# BOUNDARIES

———

Robert Helpmann (centre, in black) terrorising
Moira Shearer in *The Red Shoes*

How many movies can claim to have cast such a transformative spell on people's imaginations as *The Red Shoes*? Written, produced and directed by Michael Powell and Emeric Pressburger, drawing on a tale by Hans Christian Andersen and set in the world of 'the Russian ballet', it regularly features in roll-calls of the cinema's greatest achievements – as admired for its audacious technical originality as it is loved for its gorgeous visual compositions, its mysteriously resonant story and its memorable central performances from Anton Walbrook as the heartless impresario Boris Lermontov and Moira Shearer as the conflicted young ballerina Victoria Page.

Released in 1948 when Europe was mired in the grip of post-war austerity, *The Red Shoes* had a visceral impact. 'It aroused tremendous popular interest in ballet,' wrote Arlene Croce. 'The whole surge was extraordinary and has never been repeated.'[1] With Europe bombed out, drab and derelict, the rich intensity of its palette fed a primal human need. As the historian Lynda Nead reminds us, 'People recall those years through veils of mist and shades of grey, smog and soot choked the urban air, rubble and slag shaped the landscape.'[2] *The Red Shoes* provided an exhilarating shot of something that everyone had been missing outside the cinema: not that dull grey or even dear old English green, but colour elevated into gloriously excessive Technicolor, enhancing not only the scarlet hue of the eponymous ballet slippers, but the dazzling white marble paving and azure skies of the Monte Carlo scenes too.

The film's title symbolises a compulsion that is both creative and destructive. 'The red shoes are never tired, the red shoes dance on,' Lermontov hauntingly tells Victoria Page. He craves demoniacal control over her; she is torn between her desire to dance at the highest level and her desire for a domestic life with the composer Julian Craster. She can't have both, as Lermontov insists: 'The dancer who relies on the comfort of human love will never be a great dancer.' Art demands soul as well as body, but Victoria is driven to sacrifice herself in the face of that challenge: 'Take off the red shoes' are her last words as she lies in Craster's arms after taking her suicidal leap – the only release from her dilemma is not to dance and not to live. That is the almost paradoxical message of Victoria's fate. 'The real reason why *The Red Shoes* was such a success', wrote Michael Powell in a much-quoted passage from his autobiography, 'was that we had all been told for ten years to go out and die for freedom and democracy, for this and for that, and now that the war was over, *The Red Shoes* told us to go and die for art.'[3]

The film's influence has been widespread. It crested the high tide of ballet's popularity and indeed lifted it to a higher level, mythologising the phenomenon of 'the Russian ballet' and the mystique surrounding the man who dominated it – Sergei Pavlovich Diaghilev, the chief model for the figure of Boris Lermontov and onlie begetter of the company that went by the name of the Ballets Russes. (It is worth noting that neither Powell and Pressburger ever saw a performance by the company, and what they show relates more closely to 'the Russian ballet' as it had developed in the 1930s, after Diaghilev's death.)

As well as Hans Christian Andersen's parable, the narrative has a prime source in what had recently become known about Diaghilev's turbulent relationship with his star Vaslav Nijinsky, translated in the screenplay into Victoria Page's attempt to escape Lermontov's grip.

The film omits any overt sexual element and builds on tropes that don't falsify so much as caricature. The commissioning of avant-garde music and designs, the rows over copyright and who invented what, the small-scale British troupe pluckily competing with the grander Russian operation, as well as the figures of the enchanting but capricious Russian ballerina, the explosive ballet master drilling his slaves at the barre, the hovering ballet mother, the aristocratic lady patron, and the pompous bohemian balletomanes with their cloaks and beards – all these clichés need unpacking.

Moira Shearer herself was positively contemptuous of the film's picture of the ballet world: 'Everything was glamourised and fanciful,' she complained, 'and there wasn't a single moment which showed the real work of dancers and choreographers.'⁴ Although the use of professional ballet dancers in the cast provided another level of authenticity, the glow of glamour has ultimately proved stronger than the drudge of documentary. The image of Shearer's Victoria Page, with her flame hair, baby face and shocking-pink Jacques Fath ballgown, has retained the romance for thousands of little girls as they bash out their *tendus* and *battements*.

Beyond these fond childish dreams, the film has also transfixed adults, largely because of the uniquely surreal and wildly beautiful fifteen-minute 'Red Shoes' ballet at its heart. This unforgettable sequence moves in and out of fantasy as if to demonstrate that, in the words of Arlene Croce, 'Things that could have happened on stage were almost as strange as the things that couldn't.'⁵ 'It gave art a new meaning to me,' announced the painter R. B. Kitaj; the singer Kate Bush constructed a whole album around its themes; and the director Martin Scorsese has described the film as 'an overwhelming experience . . . something I am continually and obsessively drawn to'. Scorsese put his money where his mouth is too, leading the funding for the restoration of the original stock, first shown at the Cannes Festival in 2009.[6] Michael Powell wasn't boasting when he wrote in his autobiography, published almost forty years after the film first appeared, that 'even today, I am constantly meeting men and women who claimed that it changed their lives'.[7]

———

*The Red Shoes* stands as this book's first point of reference – an introduction to its contention that whereas opera was the most richly imaginative, fertile and powerful area of the performing arts in the second half of the nineteenth century, ballet, along with cinema, takes pride of place in the first half of the twentieth century.

Its ascent was driven entirely by Diaghilev's initiative. Combining sophisticated taste with a degree of low cunning and a range of managerial skills, he followed no prototype and had no predecessors. Many have emulated him since and some of them will be encountered at the end of this book. But while his name remains a byword, loosely applied to any buccaneering impresario who takes risks on the new – while writing this essay, I noticed Malcolm McLaren described in a newspaper as 'the Diaghilev of Punk'[8] – none has been able to match his record or his reach.

How did he do it? He was neither intellectual nor theorist, and he had no creative gift of his own – the ideas were harvested largely from others. Some even accused him of being a mere opportunist without genuine personal vision. There is some truth in this, but he was no fraud: if he jumped on to bandwagons, then he soon ended up taking the reins. Operating without a regular budget or a board of trustees (though surrounded by a band of consiglieri), he played the role of theatrical producer as God. His genius was simply practical: to spot and gather the necessary talents, to render them effective, and to get results. Without his authority, nothing would have happened.

Perhaps in a broader context Diaghilev could usefully be classified among the speculators in modernism – the dealers, collectors and patrons of the early twentieth century who took a punt on restless and marginal young artists, composers and writers in rebellion against the pieties and academies of their parents: for instance, Ambroise Vollard who traded in Cézanne and Picasso; Daniel-Henry Kahnweiler who saw the potential of cubism; Sergei Shchukin who imported Matisse to Russia; Sylvia Beach who bankrolled James Joyce; the Princesse de Polignac (Winnaretta Singer) who drew on her family sewing-machine fortune to commission Stravinsky, Satie and Poulenc.

All such figures, like Diaghilev, bought into rule-breakers cheap and early, bided their time, stoked a public appetite, and raised value in the marketplace. Sometimes their faith misled them and the investment failed, but they had the courage to take gambles based on instinct. Without them, the power would never have been connected to the grid.

Diaghilev might well have become an art dealer – the first phase of his career was based in curating exhibitions – but Russian painting had no potential to shock or enthral. His masterstroke was understanding that ballet did have that potential – it was a childish business ripe to be led to adulthood. At the turn of the century, it was moribund and infantilised, surviving either as overstuffed family-friendly entertainment for court theatres such as the Opéra in Paris, the Staatsoper in Vienna and the Mariinsky in St Petersburg, or as part of a fancy parade in superior variety halls. Out of this jejune material Diaghilev sensed the potential to make something that lived – one-act dramas that could have meaningful content, absorb recent developments in art and orchestral music, and run with the social liberations of the post-Victorian era. Now that the dust has settled, it should not be controversial to claim that works such as Nijinsky's *Prélude à l'après-midi d'un faune*, Massine's *Le Tricorne*, Nijinska's *Les Noces* and Balanchine's *Apollo* should rank alongside Picasso's *Les Demoiselles d'Avignon*, Schoenberg's *Pierrot lunaire* and Proust's *À la recherche du temps perdu* as turning points in early twentieth-century culture.

This is worth emphasising. It has always been recognised that what Diaghilev commissioned served as the main shop window for the innovations of Stravinsky, Picasso and the modernist movement before colour magazines, radio and television opened other conduits; it also pointed the way to later revolutions in theatrical language and the art installation. Perhaps even more significantly, the Ballets Russes adumbrated a new form of sensuality, challenging conventional demarcations of masculinity and femininity as well as fostering a distinctly homosexual subculture in its audience. For women, the invitation to abandon corsetry, shorten skirts, lift legs, jump, run, turn and release the entire body as an emotionally expressive, sexually alive instrument was radical. Not even tennis or athletics offered such freedom, and we tend to forget that until the 1960s even women in the first world couldn't decently walk along the street without covering themselves from bosom to knee and wearing a hat.

The appeal of ballet – like that of film, the popularity of which rose in parallel – was based in *motion*, the way it looked as it moved. This was where it crucially scored over opera. Richard Wagner had championed the concept of the *Gesamtkunstwerk*, a theatrical work of art combining musical, visual and philosophical elements, but nothing he created ever achieved that ideal synthesis. His operas might have sounded profoundly wonderful, but they looked deadly – scenically cluttered affairs in which the performers were generally poor actors who remained stationary or ridiculous however sub-limely they sang, framed by wings and backcloths painted in a style of meticulous antiquarian realism with pantomime effects and crude lighting. The young spirit of the twentieth century required something lighter, pacier and subtler: it was drawn to anything that moved fast – bicycles, aeroplanes, motor cars, the masterful-ly timed slapstick of Buster Keaton and Charlie Chaplin – and it had learned to distrust meticulous antiquarian realism. The Ballets Russes would oblige.

————

In the years following the release of *The Red Shoes*, the tide began to ebb – at least in London, the city that for a generation had been ballet's epicentre. According to the critic Richard Buckle, the first sign was a spat in the newspapers in 1951 after the flop of the new ballet *Tiresias*, choreographed by Frederick Ashton with music by Constant Lambert. The director Tyrone Guthrie wrote an article in the *News Chronicle* arguing, 'We have absorbed what ballet has to offer, and now it does not seem to be offering anything new.' This provoked, as Buckle puts it, 'a wave of antagonism to ballet'. Dun-can Harrison in the *Evening News* asked whether 'ballet is in danger of being over-subscribed'. The *Illustrated London News* followed suit with Gilbert Harding declaring, 'Ballet is a Bore', before Alan Dent returned to the subject in the *News Chronicle* with the question, 'Haven't we had a little too much ballet?' and the statement that 'grown-ups who are too fond of ballet become pampered, fractious and silly, like children who have access to too many sweets'.[9]

If this was only a journalistic flutter, soon evaporating, it was also an early warning that ballet's public image might be fading, and in the longer term, fault lines deeper than those caused by mere tedium emerged. Even if the doings of glamorous ballerinas such as Moira Shearer and Margot Fonteyn remained fodder for press interest – in the 1960s, Fonteyn's partnership with the sensational Russian defector Rudolf Nureyev became a marquee attraction – several more powerful trends were edging ballet out of its spotlit cultural position and into the wings. It maintained a loyal and sizeable audience, a minority defined by a cordon sanitaire of prejudices. But ballet began to have a problem engaging serious adult interest – to the point at which, in 1963, the influential theatre critic Kenneth Tynan could bluntly write after seeing Fonteyn and Nureyev in *Giselle*, 'As practised in Britain, [ballet] insults my intelligence and leaves my deeper sensibilities untouched.'[10]

One cause of the rot was the curse of respectability. Although the Ballets Russes had been startling, even transgressive in its frank physicality and aesthetic daring, by the 1940s the barriers had been broken and there was no more room to shock. Instead there was a retreat into the idea that ballet offered a safe haven for the polite and dainty, inhabited by revivals of nineteenth-century classics such as *Giselle*, *Coppélia*, *Swan Lake*, *The Sleeping Beauty* or *The Nutcracker*, all harking back to some lost Eden where courtly formality, tradition and hierarchy were framed by the red velvet curtain and the proscenium arch. The audience was swelled with enraptured ladies and their prim daughters turning their backs on a hard dirty rude world to live out dreams of swans and sylphs in virginal white tulle courted by slender princelings who attended to them with chivalrous deference. Attempts were made by the likes of Roland Petit in France, Kenneth MacMillan in England and Jerome Robbins in the USA to mess this fairy tale up and incorporate something closer to contemporary reality, but beyond a certain point they were hamstrung; how far could you get without spoken language and within the bounds of classical technique?

At the same time, and almost paradoxically, ballet became a scandal. Alongside these unimpeachable ladies – so the assumption ran – a conspiracy of decadent homosexuals congregated. 'It cannot be denied that there is an alarming incidence of this form of perversion among male ballet dancers,' wrote the prim (male) critic A. H. Franks in 1956. 'I have known of perfectly normal youths entering a company and becoming perverted . . . and I have heard of certain choreographers and others in authority who will not give an opportunity to a young man unless he allows himself to be corrupted into their sexual persuasion.'[11] This was something of a turnaround, because in the nineteenth century ballet had notoriously been the taste of lascivious males leching through their opera glasses at the nymphets in the corps de ballet. (When King Victor Emmanuel visited the Paris Opéra, he was overheard to enquire whether it was true that these creatures went without drawers while dancing. 'If that is so,' he sighed wistfully, 'then earthly paradise is in store for me.'[12]) But in the twentieth century, as the exposure of female flesh became more familiar, the cult surrounding the eroticised physiques of charismatic male stars such as Vaslav Nijinsky and Serge Lifar grew more intense. The posthumous revelation of Diaghilev's proclivities and his 'close friendship' with mad Nijinsky was a turning point – the first time that such relations had been openly discussed in print outside the context of a courtroom.

During the post-war years, in Britain and the USA especially, ballet suffered from the aggressive purge of homosexuality, provoked by the eugenic notion that the cultivation of a Boy Scout virility was the best defence against pollution of the nation's stock. 'Pansies' would not fight, it was thought; they were limp-wristed and weak-blooded. Men with powdered faces wearing pink tights bulging at the crotch became a theme common to crude cartoons and dreary jeremiads in the popular press. The skinny tremulous weeds who ogled them were merely pathetic. Beware.

It is impossible to deny that ballet was a magnet to queerness in all its guises,[13] and this book will be peppered with instances of it. In his memoir, John Drummond describes one exemplar – Monty Morris, a harmless Dickensian old thing, 'very thin and extremely effeminate', who

> worked as clerk for the Inland Revenue and lived in Belsize Road, down the hill from Swiss Cottage, in a room stuffed with theatrical memorabilia. He collected everything and in a small back room were piles and piles of newspapers, magazines, and programmes waiting to be sorted out. His hobby was making scrapbooks . . . He was rather deaf by the 1960s, but still to be seen everywhere at the ballet, with his piercing blue eyes, Basque beret and high-pitched voice exclaiming with outrage or delight.[14]

But the profession wasn't like that at all: and the majority of male ballet stars who emerged in the West between the end of the war and the 1960s – André Eglevsky, Igor Youskevitch, Edward Villella, Michael Somes, David Blair, Jean Babilée, Jacques d'Amboise – were married, verifiably (if in some cases not exclusively) heterosexual and robustly masculine in their stage personae. Unfortunately, this wasn't enough to stop the sniggers, and it became a cause for embarrassment and suspicion for a male to display a penchant for either watching or participating in ballet, thus preventing a lot of boys from taking up training (the theme of the film and musical *Billy Elliot*). The stigma sadly remains current, if waning.

It does not, however, obtain in Russia, where the skill of dancing well has long been an honourable accomplishment of fighting men, exemplifying the military virtues of precision, stamina and strength. The gap between the male dancers of the Bolshoi Ballet and those of the Red Army's virtuosic troupe is very small. (In Britain, one exceptional male social dancer was a naval man – Rear Admiral 'Jacky' Fisher (1841–1920), who had 'boundless enthusiasm for dancing . . . everyone else had to dance too, and there were to be no exceptions. In case his partners might not be up to his high standards, or endure his pace, he took along with him one or two Midshipmen who were expected to dance with him.'[15])

While ballet was being marginalised as decorative, vacuous and more than a bit suspect, it was also increasingly regarded as locked into an outmoded quasi-military obsession with symmetry and unity. Why the formality, why the straight lines? asked the new forces busily resisting pointe shoes and the tyranny of the barre. Schools of dance from other cultures abounded in the post-war years, with the African-American Katherine Dunham, the Indian kathakali master Ram Gopal, and the gypsy king of flamenco Antonio all making big splashes in London, Paris and New York. In every neighbourhood palais de danse, the rules and manners of Latin and ballroom dancing would yield to the gyrations of rock 'n' roll, twisting, jiving, bopping and letting it all hang out. Contemporary culture was drawn to an ever-increasing degree of physical freedom and personal expression that seemed antagonistic to the antiquated laws of ballet.

Through the 1950s New York had led 'modern dance' forward through its self-appointed high priestess Martha Graham. Her troupe toured globally throughout the Cold War implicitly promoting American freedoms and showcasing her gravely austere choreography based on the idea of tension and release, and the natural pull of gravity. Then, in 1962, a Baptist church in Greenwich Village became the seedbed of an even more radical initiative called Judson Dance Theater, where Trisha Brown, Yvonne Rainer and Steve Paxton among others explored a radically different post-modernist aesthetic. Drawing on John Cage's redefinition of what constitutes music and Merce Cunningham's fascination with dance growing out of Zen, the I Ching and the operations of chance, Judson's votaries built on basic human movements – walking, bending, jumping, running, stopping, starting – all organically combining into an anti-choreography that could accommodate the improvised, accidental and spontaneous detached from any intrinsic relation to music. In following this path, Judson left ballet behind, and some would say that it has never quite caught up.[16]

———

Diaghilev's model – also the model of the Ballet Lermontov in *The Red Shoes* – was that of an internationally itinerant body of classically trained dancers managed by benevolent dictatorship. It presented a mixed repertory of classics and new work and was sustained by a volatile mixture of private patronage and the box office. By the 1960s, this hand-to-mouth principle was no longer financially viable. Subsidy, either in the European form of central treasury grants or the American form of tax relief to donors, had become the necessary foundation, and more regulated boardroom governance demanded a level of accountancy and accountability that Diaghilev would have pooh-poohed.

Ballet's most venerable institutions – those with schools attached, such as the Kirov (now the Mariinsky) in Leningrad (now once more St Petersburg), La Scala in Milan, the Paris Opéra and the Royal Danish Theatre in Copenhagen – were paid for by the state and made part of an official high culture. It could be argued that they became sclerotic as a result, and certainly the creative force was with two much younger institutions based in London and New York: the Royal Ballet (until 1956 known as Sadler's Wells Ballet) and New York City Ballet (until 1948, Ballet Society). Each of them was blessed with a resident great choreographer, Frederick Ashton and George Balanchine respectively, both born in 1904 and active from the mid-1920s through to the late 1970s. (Balanchine died in 1983; Ashton five years later.) They have been exhaustively studied. The fame and status of their home companies have dominated the histories, and neither needs to be extensively explained or honoured here. This book will take a longer and broader perspective, examining their roots rather than their achievements. A few words are necessary, however.

Ashton's and Balanchine's relationships to the aesthetics of the Ballets Russes were complex. They grew out of them and they grew away from them; indeed, in the respect that they variously incorporated, accepted, rejected and transcended them, they could serve as case studies of the peculiar creative neurosis proposed by the Freudian literary critic Harold Bloom as 'the Anxiety of Influence' – the influence being both positive and negative, creative and destructive.

Ashton was a nostalgist and a romantic: he looked back to the nineteenth century rather than forward into his own. Although he revered one of Diaghilev's choreographers, Bronislava Nijinska, under whom he studied and whose poetics, according to his biographer Julie Kavanagh, he inherited, his artistic temperament was distinctly English in its emotional delicacy, quiet spirituality and pantomime humour. In works such as *Sylvia*, *Ondine*, *The Two Pigeons* and *La Fille mal gardée*, he revived the ethos of the ballets of the Paris Opéra that Diaghilev had disdained. He distrusted big stylistic or melodramatic statements and felt tender towards girlish prettiness, sometimes to a whimsical fault. His muse whispered to him gently; he believed in innocence.[17]

Balanchine, on the other hand, was full of complex knowledge. Emerging from Tsarist and Bolshevik Russia, Balanchine migrated via Europe to a democratic America. A rich mix! His education in St Petersburg bequeathed him a taste for imperial grandeur and its magnificent parades; later he became equally fascinated by the razzmatazz of Hollywood and Broadway that Diaghilev loathed. Balanchine was happy in several styles, but Ashton's subtleties of mood and tone didn't much interest him, and he prized form over feeling, cool wit over warm humour: 'There are no mothers-in-law in ballet,' he famously quipped in reference to its inability to communicate intricate narratives or peripheral relationships.

The principle of Diaghilev's Ballets Russes and the companies that followed in its wake had been to indulge all the senses and let rip, so an older generation often found Balanchine's more pellucid, unsentimental choreography heartlessly cerebral. This was not unfair: in parallel to Schoenberg's theory of harmony, Balanchine had a certain ruthless instinct to strip away superfluities and ambiguities, to purify ballet of its trappings and restore the honour of its basics. In contrast to Diaghilev's pursuit of the all-encompassing *Gesamtkunstkwerk* of Wagner's philosophy, he honed ballet down to the elemental: dancing to music or, as he memorably put it, 'See the music, hear the dance.' A series of perfectly achieved works including *The Four Temperaments*, *Agon* and *Stravinsky Violin Concerto* fulfilled that injunction by reducing scenery and costume to a minimum – diamond studs in the ballerinas' ears being their only concession to dazzle.[18]

The masterpieces of Ashton and Balanchine were ballet's last great hurrah. With their passing, some vital spark was extinguished, to the point that Jennifer Homans, in her superb panoptic survey of four hundred years of the art, published in 2010, could conclude with a downbeat assertion that ballet is 'dying' and the admission that she finds it hard to see how its 'decline' could be 'reversed'.[19] A comparison over a longer historical period might be verse drama, which peaked in the seventeenth century, survived into the nineteenth and then had a weak rebirth in the twentieth.

But even if all ballet's vocabulary has now been exhausted and its template can no longer yield anything but superficial surprises, it has continued to hold its own. Despite a slow shrinkage of scale and an increasingly cautious outlook caused by the diminution of state subsidy, companies on a traditional model are still functioning in most advanced economies. Over the last half-century or so, with the help of physiotherapy and sports science, dancers have been sustaining significantly longer careers with stronger and leaner bodies than ever before. An influx of young talents from South America and East Asia has swelled the ranks, compensating for a reduction in aspirants emerging from Caucasian cultures. Films such as *Billy Elliot* and *Black Swan*, set in versions of the ballet world even more fantasised than that of *The Red Shoes*, have made an impact. Kenneth MacMillan, John Cranko, Glen Tetley, John Neumeier, Jiří Kylián, Alexei Ratmansky, Justin Peck and Christopher Wheeldon are only a few of the choreographers who have continued to produce attractive, inventive and occasionally powerful work within relatively conventional boundaries. Beyond those limits, Maurice Béjart devised spectacles of staggering vulgarity that filled arenas in Europe and Matthew Bourne's poppily colourful reinventions of the classics have delighted a large public that a hundred years previously would have filled the variety halls. All-male companies such as Ballet Boyz have questioned gender roles; new media have broadened access to unaccustomed audiences. Dancers trained in classical Indian disciplines such as Shobana Jeyasingh and Akram Khan have engaged in rewarding dialogues with Western ballet; and 'modern dance' practitioners led by William Forsythe, Mats Ek, Mark Morris, Wayne McGregor, Michael Clark, Crystal Pite and Pam Tanowitz have also shown how classical technique can enrich the simplicities of the Judson legacy. (Pina Bausch, a name with a very prominent reputation, belongs to an expressionist movement that has no deep relation to ballet.) And across every continent, hundreds of thousands of tickets continue to be sold annually on a commercial basis for a small collection of large-scale narrative works – fairy tales or romances, sanitised and perfumed – that have lasting appeal to conservative and largely female audiences.

So the end is not nigh, even though at the time of writing, we confront a vast unknown – the fall-out from the unprecedented hiatus in live performance caused by the coronavirus pandemic of 2020–22. Meanwhile we must assume that ballet will continue to be ministered to by its devoted following, keeping its niche in the smaller print on the cultural menu of major cities and benefiting from some exposure through the media.

What follows here is an account of an epoch when ballet nursed much bigger ambitions. Led from the front by its mastermind of an emperor, Sergei Pavlovich Diaghilev, it set out from Russia to ravish the world.

For *The Red Shoes*, see the film as restored with commentaries on DVD (The Criterion Collection 44, 2009); Michael Powell, *A Life in Movies*, pp. 610–62; Adrienne McLean, '"The Red Shoes" Revisited'; Mark Connelly, *The Red Shoes*, Turner Classic Movie Guide; Monk Gibbon, *The Red Shoes Ballet: A Critical Study*. For Moira Shearer, see Karen Eliot, *Dancing Lives*, pp. 91–118. For more general history of ballet, see Malcolm McCormick and Nancy Reynolds, *No Fixed Points: Dance in the Twentieth Century*; Jennifer Homans, *Apollo's Angels*; and Debra Craine and Judith Mackrell, *The Oxford Dictionary of Dance*. Robert Gottlieb (ed.), *Reading Dance*, is a superb anthology of the best writing about ballet and dance. For the modernist context, see Roger Shattuck, *The Banquet Years*, passim; Christopher Butler, *Early Modernism*, passim, and Philip Hook, *Art of the Extreme 1905–14*, pp. 293–324.

## 2
# ROOTS

---

A quaint dusty fairy and her page, from the 1890
St Petersburg production of *The Sleeping Beauty*

In tribute to St Petersburg's mighty river and Charles Dickens's roistering eccentrics, they called themselves the Nevsky Pickwickians. A small fraternity of young men of the upper middle class – most of them old schoolfriends, half-heartedly studying law – they considered themselves a cut above their vulgar contemporaries, whose devotion to sports, drinking and womanising provoked them to scorn. Their own enthusiasms were more cerebral and dedicated to self-improvement of a romantic and aesthetic nature.

High-spirited and uproarious but passionately serious as only Russians can be, they met to debate the great issues of the day, the future of art, the mysteries of philosophy, advances in science. Politics they rather despised, but speech ran free, jovial minutes were kept and emotions rose fiercely in defence of truth. Whenever argument became too heated, it was the responsibility of bumbling Lev Rosenberg to ring a small bronze bell and call the meeting to order. This ritual was invariably ineffectual. 'Shut up, you old Jew,' the others would laughingly bellow,[1] in an instance of the casual bantering racism commonplace in the 1890s, where this story begins in earnest.

'Our tastes were still very far from being formed,' one of their number later recalled. 'We were enthusiastic about so many things: life was beautiful, so full of thrilling new discoveries that we could not afford the time to stop and criticise, even had we known how.'[2] Yet there was much that they could experience only through the reports of foreign travellers, piano reductions of orchestral scores or articles in foreign journals. St Petersburg couldn't be described as a backwater, but the new trends in London and Paris took time to arrive, and delay and distance gave Russian interest in them a peculiar perspective, a special glamour.

Four of this amiable outcrop of the Russian intelligentsia will play a significant part in the history of the Ballets Russes. Of these, Alexandre Benois, the natural president of the Nevsky Pickwickians, was the most sophisticated, cosmopolitan and erudite. As his name suggests, he was of French extraction – his grandfather a refugee from the 1789 Revolution, his father a well-respected architect. Their tales of the courtly culture of *ancien régime* Versailles fed Alexandre's youthful imagination, leaving him with a penchant for rococo prettiness and gilded formality, offset by an equally intense fascination with the world of fairy tale and the supernatural. Throughout his long life – he died in 1960 – he would remain a romantic conservative, absorbed in the glories of the past and sceptical of shallow modern innovation. He seems to have been a very lovable man: warm-hearted and generous in temperament, devoted to his family and loyal to his friends, Benois was held in great affection and regarded as both an intellectual authority and as a moderating force on the more wayward personalities in the club.

Among these last was the diminutive and dapper Walter Nouvel, rarely seen without a cigar between his lips. Sharply intelligent and meticulously efficient, he was a musical connoisseur, altogether bullish in his views and on occasion hypercritical. Darkly handsome Dima Filosofov was less easy to read: the most overtly literary and intellectual of the group, neither expansive nor exuberant, and sometimes caustically satirical, he would later wander off into the fogs of Slavic mysticism. Benois's friend Rosenberg was a late joiner. Bipolar, short-sighted and red-headed, secretly cursed with perverse sexual tastes, he was an upcoming art student, touched with genius as a colourist, who sought to disguise his Jewish origins by changing his name to Léon Bakst.

All of this oddly matched band were expert in the visual arts and worshipped the painting of the Old Masters. Yet they weren't reactionaries: they also knew, by repute at least, about John Ruskin and William Morris and the Arts and Crafts movement; they were versed in the ideas of Nietzsche and Ibsen's realist dramas; they venerated the figure of Richard Wagner, and longed to visit the Bayreuth Festival – every cultured young man's dream holiday destination.

But Benois and Nouvel also had another more rarefied yet low-brow enthusiasm: ballet. To their peers anywhere else in Europe, this would have been inexplicable. Scarcely afforded any status as an art form in its own right, ballet was regarded as ineffably silly, its only purpose that of feeding the erotic fantasies of lascivi-ous old gents aroused by the sight of shapely young female legs beneath short skirts. The dancing was merely formulaic; the plots were infantile pantomimes with exotic settings devoid of dramatic coherence or emotional depth. At best it provided light relief in lumbering grand operas – as in Meyerbeer's epic *Le Prophète*, in which a jaunty skating divertissement was dropped incongruously and anachronistically into the third act of a drama focused on the Anabaptist revolt of 1530. In sum, ballet had neither intellectual content nor aesthetic dignity.

But it had not always been thus. Like opera, the art form to which it was most closely linked, theatrical ballet had developed out of a Renaissance court culture that had created highly formalised mimed theatrical entertainments, grounded in French and Italian models of elegant gesture and graceful deportment. Drawing on these sources, the Milanese choreographer Carlo Blasis developed a theory, history and vocabulary of movement that he moulded into a treatise entitled *The Code of Terpsichore*, published in several languages in 1830. Defining purity of bodily line according to the aesthetics of classical sculpture and specifying technical exercises, it would remain the basis of ballet's pedagogy and philosophy throughout the nineteenth century.

In the 1830s and 1840s, ballet had enjoyed a period in the limelight, as a succession of trail-blazing female dancers took the opera houses of Europe by storm. In long skirts of layered white tulle (also known as tarlatan), they impersonated disembodied ghostly maidens who haunted their earthly lovers. Most sensationally, they jumped – and their capacity to leave the ground and appear airborne became fundamental to their myth. Acclaimed in Paris, Milan, London and St Petersburg was the Swedish-Italian Marie Taglioni, who flitted and hovered ethereally through *La Sylphide* on pointe – an accomplishment facilitated by blocking the toe of her satin slipper with cotton wads. This innovation was soon emulated by Carlotta Grisi and others in *Giselle*, another ballet with a spooky scenario co-written by Théophile Gautier, the prince of French belletrists and devotee of the dance. In contrast to these weightless other-worldly fairies, the likes of Fanny Elssler, Fanny Cerrito and Lucile Grahn presented more fiery and earthy stage personalities – Spanish señoritas, Venetian courtesans, bandit gypsies.

The young blades and dandies of the time were infatuated with them all, if fiercely partisan over their relative merits: in Paris, they were said to jostle for the privilege of drinking champagne from darling Taglioni's satin slipper; some fool in Russia stewed and chewed another of these fetishised objects, covering it in a *sauce Taglioni*; while at Balliol College, Oxford, W. G. Ward, an undergraduate of Falstaffian proportions (and subsequently a prominent

Catholic theologian) would amuse friends in his rooms by giving ludicrously camp imitations of Taglioni's will-o'-the-wisp pirouettes and dainty bourrées.[3]

The fashion did not run deep and would not survive the mid-century – the next generation of stars shone less brightly, and the storylines came to seem preposterously insipid. 'Ballet is dead and gone,' mourned Charles Dickens in his magazine *All the Year Round* in 1864. That may have been a journalistic exaggeration but, by the 1880s, it was certainly looking desiccated, as poor wizened Madame Taglioni, once the toast of the town, was reduced to teaching daughters of the aristocracy how to curtsey. In London, the programming of a whole evening of 'serious' ballet was out of the question: aside from its peripheral role in opera, it featured chiefly as a course on the menu in the music-halls, providing an interlude of cavorting between the conjurors and the stand-ups.

Scandalous cases of wretched girls in the corps de ballet prostituting themselves to supplement their pitiful wages were a staple of the tabloid press and scarcely helped the profession's reputation. In Paris, only the most strait-laced even raised an eyebrow at the idea of these vulnerable creatures being up for hire to smart young men with a laissez-passer to the notorious backstage foyer de la danse. The girls knew the deal, and nobody of any intelligence took an interest in the quality of their dancing, let alone in what they danced. A lucky few ended up 'protected' by members of the aristocracy. (Taglioni became the Comtesse de Voisins, though the marriage swiftly collapsed.)

From Milan eventually came something that woke everyone up, when, in 1881, the Teatro alla Scala staged the première of a blockbuster extravaganza – and it really was exactly that – called *Excelsior*. The conception of a flamboyant figure called Luigi Manzotti, who was blessed with a Busby Berkeley talent for organising dancers into lines and arranging them into patterns, *Excelsior* was easy to perform (the skills required by the mass of participants were on the level of parade-ground drill) and relied for its impact on accumulation of numbers and regular changes of colourful scenery. In place of the previously ubiquitous picturesque pantomimes and dainty pastorales, it introduced a more robust note of contemporary realism. Framed by a battle between the Spirits of Darkness and Light, *Excelsior* passed through a series of animated tableaux symbolically illustrating the triumphantly inexorable March of Civilisation – the latter represented by backcloths or unfurling panoramas depicting such contemporary wonders as Brooklyn Bridge, the Suez Canal and the Mont Cenis tunnel. In the manner of the hit musicals of our own day, this show would continue to tour Europe until the First World War, and its influence on popular taste was profound. In London, for instance, it set a model for two leading West End variety theatres, the Alhambra and the Empire, where big-budget 'up-to-date ballets' – such as *The Sports of England* (cricket, polo, Derby Day, etc.), *Our Army and Navy* and *Chicago* (depicting scenes from the World's Fair of 1893) – became major tourist attractions and money-spinners.

Milan also replenished Europe's stock of dancers, as teachers faithful to Carlo Blasis's principles in the school attached to La Scala turned out a succession of technically dazzling ballerinas groomed to make lucrative international careers. Key to their success, in contrast to the softer feminine appeal of Taglioni's generation, was a virtuosic ability to turn fast on pointe – a feat that would soon become a cliché, enshrined in the execution of thirty-two consecutive fouettés, in which one leg whips round the other (as in the coda to the *pas de deux* in the third act of *Swan Lake*). At the Alhambra or the Empire or its Parisian equivalent, the Eden, exponents of this accomplishment were paid handsomely and wildly applauded, smiling sweetly and displaying a long expanse of leg as they revolved like human spinning-tops.[4]

Nowhere, however, did these Milanese ballerinas radiate more glamour or command larger fees than St Petersburg, a city that had always fed its culture on expensive Western imports. Virginia Zucchi was the most significant of their number: a pupil of Blasis, she had toured all the European capitals before she arrived in St Petersburg in the mid-1880s. For three seasons – until she was banished after an amorous liaison cast her into the tsar's disfavour – she reigned on the stage of the imperial Mariinsky Theatre, extending the possibilities of the art of ballet beyond mere poppycock. What distinguished her wasn't so much her athleticism as an intensely vivid personality – to even the most vapid aquatint of a plot she brought an urgency and sincerity that could make it seem emotionally authentic. Ballet girls emulated her example and teenage fans such as Benois and Nouvel were infatuated, laying down their coats for her to walk over when she emerged from the stage door.

Ballet in Russia was a politically sensitive institution. Personally owned by the tsar, the Mariinsky – originally called, like its junior sister in Moscow, the Bolshoi – was directly managed as a department of the court. This degree of absolute direct control had both positive and negative effects. It meant that ballet had kept its dignity in ways that it hadn't in London or Paris, and nobody worried about box-office receipts – state funding was lavish. Standards were religiously maintained and the dancers were motivated by a fierce, almost regimental pride in their own integrity and excellence. But the school that fed students into its ranks taught an inflexible curriculum, and the preferences and prejudices of the imperial family could not be breached or even challenged. The entire institution was inert: although free of the taint of vulgar gimmickry that had corrupted it in the West, it was preserved in aspic and constrained by protocol, indelibly associated with the old order at a time when liberal ideas were in the ascendant.

One important tradition maintained in Russia but entirely lost elsewhere was the masculinity of ballet. In London, the male dancer had long been considered irrelevant: men might impersonate elderly or comic characters or perform acrobatic tumbles, but the roles of handsome prince or boyish suitor 'who rescued the female lead, captained the army, initiated the romance or arranged the seduction' were invariably taken by transvestite women, in the manner of the principal boys of pantomime.[5] In Paris, male dancers might also be tolerated as porters for the ballerinas, scene-swelling attendants and elderly nonentities, but no more. In a parliamentary debate on the budget for the Opéra in 1891, one wag suggested that money could be saved by replacing them with bus drivers and paying them accordingly.[6]

In St Petersburg, however, red-blooded young men in tights still danced uninhibitedly – a persistence that can be ascribed partly to the role played by dancing in the training and culture of the army, alongside fencing and drill. (Tolstoy offers wonderful evidence of this in *War and Peace*, where the hussar Denisov dazzles Natasha with his brilliant mazurka.) And although ballerinos commanded none of the attention afforded the ballerinas, this would have considerable artistic consequences.

Men ruled the roost in other respects, of course – not least in the auditorium. Ballet in St Petersburg was at the mercy of a coterie of male connoisseurs – staunchly reactionary arbiters of taste, sticklers for detail and fantastically well informed, but at some level mere voyeurs as well. 'In Imperial Russia, balletomania was by way of being a definite polite career, alternative to the Army and Navy or Diplomacy. Such and such an émigré, wishing to account for his social worth, will tell you that his father was a great general, a great

statesman or indifferently a great balletomane.'[7] In the words of Anatole Chujoy, 'The Russian balletomanes were a class by themselves, a
tightly knit group of people, most conservative in politics and artistic
taste, who considered ballet their private domain and who resented
anything that might change their status, whether it came from within or without the theatre.'[8] The memoir of Vladimir Telyakovsky, the
Mariinsky's long-serving director and a reformist, recalls his strug-
gles against their poisonous attitudes and describes their arrogant
behaviour, still all too familiar in the halls of high culture:

> They did not go . . . to the smoking rooms where plain mortals
> and simple ballet lovers gathered. During each intermission they
> congregated in the study of the chief of theatre police, where they
> stood or sat about . . . even on the desk and windowsills . . . At
> these gatherings the balletomanes usually talked very loudly . . .
> the conversation would begin with an analysis of the act just seen,
> and of course, the discussion concerned almost exclusively the
> female personnel . . . [appraising] in detail her legs and feet (for
> size and form), shoulders, waist, her whole figure, her face, smile,
> manner of holding her arms, balance at the end of a pas, self-
> control, confidence.
>
> Having finished with the dancers, the balletomanes would turn
> to actions and orders of the ballet administration, including the
> management and the Director himself . . . By disposition and
> persuasion the balletomanes were monarchists, adherents to the
> past, to imaginary traditions, actually to routine. They were very
> little interested in science and the arts and understood them still
> less. They especially shunned new music and painting.[9]

Intimately connected to the court and the press, impregnably
colonising the front rows of the stalls and eagle-eyed through their

opera glasses, this formidable coterie of whiskery elderly gentlemen – with impressive names and pedigrees, such as Prince Vladimir Argutinsky-Dolgouky, General Nikolai Bezobrazov, Sergei Niko-liaevitch Kudekhov, Konstantin Apollonovich Skalkovsky – made their opinions not only known but felt as they brokered reputa-tions, promotions and dismissals. They can be called the first true balletomanes and they were not a force for good.

The theatre was otherwise filled with subscribers from the upper echelons of society, members of exclusive clubs and fashionable regiments, with royalty and nobility occupying the central tiers of boxes. There was scant room for the commercial classes or the casual visitor, and perhaps those levels of the bourgeoisie made lit-tle demand for tickets to an entertainment that they would not have encountered or appreciated. Crammed into the gallery at the top of the auditorium, however, were some two hundred of the young-er intelligentsia, also predominantly male – Nevsky Pickwickians Benois and Nouvel among them. More than half were students, but there were also 'functionaries from the numerous ministries and other government offices, bank and office clerks' and 'a scattering of unidentifiable men in their thirties whom we, the students, sus-pected of being members of the secret police'.[10]

As passionate and erudite as the hardliners in the stalls but ready to imagine a ballet beyond the ritual observances, they held the keys to its future. What were they all watching, why were they so enchanted and who was in charge on stage?

Since the mid-century, the dominant creative figure had been a Frenchman, Marius Petipa, born in 1818 into a family of dancers. Himself a performer of some note, he arrived in St Petersburg in 1847 as squire to the dazzling Fanny Elssler. Realising that ballet in Europe was in decline, he decided to stay in Russia and developed his talent as choreographer or 'ballet master', as such professionals were then generally known.[11] Having seen off his compatriot fellow émigrés Jules Perrot and Arthur Saint-Léon, Petipa would dominate the imperial ballet into the twentieth century, despite never mastering more than pidgin Russian. Not a particularly nice man – his sketchy, score-settling volume of memoirs is positively bilious in tone as well as crowing with self-congratulation – he was something of a womaniser and as he became older and crabbier, he wasn't much liked. But he was a master of his craft, steadily productive and ready to provide what was required.

To say he relied on a formula would be unjust, but from what survives of his creations, a template does emerge: a love story in an exotic picture-book setting, evolving through a four-act structure that allows for contrast of mood and the introduction of elements of visionary fantasy or supernatural agency; a central role for a ballerina dancing on pointe, alternating regal lyricism with scintillating virtuosity, and supported from a distance by a politely attentive and self-deprecatory male admirer; a grand culminating *pas de deux* for the lovers, in which an opening slow section would be followed by two solos and a fast coda featuring applause-begging jumps and turns; shorter but technically challenging solos for secondary figures; and pleasingly symmetrical ensembles, known as *ballabili*, for a large corps de ballet, requiring the precise execution of a military drill. All these were Petipa's trademarks from *La Fille du pharaon* in 1862 to *Raymonda* in 1898, and they seem to have evolved only minimally. Petipa made choreography liquid architecture, its geometry framed by the proscenium arch in three-dimensional perspective and its intricately kaleidoscopic manoeuvres worked out through the deployment of papier-mâché figurines that he moved tactically across a board like toy soldiers in a war game.

His style was in essence that of his French education in the vocabulary of courtly grace and elegance, based on the slow unfolding of curved arms, proud head, and pliantly feline neck and shoulders, but inflected with the sharper, flashier edge of the Italians and enabled by shorter bell-shaped skirts (allowing more display of female leg) and more efficient blocked shoes (powering sharper, swifter turns, among other things). There's some guess-work involved here, because the great bulk of Petipa's work has been lost or passed down in corrupted form before it was accurately notated, but there are some important survivals too. One such is the 'Shades' *ballabile* from *La Bayadère* (1877), in which a long suc-cession of ghostly girls in identical white tutus repeatedly executes a chaste arabesque as they descend a ramp and step by step create a perfect shimmering formation on the stage – the simplest of rit-uals, but a visual mantra that becomes sublimely mesmerising in its suggestion of the infinite.

Coherent narrative, let alone plausible realism, was never Peti-pa's forte, and the plots of his ballets are generally vacuous. He was also handicapped by third-rate scores, rhythmically emphatic and thumpingly tuneful but redolent of the circus ring, and cranked out to strict order by hack composers. But Petipa hardly champed at the bit or longed to experiment. He had no desire to shock or even educate the audience's taste; he aimed merely to please it.

Only once did he seriously raise his game, in a work that con-tinues to rank as the summit of classical ballet. First performed in 1890, *Spyashchaya krasavitsa – The Sleeping Beauty –* is based on the fairy tale *La Belle au bois dormant* by the seventeenth-century French writer Charles Perrault. Compared with some of the ridicu-lous scenarios that Petipa had previously used, it was a model of clear, simple story-telling and historically accurate period detail: a fantasy, yes, but not a silly one.

The setting served as an implicit homage to the tsar by its depic-tion of the court of an absolute yet benevolent (albeit ineffectual) monarch – the ballet was bookended by tableaux of the sixteenth-century High Renaissance and the baroque classicism of Louis XIV's era, accurately reproducing all the panoply and pageantry of his court at Versailles. But it also appealed to the popular taste for pantomime escapism and imitated traits of the current hit *Excelsior* in hinging on a battle between the forces of good (the Lilac Fairy) and evil (Carabosse), as well as an episode in which a series of picture-postcard landscapes unfurled in a rolling panorama. Visually the result was almost sickeningly lavish, with settings designed and executed by a pool of in-house scene-painters, and a cast of over two hundred dancers, swelled by background rows of children and supernumeraries.

*The Sleeping Beauty* didn't set out to break new ground: it was conservative rather than revolutionary, a pure statement of an aesthetic language governed by an ideology of order, hierarchy and deference. Within that frame, Petipa did what he always did, constructing dance embroidered with all his customary tropes and creating for the imported Italian ballerina Carlotta Brianza the wonderfully varied title role of Aurora – a character who is all teenage sparkle in the first act, all veiled mystery in the second, all regal grandeur in the third.

But what elevated *The Sleeping Beauty* and inspired Petipa to his best was music of a richness and subtlety that he had never previously confronted. Its composer was Tchaikovsky, then at the height of his fame and powers (his next composition would be his operatic masterpiece *The Queen of Spades*). The task of writing for ballet might have been seen as something a little infra dig – the equivalent of writing for soap opera today – but fifteen years earlier, Tchaikovsky had tried his hand with *Swan Lake* (which sunk into obscurity until Petipa and his lieutenant Lev Ivanov overhauled it in 1895) and he knew the form. Despite his eminence, Tchaikovsky didn't baulk at Petipa's habit of dictating to his composers exactly what he wanted through a script explaining the action proposed and specifying the number of bars, tempos, metres and mood. In fact, this straitjacket seems ironically to have liberated him – this is music of incomparable dramatic vividness and melodic fecundity that imaginatively inhabits the narrative and paints the scene.

What also motivated him was that the commission came from the cultured hands of the Mariinsky's enlightened director Ivan Vsevolozhsky, a former civil servant who had lived in Paris and who was quietly determined to purge the institution of its corrosive complacency and jobsworth obstinacy. It was Vsevolozhsky – patient, tactful, dogged, Petipa's ally – who conceived and produced the entire *Sleeping Beauty* project, as well as designing many of the costumes.

The initial reception was mixed. The unprecedented sophistication of Tchaikovsky's music and the absence of the usual fiddle-faddle on stage affronted some of the more conventional balletomanes in the front stalls. The overall effect was just so much better than anything to which they had become accustomed. At least one prescient critic saw it as 'a triumph of the art in which music, dance and painting are combined', and *The Sleeping Beauty* soon turned into a massive success, appealing beyond the regular audience and recognised by those who knew as Petipa's supreme achievement.

It became one of those shows that changed people's lives and tastes. The Nevsky Pickwickians were captivated by its spell. Léon Bakst remembered that it made him live 'in a magic dream for three hours, intoxicated with fairies and princesses, splendid palaces flowing with gold, in the enchantment of the old tale'.[12] Walter Nouvel and Alexandre Benois saw it as often as they could, once six times in a week and once twice in a day. 'There was something in it that I had somehow always been waiting for,' Benois wrote, as bewitched by Tchaikovsky's music as others of his generation were by Wagner's. Looking back some fifty years later, he recalled how it 'had awakened in a group of Russian youths a fiery enthusiasm that developed into a kind of frenzy'. More soberly, he asserted that

> The delight in *Sleeping Beauty* returned me to ballet in general, to
> that towards which I had grown cool, and I passed this rekindled
> passion to all my friends, who gradually became true balletomanes.
> Thus was created one of the basic conditions which prompted
> us a few years later to become active in the same sphere, and
> this activity gained for us worldwide success. I hardly err if I say
> that . . . if I had not infected my friends with my enthusiasm, then
> there would have been no Ballets Russes and all the balletomania
> to which they gave birth.[13]

————

One day in 1890, Dima Filosofov's country cousin arrived in St Petersburg from the distant city of Perm to study law. His name was Sergei Pavlovich Diaghilev and he was keen to ingratiate himself with the exclusive band of Nevsky Pickwickians. The latter were sceptical at first of this brash young man, rather too pleased with himself and clearly determined to cut a dash in the big city. He was a puzzle, uncouth and rather too rawly Russian in style for these Westernised Petersburgers. He looked odd too, his square head being too big for his body and a striking badger-like patch of white streaking his thick black hair. His eyes were soulful, with an expression often compared to that of a bulldog, but his temperament was exuberant: when he laughed, his vast mouth opened like a cavern. Nobody ever saw him read a book. 'We thought him inferior to us,' wrote Walter Nouvel, 'and we treated him with a certain marked superiority.'[14] Benois sneered that he seemed 'completely indifferent to spiritual questions and the basic problems of existence', quite aside from his 'bad taste' for the music of Verdi and Massenet. But he did come over strong.[15] 'His constant animation,' Nouvel continued, 'his volubility and the facility with which he expressed himself, his deep booming voice – all denoted a vitality that was infectious. At the same time there was about him something definitely provincial. He lacked that ease and aplomb that distinguished the young man about town.'[16]

Serge de Diaghilev, as he affectedly styled himself, was particularly interested in Benois. One day, walking together in the country, they rested from the heat, lounging under a tree. The conversation about Russian music had become somewhat stilted when Diaghilev for no evident reason suddenly flung himself on top of Benois, playfully 'punching and pummelling' him and roaring with laughter. The strait-laced and refined Benois – educated to have 'a hearty contempt for anything that savoured of what was later called physical culture' – was appalled.[17] With a yell, he shook his attacker off. So who was this impulsive, excitable creature, and what did he want?

Diaghilev had been born into the upper middle class of landed gentry in 1872. His father Pavel Pavlovich was at that time serving in the cavalry as a colonel and would rise to the rank of major general. His mother died shortly after his birth, and Pavel soon after married Yelena, a generous-hearted woman who would become Serge's adored stepmother and give birth to Serge's two half-brothers Yuri and Valentin – all three of them reared on an equal footing in a generally contented domestic atmosphere. 'Never say "I can't",' Yelena told the young Serge. "When people want to, they can.'[18] It was advice that he heeded.

The Diaghilev family fortunes were precarious, and one can imagine Chekhov wryly recording their wayward course in one of his short stories. Serge's earliest years were largely spent in St Petersburg but, in 1878, Pavel returned to Perm in an effort to sort out the family's vodka distillery business. (Another Chekhovian link is that Perm is the city that the dramatist imagined as the setting of *Three Sisters*.) Pavel's own father had made his fortune out of vodka and become a liberal philanthropist on the proceeds, endowing many public buildings and good causes in the city. Unfortunately, he had then turned manically religious (swallowing crucifixes, according to report) and when changes in the laws relating to the sale of alcohol made vodka less profitable, bankruptcy loomed. Pavel, quixotic and irresponsible by nature, was not the man to sort things out.

Perm was somewhere and nowhere, the capital of a sparsely populated area the size of Austria, over a thousand miles to the east of St Petersburg and inaccessible by train or road. Situated at the foot of the Ural mountains, the city owed its reputation not to its smokestack industries but to its notoriety as the hub from which all convicts began the last leg of their horrific journey to the Siberian prison camps. The sight of these wretches trudging through the main street in chains was so frequent and commonplace that nobody did more than shrug, and even though the Diaghilevs held mildly progressive views (they had never owned serfs), none of their correspondence makes mention of it.

Theirs was a handsome and substantial town house of twenty rooms or so in the centre of the city. Perm was not noted for its high culture, but the Diaghilevs held regular musical soirées for the gentry, at which a small amateur orchestra and school choir supplemented the usual post-prandial songs and parlour tinkling. No doubt there was much talk of the greater glamour of St Petersburg, where Pavel and Yelena had been a well-connected couple – Yelena's sister had married a nephew of Tchaikovsky, who became a familiar of their circle, and little Serge called him uncle. (Later he liked to romanticise and exaggerate the extent of this relationship.)

The boy showed facility if not talent for music: he had piano lessons, developed a pleasant singing voice and made a tentative stab at composition. Nothing marked him out intellectually, but he was well enough educated, acquiring fluent French and adequate German and impressing his classmates with his sophisticated knowledge of literature and the theatre. Long summer holidays were spent in an idyllic dacha, and Serge's can be counted a happy childhood, throughout which the two most important people were his stepmother and his babushka nanny, in whose affections he basked: relations with his fun but feckless father would remain somewhat distant though never hostile.

As he turned eighteen, the question of his career was raised: for someone of his class, the usual options were the army or the civil service. Despite his father's rank, Serge was clearly not suited to the former and it was probably with the vague intention of passing into the latter that he opted to study law in St Petersburg. It was a course he never took seriously; he was slowly hatching other plans.

Before Serge left Perm, his father arranged for him, as was customary, to lose his virginity to a prostitute. Venereal disease ensued and, perhaps as a result, his attitude to the female body always contained an element of irrational repulsion. His childhood love for his stepmother and babushka never diminished and as an adult he would keep a handful of close women friends. He was masterly at charming susceptible grand ladies who might give him money and he had no prejudice against female artistic talent, to which he would give unprecedented opportunities. But his would always essentially be a man's world, and his erotic proclivities were entirely homosexual, specifically directed towards slender young men whom he could educate and to whom he stood in a quasi-paternal position. This was something that, strikingly, he never gloried in nor agonised over; he seems to have accepted it as simply the way he was, without pride or compunction.

Physical relations between men had a strange status in Russian society. Traditionally, they had been formally codified as criminal but largely tolerated – the idea of mature men of rank amusing themselves on the side with pretty serf boys or bathhouse attendants was as old as the hills and laughingly accepted as 'gentlemen's mischief'; even lower down the social scale, prosecutions for sodomy were generally made only in the case of rape. In late nineteenth-century St Petersburg, however, the atmosphere changed: several circles of ardent devotees of naked male beauty had emerged in high places – something of their activities is recorded in the secret diary of one member, the poet and novelist Mikhail Kuzmin – and the police and press began to take more aggressive interest in what had come to be regarded as an infectious perversion that needed to be controlled.[19]

This was in part a misreading of the new scientific study of sexual deviance, developed through the writings of Richard von Krafft-Ebing and his followers, and the first concept of 'homosexuality' as a biological anomaly. Intended to promote a better understanding of the variety of human sexual activity, these had the unwarranted effect of fostering paranoia toxically mixed with the idea of a *fin de siècle* malady of moral decadence and suspicions of Masonic conspiracy and corruption. With the risk of public exposure and scandal intensified, discretion became more imperative: Uranism was a risky business, as the murky case of Tchaikovsky tragically suggests.

Kuzmin's diary shows that Diaghilev was no stranger to the dangerous game of soliciting boys in public parks and conducting

ephemeral affairs with naive cadets. But his first significant love
seems to have been his saturnine cousin Dima Filosofov, with
whom he shared a bedroom when he first arrived in St Petersburg.
Together they embarked on several whistle-stop student budget
holidays to the cultural meccas of Europe – *la ville lumière* Paris;
the cities of Switzerland and Germany; Vienna, where Diaghilev
went to a ballet for the first time and didn't think much of it; and
Venice, which became his spiritual home – it 'secretes a poison,
and that poison lies in the way that all is real and can be sensed is
in constant contact with magic and mystery', he wrote to his stepmother[20] – and the eventual place of his death.

Money was very tight – his father's vodka business had gone bankrupt, so Diaghilev was living off a modest inheritance bequeathed
by his mother – but one meal a day and hard seats in third-class
railway carriages never stopped anyone young from having a wonderful time. Work of a conventional kind didn't play any part in this:
Diaghilev was too busy with Dima and their whirlwind artistic discoveries. Much more important to him, a youth from the backwater
of Perm, was making the acquaintance of celebrated people (one
trophy, achieved through subterfuge, was an audience with Tolstoy),
to be stylishly cosmopolitan and to develop a liberal outlook *au cour-
ant* with the most advanced trends of the day. One can assume that a
ready supply of sex must have been animating him too.

Diaghilev's primary passion was music, and at this point in his
life he nursed vague ambitions of becoming a composer – quashed
when he showed one of his effusions to a dismissive Rimsky-
Korsakov. His singing lessons didn't get him anywhere either. But
he was not easily disheartened, and his world-view was broadening
rapidly: the Russian school was all very well, but Wagner was the
acme, and he and Dima would make the pilgrimage to Bayreuth
and gorge themselves ecstatically on the operas. He also began to

develop an interest in the visual arts, buying some modern art and spending profligate amounts of his inheritance on decorating his apartment with vulgar extravagance. The refined and industrious Benois, who had a scholarly knowledge of the history of art and architecture and emitted a proprietorial stamp and snort when it came to aesthetic matters, was infuriated by Diaghilev's brash pretensions and ever afterwards maintained a decidedly ambivalent view of his talents and personality – what did he really know about anything and where was his moral core?

These would be questions that would ever remain unanswered, but Diaghilev was inexorably emerging as someone on his way to somewhere. There would be no mediocre surrender to conventional expectations: whatever the direction of his destiny, he was determined to dazzle. 'Success, my friend, is the one thing that redeems everything and covers up everything,' he lectured Benois in the course of one of their many explosive tiffs.

The psychology of their relationship was complex. Because Diaghilev held Benois's intellect and culture in sincere respect, he craved his approval – 'I even think I do everything I do just for you, or rather because of you,' he admitted[21] – while Benois felt obscurely jealous of Diaghilev's bravado and pushinesss. Later in life he would come clean and give perhaps the most sharply illuminating summary of his friend's supreme gift – the one to which all his other qualities (ambition, calculation, superstition and arrogance among them) seem subsidiary:

[He] was not a creative genius, he was perhaps rather lacking in creative imagination, but he had one characteristic, one ability, which none of us had and which made of him what he later became: he knew how to *will* a thing, and he knew how to carry his will into practice . . .[22]

'He knew how to *will* a thing.' That is to say, he knew how to galvanise others into action, he knew how to use (and discard) people, how to motivate and inspire, to cut through the Russian tendencies to bureaucratise and stonewall, to succumb to indolence and procrastination. In modern parlance, he was a superb manager; he made things happen. All pretence of graduating into the law or the civil service having been dropped, the only question was now: what things?

———

In 1895, the fun Diaghilev had experienced decorating his small apartment and buying paintings for its walls led him to the idea of mounting an exhibition or perhaps opening a private gallery. His tastes were being extended and monitored but also in some sense inhibited by Benois, who was in the process of establishing himself as a serious art critic and historian. On further trips to Europe with Dima Filosofov, Diaghilev cannily began collecting minor works from the studios of the new crop of symbolists and impressionists. Back in St Petersburg with his little haul, he puffed himself up, adopting a dandyish monocle and top hat. The persona was now finely honed. 'He had a suave address, not unlike the bedside manner of a fashionable physician,' is how Cyril Beaumont later described it. 'His voice had a soft, caressing tone, infinitely seductive. His *mon cher ami*, accompanied by an affectionate touch of his hand on your wrist or forearm, was irresistible. On the other hand, when cross, he could be brutally hurtful and arrogant, and no one could snub with more biting sarcasm.'[23] As he prepared to confront and conquer the world, Diaghilev wrote his beloved stepmother a frequently quoted letter, swaggering with shameless self-knowledge:

First of all I am a great charlatan, although one with flair; second
I'm a great charmer; third I've great nerve; fourth I'm a man
with a great deal of logic and few principles; and fifth I think I
lack talent; but if you like, I think I've found my real calling –
patronage of the arts. Everything has been given me but money
– *mais ça viendra*.[24]

Benois's two-year sojourn in Paris allowed Diaghilev some
breathing space in which to hatch his plans and make a slight
mark on the Russian art scene through newspaper critiques. When
Benois returned in 1897 to curate an exhibition of watercolours
collected by his patron, the Princess Tenisheva, Diaghilev published a bold review containing some scathing remarks about its
qualities that would surely have outraged both Benois and the
benignly munificent princess – just the sort of person whose favour
he might have been courting. Wife to a great industrialist, full of
progressive plans and enlightened principles distantly influenced
by the ethos of Morris and Ruskin, she had just made over her
estate at Talashkino to the revival and conservation of Russian arts
and crafts – an important element in the vogue for authentic native
folk culture that was in the air. It reached even the imperial court,
where fancy-dress balls were held in 'traditional' costume and the
dances were the kopak and lezginka rather than the Frenchified
gavotte or cotillion.

Within weeks of Benois's Tenisheva exhibition, Diaghilev opened
his own show of watercolours – and had the gall to write an unsigned
review of it himself. But it was evidently bigger, bolder and better,
with every last detail of the setting and what is now known as the
'visitor experience' micromanaged. Benois was of course furious
at Diaghilev's presumption, but such was their faultily wired yet
strangely affectionate connection that they soon made it up.

Throughout 1897 and 1898, subsidised by gullible plutocrats, Diaghilev mounted even more ambitious exhibitions of contemporary art with one eye on what he knew of the more cutting-edge galleries in London, Paris, Vienna and Munich. Privately he expressed impatience with the run of Russian painters – the popular sentimental-realist style of peasant-inhabited landscapes filled him with positive contempt – while evangelically claiming that he wanted to export and extol the Russian art misunderstood in the West. That aim and that traffic would remain fundamental to his activity for the next three decades.

In the wake of the exhibitions came an even more grandiose scheme – the creation of a lavishly illustrated journal along the lines of the English art nouveau monthly *The Studio*, to be called *Mir iskusstva*, 'The World of Art'. Nothing even remotely like it had ever appeared in Russia and its extravagantly glossy production values made it a major financial liability. But Diaghilev was in no mood to cut corners. Backed by Princess Tenisheva and the businessman Savva Mamontov, he put ferocious energy into corralling the best talents as contributors, using the Nevsky Pickwickians as an informal editorial committee and unpaid labour force. It was all great fun. 'The journal thrills us, we are consumed with excitement . . . there are heated debates every single day,' wrote Walter Nouvel during the heady first weeks of preparation.[25] Bakst designed the layout and supervised the graphics. After some harrumphing, Benois came on board too, lending his unique depth of knowledge to the enterprise: he may have been idly dreaming of starting something similar himself, but once again Dima's bumptious cousin from Perm had blindsided him.

The first issues struck a defiantly pretentious note in a lengthy, rambling and somewhat inconsistent manifesto that Diaghilev seems to have thrashed out in collaboration with Filosofov. Broadly speaking, it argues that art is a realm that should transcend or ignore narrow conceptions of social purpose, political nationalism or uplifting morality. This was not 'decadence', as some stiff-necked prudes suspected, but a necessary liberty. 'We must be free as gods,' it proclaimed. 'We must seek in beauty the great justification of humanity.' The nineteenth-century cliché of 'art for art's sake' perhaps sums it up, but its pages also radiate a mission to open the eyes and elevate the taste of a complacent St Petersburg public.

The scope over the next six years would be intellectually wide – essays on matters of literature, philosophy, the theatre and music were included – but the focus on the visual arts was highly selective and marked by Benois's enthusiasms for the France of Louis Quatorze and Quinze in particular and the rococo in general. The Renaissance, the Hispanic, the Flemish and the medieval were almost entirely ignored. Patriotic indulgence of those third-rate Russian realists was firmly rejected, but there was nostalgia for naive folk art and onion-dome Orthodox churches as well as the lacey fans and enamelled snuffboxes of Catherine the Great's era. In relation to the modern, its attitude was eclectic rather than astute: those who were featured approvingly included the painters James McNeill Whistler, Edward Burne-Jones and Gustav Klimt, the illustrators Aubrey Beardsley and Kate Greenaway, the architect and designer Charles Rennie Mackintosh. Impressionism made a modest impact on its pages, but post-impressionism scarcely registered at all. In St Petersburg, it may have looked avant-garde; in Europe, it would have looked mildly quaint and a bit behind the times.

Despite the absence of colour and the muddy 'photogravure' plates, each monthly issue of *Mir iskusstva*, 13 by 10 inches in size, was something to savour – a menu of rare delights in which every course was prettily garnished and prepared with thought and sensibility. Conservative factions took pot shots at what was perceived as its shallow trendiness and the circulation never rose much above a thousand copies, but overall the magazine scored a swift and resounding success – to such an extent that when Tenisheva and Mamontov withdrew their support for its rickety finances, no less a personage than the tsar himself stepped in with a three-year grant.

Never one to rest on his laurels and perhaps feeling that publishing would not be ultimately fulfilling, Diaghilev was already looking around for a further challenge. It crept up on him when a cultured and sophisticated aristocrat of his acquaintance, Prince Sergei Volkonsky, was put in charge of the imperial theatres in Moscow and St Petersburg. Volkonsky recognised Diaghilev as someone with useful contacts, and put him on to his creative team, assigning him the primary task of editing the theatres' annual prospectus – a prestige marketing tool that was also a journal of record circulated to all the subscribers. This Diaghilev managed with aplomb. Almost at once, however, he began to overplay his hand, bombarding Volkonsky with hare-brained ideas and getting up people's noses as he swanned heedlessly around a rigidly hierarchical organisation ignoring sensitive matters of status and demarcation.

One scheme proved his downfall. At this point Diaghilev had no interest in ballet – he was an out-and-out Wagnerian and opera fan, with some expertise in orchestral music and the knowledge of painting that he had swiftly been imbibing. But others among the Nevsky Pickwickians, still aglow with memories of Virginia Zucchi and the majesty of *The Sleeping Beauty*, believed that it had great potential as an art form, held back by the oom-pah-pah music that generally accompanied it. Benois had a particular soft spot for the ballet *Sylvia*. A tale of nymphs and shepherds produced originally at the Paris Opéra in 1876, it had briefly travelled to St Petersburg a decade later and Benois retained fond memories of Delibes' melodious and graceful score that had inspired Tchaikovsky. Might a new staging of this work prove to be the next *Sleeping Beauty*? Madly enthused by this idea, Diaghilev twisted Volkonsky's perhaps too yielding arm and won a commission to produce it with a team of Nevsky Pickwickians at the helm, abetted by two young choreographers with an appetite for change, the brothers Nikolai and Sergei Legat.

The prospect of a major project entirely in the hands of outsiders did not go down well inside the theatre's organisation, not least as an over-excited Diaghilev immediately began throwing his weight around, issuing unauthorised commands, brushing aside protocol and flouting the pecking order. After much heated altercation, backstairs skulduggery and unedifying rumours about homosexual carryings-on, it came to the point at which Volkonsky's own position was at stake and in order to survive he was obliged to side with the establishment. So negotiations descended to insults, push came to shove and resignation escalated into the sack. *Sylvia* was shelved, and Diaghilev's dismissal 'without right of appeal or pension' was spelled out in the cold print of the court gazette. Such wording implied disgrace, and the impossibility of re-entering any sort of government service. It was the first real setback of his life and he collapsed under the humiliation, either screaming and weeping like an infant or lying prostrate on a sofa staring at the ceiling. In the longer term, such an interdict meant that he would need to look beyond St Petersburg to advance his agenda.

A further complication would be the gradual unravelling of his relationship with Filosofov – the only one of his partners with whom he was on an equal footing in terms of age, class and status, but one whose mystical bent he did not share. Things limped on through 1902, a year in which Diaghilev and Filosofov visited Krafft-Ebing's sanatorium in Austria, presumably to find out more about his theories of the biological determination of homosexuality and its possible cure. What Diaghilev learned or experienced there, we do not know, but ever after he would remain remarkably untroubled and unapologetic about his desires. Others in his circle – including the uxorious Benois – found his refusal to adopt the customary pretences irritating and even alarming, but Diaghilev was having none of them. He wasn't out to pose as hero or martyr, or even to proselytise for the cause: he would simply be what he was. Today this seems one of the more admirable aspects of his personality.

And so he moved on. By 1904, *Mir iskusstva* had begun to bore the editorial team. The headaches related to the printing and paper stock had worn everyone down, an attempt to recruit Chekhov to oversee literary coverage had been rebuffed and with Russia now disastrously at war with Japan, money was drying up. As Benois later recalled, 'It seemed to us that everything that had to be said and shown had been said and shown. There was nothing to do now but repeat the same things over again – a prospect which hardly attracted us.'[26] Nevertheless, the magazine shut up shop with issues introducing its readership to Cézanne, Van Gogh, Kandinsky and Matisse, before Diaghilev transferred all his phenomenal energies into curating a massive exhibition of 4,000 historical portraits of Russian dignitaries and notabilities in the halls of the Tauride Palace in St Petersburg – a splendid neoclassical residence that had fallen empty. The idea for this had been Benois's, and Bakst designed the installation, but Diaghilev's unaided labour on the project was superhuman. Indeed, given that he appears to have travelled thousands of miles in search of items, accepting loans from over 500 sources (including the collection of the elderly Leo Tolstoy), as well as writing and editing the scholarly catalogue, raising the money and meticulously supervising every detail of the hanging and *mise en scène*, his achievement in opening the show on time to massive public acclaim does indeed seem almost miraculous. It was also an experience that left a profound mark on him, as indicated by a speech that he made shortly after the opening. 'The end was here in front of me,' he said as he recalled his odyssey through the estates of aristocratic and gentrified families such as his own, mouldering in crumbling mansions and no longer able to sustain their estates:

> It wasn't just men and women ending their lives here, but a whole way of life. And that was when I became quite sure that we are living in a terrifying era of upheaval; we must give up our lives for the resurgence of a new culture . . . we are witnessing the greatest hour of reckoning where things are coming to an end in the name of a new, unknown culture, one which we will create but which will in time also sweep us away. And therefore, without fear or doubt, I raise my glass to the ruined walls of those beautiful palaces, and in equal measure to the new commandments of the new aesthetic.[27]

This toast would prove prophetic, both for him personally and for Russia. In 1905 would come defeat in the war against Japan, the march culminating in the catastrophic massacre of Bloody Sunday, and a series of violent strikes and mutinies in the first wave of the revolution that would ultimately replace the monarchy with communism. Every institution, every law, every assumption, every relationship was destabilised. It is no surprise that Diaghilev's affair with Dima Filosofov should also peter out at this point, to be replaced by a less intense involvement with the art student Aleksey Mavrin, who acted as Diaghilev's personal assistant.

So Diaghilev gave up on improving St Petersburg's taste and, with his domestic reputation still under a cloud following the *Sylvia* business, he came to the canny realisation that, crudely speaking, a more profitable future lay in introducing the little-known and undervalued commodity of his native culture to western Europe. Paris would be the place to launch such a strategy, not only because Paris was the city where trends were set, but also because of Russia's close diplomatic alliance with France and his fluency in the language that made negotiations easier. (The train journey, via Warsaw or Berlin in comfortable twice-daily wagons-lits, took under forty-eight hours and was no impediment.)

His first move was to arrange another large-scale exhibition of Russian art to run as an adjunct to the Salon d'Automne, a new annual jamboree of avant-garde art held in the Grand Palais. As at the Tauride Palace, his Nevsky Pickwickian friends were again on hand to help – Benois selected many of the exhibits, wrote the catalogue and grumbled about Diaghilev's behaviour, while Léon Bakst designed both a trellised sculpture garden and a brocaded wallpaper to set off the paintings. In October 1906, the exhibition of some 750 items opened its doors.

Paris loved a novelty, and although the idea of Russia wasn't exactly that – Tolstoy's novels had been successfully translated into French and a Russian pavilion at the Exposition Universelle of 1900 had featured a kitsch reconstruction of a complete onion-dome church attended by theatrical peasants furnished with smocked blouses and long beards – the tradition of Russian art that ran from the spiritually charged medieval icons to the bold colourist brilliance of painters such as Mikhail Larionov and Nicholas Roerich came as a revelation to a public that was also busy assimilating the post-impressionists and fauvism. The curiosity of the city's cultured élite was piqued and the visiting card of 'Serge de Diaghileff' came to the attention of such luminaries of the beau monde as Proust's friends Élisabeth Comtesse Greffulhe and Robert Comte de Montesquiou – models for the characters of the Duchesse de Guermantes and Baron de Charlus in À la recherche du temps perdu.

Such contact with the *gratin*, as the top layer of Parisian society was known, might also lead to those susceptible to writing generous cheques.

But for what? Diaghilev had shot his bolt at the Salon: in terms of visual art, he had nothing more of substance to show and he always detested repetition. So he turned instead to Russian music. Again, this was something with which Paris had only the most superficial acquaintance, so in May 1907, with the help of Gabriel Astruc, an ambitious Jewish impresario – dashingly dressed, sumptuously bejewelled and a smart operator – he presented five orchestral concerts at the Opéra, introducing the city's musical public to the likes of Scriabin, Rachmaninov, Glazunov and Rimsky-Korsakov, as well as the astounding bass Fyodor Chaliapin, whose charismatically powerful presence and cavernously magnificent bass voice made a sensational impression in arias from Russian operas.

Although considerable amounts of other people's money were lost on the series, Diaghilev was undeterred: far from it. In 1908, he managed to cobble together another budget for five performances at the Opéra of a fully staged production of Mussorgsky's opera *Boris Godunov*, with Chaliapin as the tragic tsar. Given the hotchpotch of sets and costumes designed by Benois and others, a chorus rented from the Bolshoi in Moscow and the bare minimum of time for musical or technical rehearsal, 'a catastrophe', in Benois's words, 'seemed inevitable'.[28] But part of Diaghilev's genius was the ability to keep his nerve and snatch triumph from the jaws of disaster, and following superhuman round-the-clock efforts, appeals to the honour of the motherland and luck on their side, the opera's première outside Russia caused a sensation that would establish the international reputations of both *Boris Godunov* and Chaliapin. After it was all over, Diaghilev and Chaliapin walked the boulevards in a state of sleepless elation. 'We've done something tonight,' Chaliapin exulted. 'I don't know what, but we've really done something!'[29]

Diaghilev then returned to St Petersburg to plot his next foray into Paris. A more extensive season of Russian opera, with Chaliapin the star attraction, certainly. But that could be ruinously expensive. So what about filling out the programme with some ready-mixed Russian ballet too?

The basic sources for this chapter are inevitably the two major biographies: Sjeng Scheijen, *Diaghilev: A Life*, pp. 8–169, and Richard Buckle, *Diaghilev*, pp. 3–116. Scheijen's version is especially valuable for its first-hand research into Russian archives and translations of texts available only in Russian; Buckle's is the more richly and perhaps excessively detailed. I have also drawn extensively on Prince Peter Lieven, *The Birth of Ballets Russes*, pp. 21–73; Alexandre Benois, *Reminiscences of the Russian Ballet*, passim, and *Memoirs*, vol. II, pp. 37–256; Natalia Roslaveva, *Era of the Russian Ballet*, pp. 139–89; John E. Bowlt, *The Silver Age: Russian Art of the Early Twentieth Century and the World of Art Group*, pp. 161–200; Roland John Wiley, *Tchaikovsky's Ballets*, pp. 92–112; Elena Bridgman, 'Mir iskusstva' in Nancy van Norman Baer (ed.), *The Art of Enchantment*, pp. 26–43; Lynn Garafola, *Diaghilev's Ballets Russes*, pp. 147–76; Roland John Wiley, *A Century of Russian Ballet*, passim; Tim Scholl, *From Petipa to Balanchine*, pp. 21–45; Malcolm McCormick and Nancy Reynolds, *No Fixed Points: Dance in the Twentieth Century*, pp. 33–76; and Jennifer Homans, *Apollo's Angels*, pp. 245–89.

# 3

# BEGINNINGS

---

Tamara Karsavina in Fokine's *Narcisse*

Quite a lot had been happening to ballet in Russia since *The Sleeping Beauty* had awoken and Diaghilev's *Sylvia* had been aborted.

Directors had come and gone, and since 1901 the imperial theatres had been ruled by another reformer, Vladimir Telyakovsky. He was a tough character, at loggerheads with the disagreeable octogenarian Marius Petipa, sole *maître de ballet* for the previous three decades, a diehard now well past his creative best, protected by the favour of the court but made even tetchier by itching from a horrible skin complaint. A long war of attrition ensued before Petipa finally admitted defeat in 1904, slinking off to write his bilious and self-congratulatory memoirs.

One last straw for Petipa was Telyakovsky's engagement of a young choreographer from Moscow's Bolshoi Theatre called Alexander Gorsky. He is a significant pioneer in this history as the first in his profession to look outside ballet's own traditions for inspiration, refusing to be enslaved to its obsession with classical symmetry and attempting to inject some element of realism into its puerile scenarios. In Moscow, he had been close to Konstantin Stanislavsky and Vladimir Nemirovich-Danchenko, intensely admiring of their work on Chekhov's plays at the Art Theatre. What could be learned from the subtlety, detail and atmosphere that could be found on that stage? And did ballet have to be quite so silly and semaphored? Gorsky thought not, and when he was commissioned to choreograph *Don Quixote*, he avoided the cliché of an identically dressed corps dancing in unison and sought instead to create a crowd of differentiated individuals, with sets and costumes that had a plausible Spanish character. Telyakovsky loved the show, and imported it to St Petersburg, where, to Petipa's rage, it replaced his own old-school picture-postcard version of 1871.

A younger generation craving something new would take Gorsky's innovations further. In the vanguard was Mikhail Fokine, a handsome and conceited young man from a cultured background who had enjoyed his classical training in the imperial school, but whose passionate interest in all the arts left him impatient with Petipa's academicism. Early in his thirties, he began to teach and choreograph on principles that drew on Gorsky's example. 'I tried to give a meaning to the movements and poses,' he wrote later. 'I tried not to make the dance resemble gymnastics, I endeavoured to make the student aware of the music so it would not be treated as a mere accompaniment.'[1] He proposed respect for historical authenticity in design and instead of circus-stunt numbers interrupted by applause he asked for dramatic unity and integrity. Looking beyond the dominant French–Italian aesthetic of what qualified as correctly beautiful, he incorporated the sinuous curves of Asian sculpture and the rough edges of folk dance.

He was also impressed and challenged by the free spirit of the American Isadora Duncan, who had made her first visit to St Petersburg in 1904–5. Dancing alone, barefoot, bare-legged and uncorseted in a diaphanous white tunic, she opened her soul to the piano music of Beethoven or Chopin and let the music palpitate through her solar plexus into her limbs, sending her skipping and running, leaping and crouching, or even just quietly musing, all as the spirit moved her. Offstage she talked a lot of airy nonsense about Ancient Greece and nature and the Muse Terpsichore. She was certainly highfalutin; yet there was something magical about her disdain for the conventions that made all sorts of things suddenly seem possible.[2]

Fokine was ready, when appropriate, to remove the ballerina's blocked shoe and even to let her run barefoot, but he never accepted Isadora's renunciation of rigorous balletic technique. There was in truth nothing very sophisticated about the way she moved, and this ultimately limited her expressiveness. In his own early work, Fokine would take advantage of her liberties, but offered another more fruitful direction for revolution: instead of Petipa's lumbering, over-stuffed four-act structures that filled an entire evening in imitation of grand opera, he would create succinct one-act works following either a single narrative, in which the dancers functioned as silent actors, or a suite of dances presented within a coherent pictorial frame. Another radical departure was his refusal to construct everything round a perspective that directed everything head on at the audience – a hangover from the court of Louis XIV, where it was treasonably impertinent to turn one's back on royalty. Instead his dancers played to each other, inside the drama, even if that meant turning their backs on the auditorium.

To realise these and his other reforms Fokine needed dancers as excited as he was by the new possibilities – artists ready to collaborate creatively rather than merely follow a grouchy old ballet master's orders. Here he was fortunate; things had changed since the 1890s. Imported Italian stars had gone out of fashion because a young generation of Russians had learned all their tricks: insisting on a mercilessly tough physical curriculum that survives to some extent today, the Mariinsky had now schooled its own stars – among them the scheming Mathilde Kschessinska, once the tsar's mistress, still highly placed at court and always ready to use her influence there to get what she wanted, and Pavel Gerdt, a superb male dancer, famous for his mime, who became a much-loved teacher.

But Fokine would be closer to another junior group – one might call them the 1905ers, united by their participation in an unprecedented strike they held in that politically tumultuous year. As well as petitioning Telyakovsky for better pay and conditions and more voice in artistic decisions, they actively disrupted performances by running through dressing rooms calling on dancers to remain offstage. The rebellion – widely regarded as shocking *lèse-majesté* – tragically petered out after one leading delegate, Sergei Legat, killed himself in uncertain circumstances (his brother Nikolai later described him as 'highly imaginative and temperamental'). But a powerful desire for change had been unleashed.[3]

Beginning with little confections for charity matinées, school concerts and private parties, Fokine began to hone his style. One of his first efforts was *Chopiniana*, a fantasia danced to Chopin's music and based on that composer's dreams and nightmares – after several different incarnations, it would evolve into one of his most durable works, *Les Sylphides*; another, *The Animated Gobelin*, in which figures on a French tapestry spring to life, eventually became *Le Pavillon d'Armide*. Both of them were taken into the main Mariinsky repertory in 1907–8, with sets by Benois, and both survive in some form today. Although, ironically, they look more quaintly dated than the classical pantomimes of Petipa they were intended to supersede, they have enormous significance in this history, not least because of their association with three extraordinary dancers who require some introduction.

Two of them were young ballerinas, signatories to the 1905 petition.

Anna Pavlova, born illegitimate in 1881 of doubtful parentage (she may have been Jewish on her paternal side), was a sickly child.[4] Like the Nevsky Pickwickians, however, once she had seen *The Sleeping Beauty*, there was no question of her destiny. Weak ankles and pitifully thin legs did not bode well for a professional career – she struggled to be accepted into the imperial school and then suffered because her spindly physique did not adapt to a training regime designed for frames more robust than hers.

Having realised that her body would never allow her to master the flashy spinning-top tricks of the Italians, she cultivated instead an idiosyncratic style of ethereally weightless fluency that made her seem a creature more of the air than the earth. Neither classical perfection nor regal grandeur was her style, and she was never one to blend with others into a bigger dramatic picture: she was best seen alone in the spotlight as a fluttering dragonfly, a melting snowflake, a winsome dryad, a will-o'-the-wisp – and, most famously, a dying swan, her arms quivering with a frustrated desire to take wing as the life force fades, in a four-minute solo choreographed for her by Fokine that she is said to have performed over 4,000 times around the world, imprinting on ballet one of its archetypal images. Perhaps there was something of Taglioni in her, and something of Isadora too.

Kind to animals, smiling to children and gracious to her fans, Pavlova was less enamoured of the rest of humanity: her massive ego and dimples of steel meant that she was a law unto herself, her male partners, frequently discarded and replaced, being regarded as only a necessary evil, their sole function to enhance the illusion of herself that she wished to create. But she had pure genius – the gift of apparent spontaneity – and she danced like a dream.

Four years her junior, Tamara Karsavina was an entirely different personality: highly intelligent and literate, a steadfast friend and reliable colleague, queenly but gracious; she was universally respected and would later enjoy the sort of ordinary life outside the theatre that Pavlova would have dreaded. If there is a beacon of honest goodness in this book, then it shines from her.[5]

Her father, Platon Karsavin, had been a fine dancer whose progress had been arrested by Petipa's disfavour. Subsequently he became a teacher and little Tamara his pupil. Tamara was then admitted to the imperial school, and her enchanting memoir *Theatre Street* gives a vivid picture of life as a boarder at this élite institution, which delivered a rounded education free of all charge but expected lifeblood in return. Whatever its rigours and demands, the quality of pedagogy was second to none. Particularly venerated were the Italian Enrico Cecchetti, whose 'method' provided the solid foundations, and Christian Johansson, a nonagenarian Swede, blind in one eye and fearsomely candid, who, despite being chair-bound and doddery, taught the older students the finer points in what was known as *la classe de perfection*.

With her darkly expressive beauty, dramatic versatility and poetic imagination, the dancer who emerged from this chrysalis was a more warmly human creature than Pavlova – somebody who could communicate emotional realities as well as elusive fantasies. Not surprisingly, Pavlova did not care for her junior one bit, beadily watching her ascent through the ranks; there would not be room for the two of them for long.

Karsavina and Fokine fell for each other in a calf love that never – so they claimed – went beyond long walks and soulful glances. Both would marry elsewhere, but their professional relationship was more fruitful, and enriched by the third of these outstanding figures – someone who justifies the cliché of 'a legend in his own lifetime'.

Born in Kyiv in 1889, Vaslav Nijinsky was of Catholic Polish ancestry, with perhaps some Tartar blood in the more distant mix.[6] His parents were professional dancers, touring the Caucasus and Ukraine, where the young Vaslav learned wildly athletic, high-jumping, back-flipping folk dances such as the kopak and lezginka.

Schooled into ballet in St Petersburg, despite a poor academic record he was fast-tracked through the system and was partnering all the star ballerinas by the time he was eighteen.

He was always an oddball. With an explosive temper yet self-contained to the point of narcissism, obsessively tidy and compulsively meticulous, he remains a psychological conundrum: today he might be diagnosed on the autistic spectrum. One dancer, Lydia Sokolova, later recalled, 'Although he was virtually never alone, he was as it were always alone with himself. He could not mingle in any way, he very rarely addressed anyone in conversation. If he did it was with somebody with whom he was dancing and then he spoke so shyly and softly, without looking at the person as he spoke, and would get away as quickly as possible.'[7] As his sister Bronislava put it more bleakly, 'He never had a friend.'[8]

Igor Stravinsky later noted 'curious absences in his personality',[9] while others were struck by the uncanny transformation that took place when he put on a stage costume and became someone else – as if a void had been filled. Those encountering him outside the theatre were often flummoxed by his sullen, downbeat ordinariness and even in rehearsal he could be so self-effacing as to leave no impression. Not obviously handsome, he could casually be mistaken for a barrow boy or a labourer; only if you looked more closely did he radiate the dangerous allure of the untamed animal. He was hard to read, harder to define: his manner could seem either predatory, or forbidding, or vulnerable, or merely a blank, and in a culture in which masculine and feminine were clearly defined and demarcated qualities, his erotic aura exuded a disturbing perfume of the Uranian 'third sex' – languid, curvaceous, limp-wristed, rose-coloured.

His physique was bizarre, and goes some way towards explaining his abilities: about 5 foot 4 inches tall, he had a thick neck, narrow

sloping shoulders, a slender upper torso and a wasp waist supported by rock-solid thighs and bulbous calves. By some alchemy, this
stockily muscled and prosaic frame could become supernaturally
airborne, or exotically sensual, or the epitome of poetic yearning.
His partners on stage were aware of the effort behind the illusion, and even a certain compulsive joylessness behind the effort:
Sokolova noticed how he would 'puff and blow so much . . . I have
never seen the spark of true enjoyment in his eyes . . . he danced
because he could, and couldn't do anything else.'[10] The teacher
Nikolai Legat noted that by 'tightening his leg muscles, especially
those of the thighs in the air, he made all his moderate jumps fairly high. During the leap he held his breath in, i.e. he breathed in
shortly before the spring and breathed out as soon as he was down
again.'[11] But the most precise description of his technical powers –
if not the source of his fabled ability to give the illusion of hanging
flat in the air while jumping – was provided by his friend Marie
Rambert:

No one held more firmly to the ground in order to obtain that
fabulous spring. He had an exceptionally long Achilles tendon
and was one of the very few people who could do a full *plié* (that is
until the thighs became horizontal) in the fifth position (i.e. with
his feet turned out at right-angles). In addition to that, in every
*grand jeté*, whether it was straightforward or *en tournant* he did the
*battement* with the second leg without dropping the first, and for
a moment held that position in the air . . . There may be other
dancers who actually jumped higher, but with them you measure
the distance from the ground; Nijinsky came nearer the stars and
made you forget the earth altogether.

His pirouettes were brilliant, but it was not so much the amount
of actual turns that he did in a pirouette that mattered – of those

others may do more – but the incredible lightness and swiftness of his head movements.

His feet were extraordinarily supple. I remember him showing me – having taken off his shoe – how to hold the foot *sur le cou-de-pied*. He said to me, 'Clasp it as though with the hand,' and indeed his foot had the intelligence and sensitiveness of a hand. This probably determined his touch on the ground. Few people realise that the touch of the foot on the ground is as important with a dancer as the touch of a pianist's fingers on the piano, and it was the perfection of this touch that he possessed to a supreme degree.[12]

These jewels – Pavlova, Karsavina and Nijinsky – dancing Fokine's one-act ballets, as well as the mighty bass voice of Chaliapin, would be Diaghilev's treasure trove, the Unique Selling Point he would offer Paris. Some hint of what was to come was already in the air. Little posses of Russian dancers had already begun to tour European capitals and resorts, but they were presented essentially as vaudeville turns offering a *pas de deux* sandwiched between performing dogs and jugglers. A Finnish impresario called Edward Fazer had in 1908 taken a rather larger contingent to Helsinki and Berlin. But Diaghilev's ambitions were much grander: he wanted to transport not only stars in costume, but an entire theatrical and musical culture. For that he would need jaw-droppingly large sums, and raising them would be a persistent headache.

Potential donors inconveniently died, promises were reneged on, a sympathetic philanthropist who had made a fortune out of rubber goods went bust, and the tsar capriciously withdrew his offer of a grant (possibly at the behest of his witchy ex-mistress Kschessinska, who resented anything that might end up promoting her arch-rival Pavlova). Programming had to be changed in consequence, and Diaghilev was left reliant on a wing and a prayer and the generosity of his closest woman friend – the Polish-born Misia Edwards, estranged wife of a newspaper mogul and an inspiration for Proust's slyly satirical portraits of Madame Verdurin and Princess Yourbeletieff. Diaghilev and Misia were like siblings, constantly giggling, bickering and rowing, secure in the knowledge that their relationship was unassailable. His other lifeline, acting as his French business agent and proxy, was the impresario, backer and fixer Gabriel Astruc, whose commercial canniness and access to the ins and outs of the theatrical world were essential resources.

In St Petersburg, Diaghilev planned his Parisian *Saison Russe* of opera and ballet. Sergei Grigoriev, the ballet master, rehearsal director and company manager who would become one of his most long-serving and long-suffering deputies, left a pleasant but deceptively collegiate picture of a meeting of his first kitchen cabinet – consisting largely of Nevsky Pickwickians such as Benois, Bakst and Nouvel:

Sitting in the dining room, a small room with an oval table. On the table to Diaghilev's right stood a samovar, and his valet Vasili poured out tea. There were biscuits and jam on the table, and several plates of Russian sweets. In front of every member of the company lay a sheet of paper and a pencil. Diaghilev had a large exercise book in front of him ... Any friend of Diaghilev who happened to call during the sittings was made welcome and took part in the discussion, expressing his opinion and giving his advice. Diaghilev took notice of what everyone had to say.[13]

Or did he? Like all the best generals, the truth was that he was receptive to ideas and good at listening to a trusted few, but ultimately all major decisions were taken by himself, without heed to majority votes or democratic procedures. Nor could he be bothered with accounts. 'No books or ledgers even were kept,' noted Peter Lieven. 'There were only small torn bits of paper with scribbles which nobody but Diaghilev could decipher . . .* He was the antithesis of a money-grabber,' Lieven continued; 'he had no respect for money, either his own or other people's.'[14] It was simply a means to an end, and with the help of jottings made in a little black exercise book, he operated on the principle of the French army: '*On se débrouille.*' (We'll muddle through somehow.)

As Chekhov observed, Russians have a weakness for endless musing and dithering; Diaghilev, however, could always cut to the quick. And he needed to: the gamble was immense, and an opera and ballet company of 250 and an orchestra of 80 – drawn ad hoc largely from personnel of the imperial theatres whose contracts left them at liberty during their summer vacation – had to be signed up, instructed and rehearsed.

In May 1909 the dancers arrived in Paris by train. Diaghilev set himself up, as he always did, in a hotel suite, 'encumbered by trunks always half packed, the tables cluttered up with letters, programme proofs and box files, canvases and drawings on the chairs and against the walls'.[15] The idea of home never interested him, nor the accumulation of worldly wealth; a happy nomad, he liked eating in good restaurants and ran up huge bills in a lordly fashion – someone would pay them somehow, some time – but his clothes were often embarrassingly threadbare and he never fussed about luxuries. Everything he had, spiritually as well as materially, was invested in the art he produced.

---

* This was only a slight exaggeration. An exasperated London solicitor, delegated to sort out one mess, complained, 'It is really very difficult to deal with your affairs, unless you will give them your attention.' (Ekstrom Collection, V&A Theatre Museum, 7/1/1/8.)

The dancers were more modestly accommodated in *hotels garnis* along Boulevard St Michel. Few of them had ever been out of Russia; painfully conscious of their provincialism, they were more bemused and intimidated than entranced by the glamour of *la ville lumière*. 'So exaggerated had been my idea of its inconceivable elegance', recalled Tamara Karsavina, 'that in my heart of hearts I expected the streets to be like ballroom floors and to be peopled exclusively with smart ladies walking along with a frou-frou of silk petticoats . . . I was terrified of seeming provincial.' But there was scarcely time for her to disabuse herself. Astruc was housing the company in the centrally located but rather down-at-heel Théâtre du Châtelet, best known for a long-running musical spectacular *Around the World in Eighty Days* and special effects facilitated by its sophisticated stage machinery. Diaghilev decided to renovate and re-carpet the foyers and auditorium, so the poor dancers and musicians had to struggle in rehearsal against hammering and dust. 'The stage hands regarded us all as lunatics,' Karsavina continues. 'The fortnight preceding our performances [was] arduous, feverish, hysterical.'[16] But perhaps quite fun too, with *esprit de corps* sustained by buffets of delicious food laid out on packing cases. (Ballet dancers in those days weren't as obsessed with stick-thinness as they are today, and they had appetites like horses. 'I always ate *everything*,' Karsavina insisted.[17])

With all expenditure being put on tick and the box office incapable of delivering enough to cover costs, utter disaster and ruin seemed a hair's breadth away. Yet a mood of heady optimism sustained the enterprise – an optimism that would seldom fail thereafter and at some critical points saved it. It was Paris in the spring, and after a successful dress rehearsal, there was a celebratory supper at which toasts were proposed and hopes ran high. 'Everybody was in an exalted state of mind. Nobody doubted that success awaited them,' writes Lieven. 'They went into the battle as if it were already won.'[18]

On their side were Parisians' endemic curiosity and receptiveness to the new, in a cultural atmosphere in which dance was becoming fashionable as never before. This must be emphasised: today it has become commonplace to assert that Russian ballet exploded over Paris like a volcanic eruption, changing the odds for art in one overnight convulsion. But that is not the case: warning tremors had been felt for years.

Although it is true that by the turn of the century formal ballet at the Opéra had fossilised into fustiness and daintiness, much more animated and uninhibited danced entertainment was being programmed at the Folies Bergère and variety theatres such as the Casino and the Olympia – one can sense something of their energy and character in the art of Toulouse-Lautrec. Also on show was a steady stream of exotic imported novelties, including Isadora Duncan and her barefoot Greek frolics; another American pioneer, Ruth St Denis, who had a fascination for Indian dance; the acrobatically flexible Spaniard Alda Moreno; the winsomely fluttering Hanako, previously a geisha; and the troupe of Cambodian temple dancers, evocatively drawn by Rodin. Such novelties stimulated the market's appetite.

So at this point Diaghilev should be seen not so much as a radical innovator but as someone shrewdly riding the crest of a wave, bringing something bigger but not essentially challenging to an audience that was predisposed to approve. An extensive promotional campaign bolstered him. Beyond the obvious fly-posting and feeding titbits to journalists, the impresario Astruc drew an A-list of dignitaries, celebrities, opinion-makers and eye-catchers to the first night. 'I offered seats in the front row of the Dress Circle to the most beautiful actresses in Paris. Out of 52 invitations, 52 answered yes. I took the greatest care to alternate blondes and brunettes,' he famously bragged.[19] Whether this was mere *blague* or not, we shall never know – there are sadly few convincingly detailed first-hand accounts of the performance on 19 May 1909 – but the occasion was clearly an outstanding success, with the refurbishment of the auditorium and glamour of the audience causing almost as much excitement as anything on stage.

The repertory was carefully tailored to appeal to Parisian sensibilities. The programme for this first night consisted of Fokine's *Le Pavillon d'Armide*; the sung second act of Borodin's opera *Prince Igor*, containing a sequence in which Polovtsian warriors dance like furies; and *Le Festin*, a mixed bag of short items that served as a tantalising sample suggestive of the riches left behind in St Petersburg. Some specific calculations were being made here.

*Le Pavillon d'Armide* can be read as St Petersburg's compliment to Versailles, symbolic of a deep artistic entente between Russia and France. Based on a tale by Théophile Gautier set in the grounds of a chateau, it was all rococo elegance and fantasy, conservative in spirit to the point of nostalgia for autocracy, and sumptuously designed in the manner of a Fragonard painting by Benois – a Russian of French name and ancestry as well as sympathies.

Yet it was Russian music (by the young composer Nikolai Tcherepnin) and Russian dancers that brought it to life – literally so, as they embodied the figures in the Gobelin tapestry. Here was born one of the legends of the Ballets Russes: Nijinsky's supernatural hovering jump, powered by his muscled legs and springy toes, perceived by audiences who had never previously given much thought to men dancing at all as miraculous, and crowned, often on a whim of the dancer's own, by a trajectory into the wings that rose to its highest point just as he vanished from view and left an impression of ever increasing altitude. The critic Cyril Beaumont talked of his 'freedom of the air', the sheer naturalness of his ascent: 'No flurry, no seeming preparation . . . he vaulted upwards or bounded forwards with the effortless ease of a bird taking flight.'[20] Nobody ever measured or filmed this miraculous illusion. As balletic technique has in many respects advanced over the past century as physiological development has become more scientific, it is doubtful that we would find it so impressive today. Even in his own times, there were a few sceptics: Nikolai Legat wrote of a dancer in Moscow called Damashoff, uncommemorated elsewhere in the annals, who made what Nijinsky did look like 'child's play'.[21] Indeed Nijinsky himself always downplayed the whole business. It was simply something he had learned to do, like backflipping through hoops or juggling balls. 'No! No! Not difficult,' he would say when interrogated. 'You just have to go up and then pause a little.' But he was about so much more than his headline ability to jump very high.

*Le Pavillon d'Armide* also introduced Paris to the enchanting Karsavina – lustrously beautiful, vividly responsive to music and character. Nijinsky was too self-absorbed to be a naturally generous partner, but she understood his vulnerability and could handle him. Together they returned at the end of the programme to light up *Le Festin*'s banquet of balletic divertissements with a gloriously virtuosic *pas de deux* that enhanced the glory that they had already earned separately.

The other sensation of the evening was something in bold contrast that channelled the intense fascination that 'civilised' western Europe felt at the spectacle of 'primitive' instinct: Fokine's Polovtsian dances from *Prince Igor*, to the music of Borodin. In place of the gentilities of *Le Pavillon d'Armide*, this offered an image of Russia at its most intoxicatingly wild and raw – instead of pink ballet slippers and classical decorum, here was a frenzy of barbaric exoticism, primary in its colours and accompanied by the singing of an exuberant chorus with a black-toned baleful bass, culminating in a thunderous murderous charge of fired-up warriors led by the

electrifying figure of another great Russian male dancer, Adolph
Bolm. Like Chaliapin, Bolm could inspire awe and terror without
the ambiguities or introversions of Nijinsky – he was a blazing-
ly virile presence seemingly ready to leap off the stage over the
footlights to rape the ladies and slaughter the gentlemen in the
auditorium. No wonder that the Polovtsian dances were an immediate and durable smash hit.

So much for the first night. The reviews were generally enthusiastic. The orchestra sounded wonderfully red-blooded, the dancers
were remarkably energetic, the decor had an almost impressionistic
panache far removed from the fusty meticulous realism of ballets
at the Opéra – but there is also a sense of shock, as if the critics
didn't know quite what to make of it all. Astruc, never one to miss
an opportunity to puff, gave public opinion a sharp push by writing
a letter to *Le Figaro*, extolling 'Serge de Diaghilev' and proclaiming
their shared triumph:

> Please make it known, I beg you, that it was [Diaghilev's] brilliant
> initiative, his iron will and his remarkable understanding of
> the theatre which have made it possible for me to present the
> Parisian public – and what a public it is – with these unique and
> unforgettable spectacles. For a year he has laid the foundations
> of victory, marching on, heedless of every obstacle, and I thank
> him for having associated me with one of the most beautiful
> phenomena ever to appear before the eyes of Paris.[22]

Over the coming weeks, such hype would prove justified: the
Russians continued to amaze and enthral. Chaliapin was fearfully
mesmerising as Ivan the Terrible in Rimsky-Korsakov's opera *The
Maid of Pskov*. Then came two more ballets by Fokine, again geared
towards French taste.

What in Russia had been called *Chopiniana* was recast as *Les Sylphides* – a mistily aquatinted reverie of desexualised womanhood evoking Parisian ballet in its heyday in the 1830s, when Taglioni and her sisters danced in shimmering white tulle, and Chopin's haunting piano music (for the purposes of the ballet, rather flatly orchestrated) provided the fashionable melodies. Fokine offered no plot: only a mood, an atmosphere, a tableau in constant evanescent motion. The scenery designed by Benois showed a ruined Gothic abbey in a forest clearing where the eponymous lady phantoms, led by Karsavina and Pavlova, materialised in pallid moonshine. Flitting like fireflies, wafting and wisping and resting in exquisite soft-edged poses, they shyly evaded the tender grasp of the male dreamer of this romantic vision – a long-haired poetic youth in a black velvet jerkin, incarnated by Nijinsky with a previously unsuspected delicacy and restraint, as well as effortless musicality.

Any whiff of eroticism in *Les Sylphides* was refined and fully clothed; in *Cléopâtre*, which followed it, the sexiness was uninhibitedly sensationalist, taking things just about as far as they could go without the police being called. Fokine's Cleopatra was not the queen of Shakespeare's tragedy, but of Pushkin's fragmentary fable *Egyptian Nights*, in which she offers a night of ecstatic love to any man who will agree to pay the ultimate price by drinking fatal poison the following morning. This theme was popular at the time – the subject of numerous quasi-pornographic poems and paintings, adapted by Colette and her lover Missy only months previously for a saucily lesbian (and perhaps tongue-in-cheek) mimed play they devised for the Moulin Rouge. Fokine's version was more extravagantly melodramatic in tone, and although the music was nothing but a medley culled from six different composers, the decor by Léon Bakst was of stunning magnificence: vast basalt statuary framed a view of a pink-pillared temple, behind which the Nile glittered in the violet twilight, with costuming of barbarically gilded splendour, intricately detailed and deep-dyed in colours of a richness and brilliance that even the great avant-garde colourist painters of the time – Matisse, Gauguin, Derain, Delaunay, Kandinsky – could not match. Somehow it managed to be more than just an exercise in decadent *fin-de-siècle* sensuality: in Arnold Bennett's words, it was 'saved by a sort of moral nudity, and by a naive assurance of its own beauty . . . too fresh, zealous and naive to be perverse'.[23]

Pavlova, Karsavina and Nijinsky danced exotic slaves and the corps let rip in a bacchanal, while Fokine himself was Amoun, the nobleman who can't resist the fatal offer. Yet the star of this show wasn't a dancer at all but a Russian Jewish woman of startling beauty and limitless wealth – her father owned banks, sugar mills and breweries – who had taken a few ballet and acting lessons in St Petersburg and began her professional career as something approximating a high-class striptease artiste. Ida Rubinstein had flouted the orthodoxy of her family not only by going on stage, but even more brazenly by appearing nude in public.[24] As Salome, she shed all seven veils and fell foul of the censor; as Cleopatra in Paris, she was carried mummified from an ebony and gold sarcophagus, and held upright as attendants ritually unwound her body from eleven embroidered sheets of differing hues, until she herself whipped off a twelfth sheet of midnight blue and revealed herself in almost transparent shimmering *déshabillé* – a tall and willowy figure, imperious yet vulnerable, her jet-black eyes framed by kohl, her cheeks pallid, her lips slightly parted, her head crowned by a powder-blue wig with gilded braiding.

In other respects Rubinstein was not egregiously talented: in Lieven's words, 'The question of good taste did not trouble her.'[25] Her training in ballet and acting was exiguous; what she relied on instead was the ability to mime and vamp in a style known as '*plastique*' that involved the striking of expressive statuesque poses. She also knew how to draw attention to herself, from an entrance to an exit: 'She didn't dance, she walked,' commented Benois. 'But how she walked!'[26] Alongside this went a gift for self-advertisement through fanciful newspaper coverage. One myth that did the rounds was her habit of drinking champagne out of the cup of Madonna lilies; and like her inspiration Sarah Bernhardt, she had a penchant for keeping ferocious wild cats as domestic pets.

By the time the six-week season of a dozen performances ended in mid-June, Diaghilev was plotting a return to Paris in 1910. Every door was now open to him; all his calls were answered. Maurice Ravel was commissioned to compose *Daphnis et Chloé*, to be choreographed by Fokine, and future projects were being discussed with that eager young beaver, nineteen-year-old Jean Cocteau, and Marcel Proust's intimate, the composer Reynaldo Hahn. The élite had been alerted to the gestation of something of remarkable quality and originality, and a new audience had been seeded for a branch of dance that had been widely written off as a valid, vital art form. Proust wrote in *La Prisonnière* of '*une invasion charmante*' that caused '*une fièvre de curiosité* . . . less bitter, more purely aesthetic, but perhaps quite as intense as the Dreyfus Affair'.[27] As that cosmopolitan Anglo-German diplomat and connoisseur Count Harry Kessler – friend to Richard Strauss and Hugo von Hofmannsthal, to Auguste Rodin and Edvard Munch, a man who could savour all the rich complexities of Middle European high culture – wrote in his diary, 'All in all, this Russian ballet [is] one of the most remarkable and significant manifestations of our time . . . We are truly witnessing the birth of a new art.'[28] That judgement would soon become the stuff of journalese.

At the heart of the initial success of the *Saison Russe* was a fascinating paradox, noted by Benois: 'Our wild Russian primitiveness, our simplicity and *naïveté* had proved to be more progressive, more elaborate and more refined than all that was being created in Paris – the most cultured of cities!'[29] Of course, that primitivism was something that had been thoroughly theatricalised and carefully cooked up to please the market, but something had shifted – and Diaghilev had been given his cue to proceed in a more aggressively creative direction.

There was only one unresolved question: money. Although Diaghilev had proved what Lieven called his 'genius for creating an atmosphere of intellectual snobbery around his enterprise',[30] the adulation of the élite was not enough to fill all the seats or pay all the bills. Expenditure on the Paris season had exceeded income by 86,000 francs. Astruc, as Diaghilev's agent, was the first port of call for creditors. He also discovered that, before any debts were paid off, Diaghilev had been secretly negotiating with the Opéra to present a 1910 season. Understandably livid at the Russian's ingratitude and disloyalty, he seized all the sets and costumes in distraint and attempted to declare Diaghilev bankrupt. He then wrote a violently incriminating letter to the tsar's office scuppering any chance of the court exchequer providing Diaghilev with further subsidy. By the end of the year, things had been patched up and a new agreement with Astruc signed, but this nasty episode reminded everyone what a cliff-edge business the importing of Russian opera and ballet was.

Something else was going on behind the scenes, much whispered about and much more personal. In Paris Diaghilev's secretary Alexei Mavrin had disappeared suddenly – gone off with the ballerina Olga Fedorova, it was said. Diaghilev had now taken Nijinsky under his personal protection, and they were occupying adjoining hotel rooms with a connecting door. Nijinsky had acquired a platinum ring set with a huge sapphire, and he alone among the dancers would be invited to the choice suppers at the Restaurant Viel that

Diaghilev hosted after performances (events that, as a sociopath, he must have found an ordeal). Over the summer, before returning to St Petersburg, they travelled together to the spa at Carlsbad – Nijinsky was recuperating from a bout of typhoid – and to Venice. Everyone knew what was going on and worried about the implications, but once eyebrows had been raised, the relationship wouldn't have been openly discussed.

The affair had started in St Petersburg, and Diaghilev wasn't Nijinsky's first lover. A couple of years earlier, the dancer had been taken under the wing of Prince Pavel Lvov, a wealthy, worldly thirty-something man about town, madly social and enthusiastic about racing motor cars. Lvov appears to have used the classic tactic of sending his card round to the dressing room after a performance and inviting the boy to dine with him and a lady friend. But there was no lady friend. Seducing him with extravagant generosity that included establishing him in a luxurious apartment, paying for extra ballet lessons and showering his impoverished mother and sister with hampers of food, Lvov seems also to have been genuinely kind and fond of the strange lad. 'Gentlemen's mischief' was not unheard of and few questions would have been asked.

At some point Lvov tired of Nijinsky, who was not homosexual and perhaps only politely compliant in the bedroom. For a party-goer like Lvov, he can't have been much fun downstairs either, given his monastic ballet regime and difficulties in relating to other people: nobody would ever claim that Nijinsky had a ready sense of humour. So in a transaction common among homosexual coteries at the time, Lvov passed him over first to a Polish count and thence to Diaghilev.

In the diary he wrote a decade later while suffering from extreme psychosis, Nijinsky recalled that their first encounter was a telephone call. This may not have been the case, but there is no reason to doubt that Diaghilev asked him over to his hotel, and there began Diaghilev's passionate infatuation. Nijinsky, an ambitious, naive youth of low social class, was not in any position to resist: the relationship might not have been what he wanted, but it was what he needed. Through the crossed-wire chaos of his madness, one senses how it must have felt for him:

I hated Diaghilev from the very first days I knew him, because I knew Diaghilev's power. I did not like Diaghilev's power, because he abused it . . . I hated him for his voice which was too self-assured, but I went in search of luck. I found luck there because I immediately made love to him. I trembled like an aspen leaf. I hated him but I put up a pretence, for I knew that my mother and I would starve to death [otherwise]. I understood Diaghilev from the first moment and pretended therefore that I agreed with all his views. I realised one had to live and therefore it did not matter to me what sacrifice I made. I worked hard at dancing and was therefore always tired. But I pretended I was cheerful and not tired in order that Diaghilev should not be bored. I know that Diaghilev felt it, but Diaghilev liked boys and therefore found it difficult to understand me. I do not want people to think that Diaghilev is a scoundrel and that he must be put in prison. I will weep if he is hurt.[31]

But there would be much weeping, and much hurt.

———

Following Astruc's letter complaining about his financial mis-conduct, Diaghilev was yet again in embarrassing disgrace in St Petersburg and could no longer count on support from the tsar.

Undaunted, he joined forces with a balletomane Jewish banker and heir to a large fortune, Baron Dmitri Günzburg, who was happy to stand collateral and negotiate loans in return for an informal role as finance director. Never interested in balance sheets, Diaghilev readily handed him the brief and charged ahead. Although plans to present more opera starring Chaliapin – who had caused as explosive a sensation in Paris as Njiinsky – had to be shelved, there was no question of Diaghilev resting on his laurels or playing safe.

His programming was shrewd. To mollify Benois's sentimental affection for French romanticism and follow up on the success of the similarly perfumed *Les Sylphides*, a revival of *Giselle* was announced as a showcase for Pavlova. The novelty would be *The Firebird*, concocted and choreographed by Fokine on the basis of several folk tales, designed in fantastically colourful style by Alexander Golovin, with music by a rookie composer called Igor Stravinsky, on whom Diaghilev took a sharp punt after more experienced hands had let him down. Rooted in national ethnicity, it would be, as he put it, 'the first Russian ballet – for there aren't any'.[32]

But Pavlova dropped out. After one contract with Diaghilev, she had cynically realised that she could keep more control and make more money with less effort by abandoning all artistic ambition and throwing integrity to the wind. She would henceforth organise her own little touring troupe, available to dance the balletic equivalent of cheap confectionery on any stage or end of the pier that would pay the requisite fee. For the next twenty years, audiences the world over happily flocked to her tatty shows; miraculously, the magical quality of her dancing persisted.

The beneficiary of Pavlova's defection was loyal Karsavina, who could have gone the same way as her rival but chose the nobler path instead. Despite her exquisite performance in the title role, *Giselle* would prove a damp squib, regarded as nothing more than an insipid period piece. But blessed with gorgeous picture-book designs, Stravinsky's thrillingly vivid score, and Karsavina as the volatile creature who helps a young prince out of a tight spot in return for her liberty, *The Firebird* made a more enduring impact.

Two further new ballets by Fokine in that Paris season of 1910 mark a high point of his creativity. One was *Scheherazade*, a drama suggested by the *Thousand and One Nights* and danced to a short-ened version of Rimsky-Korsakov's symphonic suite. Capitalising on the taste for orientalist eroticism created by novels such as Flau-bert's *Salammbô* and Anatole France's *Thaïs*, it was choreographed in a style closer to the flamboyant mime of early cinema than to classical ballet. Violently sadistic and uninhibitedly decadent in temper, it caused an instant sensation, offering Ida Rubinstein as the lascivious Sultan's wife Zobeide a second opportunity to strike provocative poses that radiated *femme-fatale* glamour and Nijinsky the role of her secret lover the Golden Slave – 'a stallion', wrote Fokine, whose arrival, 'overflowing with an abundance of power', precipitates a climactic orgy.[33]

Aside from the flesh and sweat of the dance, the spectacle *Scheherazade* presented was one of awesome splendour: in his first major theatrical commission, the eccentric Nevsky Pickwickian Léon Bakst, formerly best known as a portrait painter, conjured up an extravagant fantasy of a harem. In place of the customary flat backcloths and wings came great swags of curtain, mounds of undulating cushions, pendant lamps and Turkish carpets; the cos-tumes tantalisingly concealed as much as they revealed; and the colour scheme was a peacock riot. 'There are reds which are tri-umphal and there are reds which assassinate,' he wrote. 'There is a blue which can be the colour of a St Madeleine and there is a blue of Messalina.'[34] Bakst used them all, hotly and gorgeously. Benois was furious about the whole thing: the ballet had been his idea, he claimed, and he should have been allowed to design it. His rage increased when Diaghilev commissioned Bakst to ginger up Benois's rather vaporous sets for *Giselle* – a production that in any case was unsuccessful. Another rift ensued.

As Benois had to admit, Diaghilev had 'the habit of success' and he was forced to forgo his pique when he saw *Scheherazade*. 'A production that is truly amazing . . . I have never seen such absolute harmony of colour on the stage,' he wrote generously, in a review published in the Parisian journal *Rech*.[35] The ballet was unstoppable: no other work of the Diaghilev repertory would captivate such a wide audience or exert such extensive cultural influence. Bakst's 'absolute harmony' of vibrant contrasts was slavishly imitated by fashionable domestic decorators, while couturiers such as Paul Poiret were inspired by the bird-of-paradise exoticism of the women's costumes of turban, loosely cut pantaloons and blouses adorned with ropes of pearls. Mayfair's 'pale pastel shades were replaced by a riot of barbaric hues – jade green, purple, every variety of crimson and scarlet, and above all, orange'[36] – a high style that filtered down so that 'soon there was not a middle-class home without its green and orange cushions on a black carpet',[37] and manufacturers adopted such colours for 'felt hats and cotton dresses and woollen sweaters'.[38] Beyond its purely visual impact, in the years before the First World War *Scheherazade* became a benchmark of taste among progressives and the bohemian young. Not to have thrilled to *Scheherazade* was to be outside the cultural loop.

The other new Fokine ballet was a much subtler affair, one for connoisseurs: danced to Schumann's music of the same title, with Biedermeier costumes designed by Bakst, *Carnaval* was a romantic frolic with bittersweet undercurrents, in which the traditional *commedia dell'arte* figures of Harlequin, Colombine, Pantalon and

Pierrot become role-players at a ball; real and feigned emotions, masks and disguises, hints and evasions, leave everything in a state of delicious ambiguity.

Despite the absence of star draws such as Pavlova and Chaliapin, this second season was a box-office success: given the decision not to import a Russian orchestra and the absence of opera's cash-voracious demands, the balance sheet lurched into the black. Relations with Astruc, whose address book and *savoir faire* remained so extremely useful, were patched up amicably. On this foundation, slender as it was, Diaghilev now felt empowered to up his game by forming his own year-round company, rather than engaging dancers from the Russian imperial theatres during their summer vacations when they were off contract and free to accept outside engagements.

There were obstacles. One problem was that his 'habit of success' in Europe caused toxic envy in Russia, and his high-handed and often manipulative behaviour did nothing to assuage it. The idea circulated that Diaghilev was more interested in lining his own pockets than in promoting the art of his homeland: whatever the dimensions of his ego, this was patently untrue, but it became the common prattle in St Petersburg, discouraging anyone from sponsoring him and confirming the official line that he wasn't to be trusted.

Another problem that was to dog him continually was the number of other impresarios jumping onto his bandwagon or offering his leading dancers bigger fees than he could afford. Two of his prime stars were now in a position to call their own shots. One was Pavlova, dancing garbage exquisitely and ubiquitously; the other was Ida Rubinstein, so wealthy that she could bankroll her own showcase and park it right on Diaghilev's pitch. Moving base to Paris, she commissioned Gabriele D'Annunzio to write her a 'mystery play' *Le Martyre de Saint Sébastien*, to be designed by Bakst and choreographed by Fokine with musical interludes composed by Debussy. Fortunately for Diaghilev, it would flop.

A deliciously farcical turn of events played into Diaghilev's hands. In January 1911, Nijinsky – still ranked as a relatively junior dancer in Russia – made his St Petersburg debut as Albrecht in *Giselle*, in the presence of the tsar's mother and other elderly duchesses, as well as several courtiers who had their knives out for Diaghilev. Nijinsky was always compulsively fussy about what he wore on stage and he insisted on wearing the same Renaissance-style costume, modelled on figures in the paintings of Carpaccio, that Benois had designed for him in Paris, consisting of a jerkin and tights. For some reason, he neglected that night to wear mitigating baggy trunks or a support strap, leaving the bulges of both his genitals and his buttocks exposed. Accounts of what followed vary, but it seems that the tsar's mother and her ladies were scandalised and a message was relayed backstage during the interval that unless decency was brought to bear, they would depart. Nijinsky, never one for a tactful compromise, refused and went on to dance the second act unencumbered.

The next morning he was fired from the Mariinsky for *lèse majesté*. On being told that an apology could see him reinstated, Nijinsky huffily announced that he considered himself to be the one requiring an apology, and that henceforth he considered himself to belong only to Diaghilev. The dismissal left him eligible for military service, so the upshot was that he would have to leave Russia for the foreseeable future to avoid it. Diaghilev was delighted by the ensuing furore in the press and telegraphed Astruc in Paris to spread the deliciously titillating story: 'Appalling scandal. Use publicity.' Other dancers with an eye to the main chance as well as artistic adventure followed Nijinsky and resigned, including his brilliantly talented sister Bronislava and the awesome Adolph Bolm. Diaghilev also mollified Fokine and Benois – neither of them a hundred per cent loyal to him – by giving them senior honorary positions in the year-round company to be known as 'Les Ballets Russes de Serge de Diaghilev'.

With a company of dancers picked up from various sources and drilled into unity by the revered Italian ballet teacher Enrico Cecchetti, Diaghilev set up a base in Monte Carlo that would serve for rehearsal and as a testing ground for new works. Debut engagements in Rome and London, as well as a return to Paris, were in the diary, and among the new works commissioned, two would prove of lasting significance, both of them choreographed by Fokine and focused on the genius of Nijinsky.

The first was *Le Spectre de la rose*, a nine-minute *pas de deux* based on a poem by Théophile Gautier and danced to the banal lilt of Weber's *Invitation to the Waltz*. Designed by Bakst in sweet-toothed Biedermeier style, thrown together in a hurry and to some extent improvised by the two dancers concerned, its premise could hardly have been simpler. A virginal girl (the exquisite Karsavina) returns home from her first ball and falls asleep in a chair, cherishing a rose handed to her by an admirer. Through an open window materialises the spirit and perfume of the rose – a projection of all her innocent fantasies, rousing the girl into a somnambulistic duet before it leaves her in a final upward parabola of a leap back through the window into the night. The girl wakes from her dream and kisses the rose.

In a cap, leotard and silk tights adorned with pink, red and purple petals, his face painted to resemble some exotic insect, Nijinsky evoked a creature less than human and neither male nor female: not until the rock-star provocations of Mick Jagger and David Bowie more than half a century later would an image of androgyny be so overtly and alluringly expressed.* Flitting and darting, his arms sensuously curved and sinuous, he danced as if entranced, before making that last supernatural ascent into the ether that became the essence of his legend. That jump was, of course, only a carefully rehearsed and calculated illusion, fostered by a false perspective in the scenery that exaggerated the impression of height. Its physical reality was a simple feat of muscular propulsion that left the dancer collapsed in the wings, panting with exhaustion like a winded boxer and attended by a backstage crew offering water and towels. But audiences witnessed it as a miracle, and demand became so relentless (over a hundred performances in 1911–12, according to Peter Lieven[39]) that Nijinsky became bored with it. Never, as Joan Acocella wrote, has 'so much artistic fame' been 'based on so little artistic evidence'.[40] Or, one might add, so little substance.

The other durable new work of 1911 was *Petrushka*, perhaps the finest achievement of the pre-First World War phase of the Ballets Russes. It was certainly typical of its simultaneously nationalistic and cosmopolitan outlook in being based in Russian folk culture and produced, created and performed by Russians, while being composed, choreographed, rehearsed and performed in Europe.

Its roots lay in the ongoing tensions between Diaghilev and Benois, the blame lying with six of one and half a dozen of the other: Diaghilev always genuinely wanted Benois on side, but he was often tactless in his manners and drawn towards new artistic territory of which the conservative Benois did not approve; the artist was quick to take offence and enjoyed licking his wounds. In an

---

* For a masked ball in St Petersburg, Nijinsky wore 'a lady's costume of the eighteenth century . . . with all the jewellery and laces . . . he looked as if he had walked out of a Watteau . . . nobody could have told that this charming masquerader was not really a girl' (Romola Nijinsky, *Nijinsky*, p. 60).

effort to repair their latest rift, Diaghilev asked Benois to devise and design a work for which music was being written by the composer of the moment, Igor Stravinsky. Benois sulked and hummed and hawed, but in the end could not resist a scenario (sketched out by Stravinsky and Diaghilev) that appealed so deeply to his memories of childhood in St Petersburg, where the rigours of winter had been enlivened by a colourful and bustling Butter Week frost fair.

*Petrushka*'s opening scene presented the fair on stage through a brilliantly detailed, action-packed tableau in which the corps de ballet became a crowd of imaginatively individualised people of all classes – coachmen and hawkers and drunks, elegantly promenading ladies, jolly nannies with prams, crisp army cadets, street dancers, mischievous children – milling about, laughing and jostling, buying and selling. Their attention is drawn to a booth in which a sinister conjuror presents a traditional puppet show. Here Petrushka is not the wife-beating Mr Punch of British seaside notoriety but something more like a melancholy Pierrot, mechanically dancing for the gawping public alongside an empty-headed ballerina doll and a brutish Moor (caricatured in a blackface manner that would now be deemed unacceptably racist). The second scene takes us backstage, where these painted-wood and straw-stuffed puppets, enslaved by the occult powers of the conjuror, assume a quasi-human life of their own. In his cell Petrushka pines after the ballerina, who has eyes only for the scheming Moor. Tragedy follows as the Moor murders Petrushka; a final arresting image shows Petrushka's ghost (was he, or was he not, only a puppet after all?) appearing above the booth and stretching his arms out in mute appeal before collapsing in a limp heap.

Preparations were fraught, especially because of Stravinsky's intense dislike of Fokine, who found the modernist irregularities of the score's rhythms as hard to master as the dancers did. Further complications included a terrible heatwave during rehearsals, and another fit of pique by Benois, at last given his big chance to shine but suffering from a painful abscess on his arm. Shortly before the ballet's première in Paris, his scenery arrived from St Petersburg. Some of it had been manhandled en route, and particular damage was caused to a portrait of the conjuror that hung menacingly in Petrushka's cell: the incapacitated Benois gratefully accepted Bakst's offer to repaint it.

But he melted with horror and rage when he saw that Bakst had completely altered his concept, showing the conjuror 'in profile, with his eyes looking sideways'. The explosion that followed was all too typical of the internal dramas that regularly rocked the Ballets Russes. In his memoirs, written a quarter of a century later, Benois gives a rueful account of his own behaviour that is worth quoting at length, even though it does not mention the anti-Semitic abuse that some witnesses insist that they heard him utter:

Had I been in good health, I would of course have tried to arrange it all in a friendly way; Bakst had probably no evil intentions at all and had only exhibited too much zeal. But I had come to the theatre with a temperature and unbearable pain, the atmosphere of the rehearsal was tense – in short, I considered the alteration of my portrait an unpardonable outrage . . . my fury expressed itself in a loud shout across the theatre, filled with a highly select audience: 'I shall not allow it! Take it down immediately! I can't bear it!' After which I flung my portfolio full of drawings on the floor and rushed out . . . My state of fury continued for two days . . . it was in vain that [Walter] Nouvel kept coming to explain that it had been a misunderstanding and that both Seriozha [Diaghilev] and Bakst were very sorry . . . I would not listen, nor give in . . . I sent in my resignation to Seriozha, giving up my post . . . I even began to threaten (without really meaning it) to take Bakst to court.[41]

Even though the offending portrait was replaced by the original, the bad blood would fester for over a year, and although things were eventually patched up, this was an episode that further alienated Benois from Diaghilev's inner circle.

Nor was it the last of *Petrushka*'s birth pangs. In another episode all too typical of the Ballets Russes and its hand-to-mouth finances, Diaghilev ran out of credit on the day of the première and the costumier refused to deliver his last batch until he had been paid. The story goes that only minutes before curtain up, Diaghilev rushed sweating into the box of his chief sponsor, Misia Edwards, and prostrated himself with a plea for the missing 4,000 francs. She duly sent her driver off to pay the importunate man.

Despite all this, it was worth it. *Petrushka* was an instant triumph – for Stravinsky and his marvellously animated and inventive score; for Fokine, who here most fully realised his principles of using dance as an authentically expressive instrument in a coherent wordless drama; and for Nijinsky, always at his most inspired when performing on the cusp of what is human, who excelled himself in suggesting a stiff or flopping doll uncomfortably burdened with a heart and a soul. (Later, some would interpret the figure of Petrushka as a reflection of Nijinsky's own troubled psyche; others would see the character more broadly as a symbol of the Russian Everyman oppressed by autocracy.) The sum of it was something felt to be unprecedented: as Georges Banks wrote in the modernist journal *Rhythm*, 'I have never seen anything which suggested sentiment, passion and the inevitable sequence of things, produced by movement and sound alone without consciousness of the elimination of dialogue as this production does.'[42]

———

The company now moved to London, where appreciation of dance was markedly less sophisticated than in Paris. Vain efforts had been made over the years to raise the tone: the proselytising insistence of a wonderfully eccentric parson called Stewart Headlam that dance was 'an outward sign of an inward and spiritual grace ordained by the Word of God' fell on deaf ears;[43] Isadora's diaphanous cavortings made some mark whenever her tours touched down; and the Canadian mime Maud Allan's 'artistic' discarding of Salome's Seven Veils caused a few months' sensation. But these were phenomena of only passing concern: what the market persistently wanted was colourful musical pantomime involving graceful poses and tee-totum spins and the titillating exposure of female flesh – cravings met by the larger West End variety theatres such as the Alhambra, the Empire, and the still extant Coliseum and Palace.

These institutions had long relied on solo ballerinas imported from Milan, but when this well dried up and other home-grown talents had moved on to richer pastures in the USA, luminaries of St Petersburg granted summer leave began to replace them. First to arrive in 1908 had been the exquisitely beautiful Lydia Kyasht, engaged for a month at the Empire. Her weekly fee might have been enticing – £150, compared with the £7 she would have earned in Russia (chanteuse Marie Lloyd, however, at the top of the bill, was on an astronomical £600) – but the drawbacks were considerable, not least the requirement to perform twice nightly. Kyasht soon ruefully came to realise that scant respect would be shown for her artistry. 'English people do not really understand ballet,' she later wrote in her memoirs. 'They imagine they do, but the truth is they like to come to a theatre and see a dancer kick her legs.'[44] Her regal manner on stage was sometimes met with derision – in the course of one of her more sublime numbers, a slave girl laid a bowl of fruit at her feet. ''Ave a banana!' shouted a wag from the gallery.

In Kyasht's wake came several of her colleagues and in the summer of 1910, West End audiences could take their pick between Pavlova at the Palace, Karsavina at the Coliseum (in a potted version of *Giselle*), Olga Preobrajenska at the Hippodrome (in *The Lake of Swans*) and Yekaterina Geltzer at the Alhambra. The critics pronounced them neat, dainty, graceful and effective: one may assume that audiences were pleasantly diverted. But they made no deeper impact than the Chinese conjuror, performing dogs and newsreels that flanked them, and Diaghilev knew that he would have to proceed with caution.[45]

Fortuitously he arrived in London in time to justify Virginia Woolf's celebrated gnomic remark that 'on or around December 1910, human character changed'.[46] What she meant by this has been much debated: she could have been playfully referring to a sense of liberation following the death of Queen Victoria's son Edward VII, to the suffragettes, to startling developments in travel by air and automobile, to polar exploration, or to her friend Roger Fry's exhibition of post-impressionism at the Grafton Gallery. Perhaps all, or perhaps none of those things: yet something was in the air, and what was initially billed as 'The Imperial Russian Ballet' deserves a place in this catalogue of change too.

The company had arrived after its spring season in Paris to serve as the centrepiece for a gala at Covent Garden marking the coronation of George V. It was a magnificent occasion, assembling the world's royalty in all its ceremonial pomp and glittering parures: '*élégance indescriptible*' read Diaghilev's telegram the next morning to Astruc. The press had primed the public that these productions were all the rage in Paris, and the critical and public reception was duly enthusiastic. But Diaghilev was playing it safe: sensing London's relatively uneducated taste, he programmed neither of Fokine's ground-breaking ballets to music by the 'difficult' modernist Stravinsky. Instead Karsavina and Nijinsky danced exquisitely in the romantic *Le Pavillon d'Armide* and *Carnaval*, and the evening concluded with the rousing *Polovtsian Dances*. *Les Sylphides*, *Cléopâtre* and *Scheherazade* followed the next week, by which time London was slavering. 'It was like discovering America, paradise rather,' recalled the otherwise dry-as-dust imperial civil servant Ralph Furse in his memoirs.[47] The tectonic plates had shifted and the cultural crust was seismically cracked. An anonymous commentator in the high-society magazine *Bystander* immediately noted that 'mere opera' had been put 'into quite suburban shade' by 'the apotheosis of the Body Beautiful which Puritanism and the Victorians banned and banished as not fit or, at any rate, not a quite nice food for the worship of a respectable middle-class nation'.[48] The *Daily News* concurred: 'Judging from the behaviour of the audience at Covent Garden, the Russian term for enthusiasts for the ballet, BALLETOMANIACS, will have to be incorporated into the language.'[49] (Indeed, the *Oxford English Dictionary* confirms the arrival of 'balletomane' in 1919.)

The groundwork was now laid. By the end of 1911, and brief seasons in Berlin, Rome and Monte Carlo, the Ballets Russes had become the fashionable talk of Europe and Diaghilev could name his terms. Having formed a tactical alliance with the previously antagonistic Mathilde Kschessinska, the ballerina who held the keys to the favour of the tsar's court, he also had high hopes of bringing the company home to St Petersburg with a triumph that would rout his enemies. But it was not to be: the theatre he had booked burned down and there were problems over Nijinsky's status following his dismissal.

So Diaghilev began to look elsewhere, and what had been the dream of showing the best of Russia to Europe became a more open commitment to risk and experiment that transcended nationalism.

Whether human nature changed or not 'around December 1910', it is surely significant that the *Oxford English Dictionary* records the first instance of the term 'avant garde' as occurring in that year. Until this point, the productions of the Ballets Russes had been carefully tailored to reflect trends rather than to innovate them – even the Stravinsky ballets were fundamentally exercises in nostalgic folklore. Now Diaghilev began to push the envelope, pursuing conversations and making commissions that would lead him to the forefront of modernism.

The basic sources for this chapter are Tamara Karsavina, *Theatre Street*, pp. 139–240; Romola Nijinsky, *Nijinsky*, pp. 32–99; Prince Peter Lieven, *The Birth of the Ballets Russes*, pp. 74–105; Alexandre Benois, *Memoirs*, vol. II, and *Reminiscences of the Russian Ballet*, passim; Michel Fokine, *Memoirs of a Ballet Master*, pp. 87–139; Natalia Roslaveva, *Era of the Russian Ballet*, pp. 167–89; Boris Kochno, *Diaghilev and the Ballets Russes*, pp. 5–55; Richard Buckle, *Diaghilev*, pp. 91–18; Arthur Gold and Robert Fizdale, *Misia: The Life of Misia Sert*, pp. 130–265; Richard Buckle, *Nijinsky*, pp. 7–161; Bronislava Nijinska, *Early Memories*, pp. 3–316; Lynn Garafola, *Diaghilev's Ballets Russes*, pp. 3–49 and 177–200; Malcolm McCormick and Nancy Reynolds, *No Fixed Points: Dance in the Twentieth Century*, pp. 33–76; Sjeng Scheijen, *Diaghilev: A Life*, pp. 111–205; Jennifer Homans, *Apollo's Angels*, pp. 245–89; Jane Pritchard (ed.), *Diaghilev and the Golden Age of the Ballets Russes 1909–1929*, pp. 15–70; and Lucy Moore, *Nijinsky*, pp. 1–52.

# 4

# TRIUMPHS

IT HAS BEEN REMARKED THAT HITHERTO IN THIS COUNTRY THE MASCULINE DANCER HAS ALWAYS LOOKED MORE OR LESS FOOLISH, AND GENERALLY TAKEN REFUGE IN FRANKLY ECCENTRIC CREATIONS. NIJINSKY, MORDKIN AND OTHERS HAVE SHOWN US THAT A MALE CAN BE MANLY THOUGH GRACEFUL. THIS DISCOVERY MAY HAVE FAR-REACHING RESULTS, AS DEPICTED ABOVE.

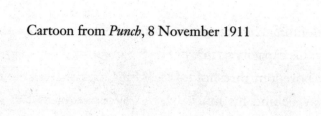

Cartoon from *Punch*, 8 November 1911

One defining characteristic of Diaghilev's personality, complementary to his capacity to make things happen and get things done, was a low boredom threshold. It was this almost irritable restlessness that lay behind his much-quoted exhortation to the young poet Jean Cocteau, a tiresome opportunist hanging on to the Ballets Russes's coat-tails in Paris as he angled to be given his big chance. '*Étonne-moi, Jean*,' Diaghilev challenged him, perhaps with a note of impatience. Buzz off until you can show me something fascinatingly different. Cocteau would certainly try.

By the beginning of 1912, London and Paris were conquered territory, and throughout that year the Ballets Russes would also lay siege to the Middle European cultural centres of Berlin, Vienna, Dresden and Budapest as well, with tours of the Americas on the horizon too.

But Diaghilev already felt that the product was stagnating. He was bored by the shenanigans of star dancers such as Pavlova, Kschessinska and Ida Rubinstein, who were either disloyal or greedy or narrowly self-interested, or all three. He was bored by attempts to resuscitate dainty white-tulle ballets such as *Giselle*, just as he was bored by Benois's nostalgic infatuation with the court of Versailles and Renaissance Italy. More problematically, he was also beginning to be bored by one of his greatest assets – the choreography of Michel Fokine, which had to date provided virtually all the company's original work.

95

Fokine's ballets for Diaghilev had been brilliantly varied in subject matter and atmosphere – from the folkloric *Petrushka* and *The Firebird* to the subtle salon perfume of *Carnaval* and the exoticism of *Scheherazade* – as well as offering showcases for the talents of Karsavina and Nijinsky. Yet his newer creations palled: the classically themed *Narcisse* proved insipid, while two orientalist fantasies, *Thamar* and *Le Dieu bleu* (based on a scenario that was Cocteau's first vain attempt to meet Diaghilev's demands for *étonnement*), contained nothing original or striking, despite Bakst's fabulous designs. Worse, Diaghilev insultingly short-changed Fokine's work on *Daphnis et Chloé* and the exquisite score that had been commissioned from Maurice Ravel; its rehearsal schedule was curtailed and the première postponed.

Now was the time to rewrite some of the rules – to turn on his paymasters by taking them out of themselves and showing them what they didn't know they wanted. His twenty-three-year-old lover Nijinsky would lead the charge. In him Diaghilev had detected, on nothing but a hunch, a genius that went beyond his capacity to incarnate other identities and leap like a big cat. Nijinsky danced to a different drummer as he inhabited his mysteriously unconventional view of the world. Could he be the choreographer to push ballet out of the realms of fairy story and lurid romance into uncharted aesthetic territory? In private, their relationship was becoming tetchy – Diaghilev twitchily jealous and possessive, Nijinsky uncommunicative and sexually reluctant – but over the next year they would be intensely engaged in a great adventure.

Much of the initial impetus for Nijinsky's first creative essay came directly from Diaghilev. It was he who selected Debussy's voluptuous tone-poem of 1894, *Prélude à l'après-midi d'un faune* (only ten minutes long, and therefore damage-limited) as the music he should use; it was he who introduced Nijinsky to the new philosophies of theatre proposed by Adolphe Appia and Edward Gordon Craig, with their focus on light and movement rather than fixed text and scenic realism; and it was he who led Nijinsky to Hellerau, a garden-city suburb of Dresden. Here, in a theatre modelled on Athenian lines, the Swiss guru Émile Jaques-Dalcroze taught eurhythmics, a form of dance not dissimilar to that practised by Isadora Duncan, based on an instinctive and improvisatory response to music.

But Nijinsky had own ideas. If these influences were absorbed, something quite different from them emerged from the maelstrom of his imagination. Articulating the intensity of his vision would be the problem. Never easy with words or social interaction, he seemed in rehearsals – of which there were something like a hundred – to have very precise ideas of what he wanted without being able to explain to the increasingly exasperated and exhausted dancers what they might be.

Certain aspects of the piece were not original: the idea of moving in profile with the palms of the hand held flat, evoking figures on Ancient Greek vases or friezes, was even something of a cliché (prevalent, for example, in a ballet by Fokine for Wagner's opera *Tannhäuser*, in which Nijinsky had himself appeared). Amorous fauns and shy nymphs in laced sandals weren't unfamiliar either.

What was unprecedented, however, was a ballet in which all the rules of classical elegance of line were entirely flouted. There were no graceful poses here, no curving of the arms or rolling of the neck, no pirouettes or *jetés*, indeed nothing that would commonly be called dancing. With their feet rocking flatly between heel and toe, the dancers seemed to jerk robotically rather than bend and stretch fluently. Conveying no emotion through their mime, they moved without any direct relation to the metre of the music, which provided an atmospheric background soundtrack rather than a series of beats that cued steps.

What also shocked was an eroticism far more perverse than anything in *Scheherazade*: played by Nijinsky himself costumed in a fig-leaf body-stocking designed by Bakst, the faun was presented as an amoral animal with pointed ears and stubby phallic tail lounging in a rocky landscape, indolently self-absorbed until his eye lands on nymphs in search of a bathe. As the one singled out as the object of his desire flees his unwelcome advances in fright, she drops her shawl. The faun picks it up and caresses it, before laying it on the ground, lowering himself on top of it and graphically arousing himself to orgasm. The overt representation of masturbation – with further phallic overtones suggested by the pipe on which the faun idly blows – was too much for the first-night audience to stomach, and the final ecstatic spasms were subsequently toned down.

Diaghilev positively wanted a scandal and, with the help of Astruc's address book, that is what he got. Tactics were carefully planned. Few dress rehearsals can ever have been packed with more A-list celebrities – Jean Cocteau, André Gide, Pierre Bonnard, Édouard Vuillard, Aristide Maillol, Hugo von Hofmannsthal and Max Reinhardt among them – invited in order to talk the ballet up in fashionable circles; and two days later, the audience for the première at the Châtelet would be graced with a glut of high society. Gratifyingly, they greeted Nijinsky's first ballet with wild cheers mixed with hissing catcalls and, as if to ratchet up the furore, Diaghilev appeared before the curtain to order an immediate repetition of the performance. Over the following days, the press divided, with the editor of *Le Figaro* leading the attack and deploring *L'Après-midi*'s obscenity, while an article in *Le Matin* signed (but not written) by the elderly Auguste Rodin took up the cudgels in its defence. In commercial terms, it all worked a treat: the theatre was soon sold out.

This electrifyingly strange work marks a watershed in the story of the Ballets Russes. Its sensational success left Fokine feeling old hat, and in the words of his friend Sergei Grigoriev, it became 'almost impossible to work with him'[1] – not least as the short-changed *Daphnis et Chloé*, on which he had sweated, opened ten days later only to be received without *éclat*. So when he flounced out in high dudgeon, many in the company, sick of his tantrums and para-noia, thought it good riddance. Ever afterwards, he would declare himself dismayed by what he regarded as the wrong direction on which Diaghilev had embarked, presenting himself as a conserva-tive reformist, upholding the canons of good taste and seasoned experience, in contrast to the greenhorns resorting to ephemeral, jejune gimmickry. But Fokine would live to have the last laugh: a clutch of his creations, the heart of the Ballets Russes's first wave of success, would remain box-office bread and butter throughout Diaghilev's life and sustain their popularity worldwide for a further generation. Nijinsky's work survived only in fading memories and passed into legend. A century on, it is a moot point which of them has left the greater legacy.

Henceforth, the Ballets Russes would divide opinion, in a man-ner that has remained typical of audience response to high culture. A majority continued to crave ballets like Fokine's, offering an essentially nineteenth-century approach to narrative coherence, characterisation and the demarcation between fantasy and realism, as well as adherence to a concept of bodily beauty dating back to the Renaissance, whereas a minority responded to work that stretched the rules to breaking point and sought new forms that subverted or inverted tradition. Majority and minority would coincide in their enthusiasm only rarely.

*L'Après-midi d'un faune* also represents a decisive shift west. Such a ballet could never have been presented in prim St Petersburg. 'We'd be hauled off at once to the . . . lunatic asylum, or sent to Siberia for hooliganism,' Diaghilev admitted.[2] As the political situation in Russia continued to degenerate, he began to consider emigrating permanently. Among his ambitions had been returning in triumph with his Fokine repertory to cock a snook at the court establishment that had thwarted him – but now it faded.

Diaghilev signed up the modernists. An attempt to bag Arnold Schoenberg in the wake of his atonal expressionist monodrama *Pierrot lunaire* came to nothing, but thanks to the mediation of the well-connected Count Harry Kessler, Richard Strauss, supreme on the European musical scene after his operatic hat-trick of *Salome*, *Elektra* and *Der Rosenkavalier*, was commissioned to write a score on the biblical theme of Joseph and Potiphar's wife – to a scenario Kessler co-devised with Hugo von Hofmannsthal.

Meanwhile two ground-breaking works by Debussy and Stravinsky were germinating for the 1913 season. Debussy's *Jeux* ('Games', or perhaps 'Playtime') seems to have been based on an idea concocted jointly by Diaghilev and Nijinsky, possibly inspired by a tennis party witnessed by Nijinsky while visiting Lady Ottoline Morrell in the gardens of Bloomsbury's Bedford Square. ('*Aimez-vous Platon?*' the gushingly earnest Lady Ottoline had asked a bewildered Nijinsky.[3]) Bakst's setting showed a glade adjoining a tennis court in moonlight; the date was specified in the programme as 1920. A ball was thrown on to the stage (not a tennis ball, oddly, but something more like a football), and two women and a man (Nijinsky himself) chase it. Dressed in sporty white flannels and wielding racquets, their arms rotating as if for a serve or a golf swing, they flirted and bickered in an unmotivated, undeveloped, understated sexual rivalry. Thoughts of leaving the genders of the three dancers indistinguishable, with Nijinsky dancing like the women on pointe, and of bringing the action to a climax with a cardboard Zeppelin airship crashing apocalyptically to the ground, were abandoned; instead all three performers moved neither on the ball of their foot nor on pointe but awkwardly in between – and the close appears to have been marked only by an open-ended suggestion of a *ménage à trois*, with 'each girl resting her head on the young man's shoulder', according to Cyril Beaumont.[4]

To Paris and London audiences in 1913 *Jeux* was a cryptic puzzle that bemused rather than scandalised, and it vanished after a handful of performances. Debussy's slippery seventeen-minute score had no discernible shape or logic – the music simply flowed on through constant subtle changes of tempo without repeating or reinforcing itself melodically. As for the choreography, not even the dancers involved had a clear sense of what Nijinsky intended – 'He was at a loss to explain what he wanted of me,' Karsavina recalled[5] – and rehearsals were bad-tempered. Debussy disapproved of the way his music was interpreted; paid-up fans such as Kessler thought it 'more or less a failure, and boring',[6] and the Fokine camp heartily concurred – Lieven, for instance, saw it as 'mere stupidity, completely devoid either of common sense or of artistic value'.[7] Posterity has remained ambivalently curious.

In the incoherent journal that he scribbled during his mental breakdown in 1919, Nijinsky tantalisingly revealed that '*Jeux* is the kind of life Diaghilev dreamt of . . . Diaghilev wanted to make love to two boys at the same time and wanted those boys to make love to him. The two boys are two young girls, and Diaghilev is the young man. I camouflaged these personalities on purpose.'[8] Allowing for Nijinsky's unreliable state of mind, this sounds plausible enough. But more significant than any erotic subtext is the fact that *Jeux* represents the first tentative attempt by the Ballets

Russes – by ballet, indeed – to draw on the material of ordinary contemporary life and the fluidity of gender and identity. As such, it proposed ideas that became a preoccupation of modern dance half a century later.

*Jeux* suffered from a shortage of rehearsal – it seems that its final minutes were never quite finished – as Nijinsky had simultaneously been working flat out for months on a larger project, wedded to a madly ambitious new score that Stravinsky had been gestating since 1910. Sketched out at Princess Tenisheva's artists' colony at Talashkino, but written largely at an upright piano in the composer's apartment overlooking Lake Geneva, *The Rite of Spring* (*Le Sacre du printemps*) emerged as a thirty-five-minute ballet in two scenes.[9] It had been conceived in collaboration with the polymathic painter, mystic philosopher and amateur archaeologist Nicholas Roerich, who had conducted ethnographic research into the 'barbaric' Scythian cultures of the steppes. Out of his findings he developed a scenario focused on an imagined pagan ceremony, during which a patriarchal tribe celebrates the earth's renewed fertility, culminating in the blood sacrifice of a female virgin.

*The Rite of Spring* had originally been pencilled in for Fokine to choreograph, but he had stomped out of the Ballets Russes and in any case Stravinsky had come to detest him as 'easily the most disagreeable man I have ever worked with'.[10] Tentatively, Diaghilev handed the enormous challenge to Nijinsky. To help him communicate more clearly with the dancers and navigate his way through the unprecedented complexities of the epic score, Diaghilev hired a vivacious young teacher trained in Dalcroze's eurhythmics. She was Cyvia Rambam: like Nijinsky, her mother tongue was Polish, and with her name softened to Miriam Ramberg and then to Marie Rambert, she later became a formative figure in the history of British dance.[11]

Between December 1912 and May 1913, including six solid weeks at the Aldwych Theatre in London, there were at least 130 rehearsals, all of them fraught. Scored for a vast orchestra, often violently dissonant and strident, the music had a hammering intensity like nothing that anyone had heard before. In the studio, bashed out on a piano, its syncopations, polyrhythms and irregular time signatures were incomprehensible and it hardly helped when Stravinsky came in to play the music himself, banging his feet and fists as he shouted out the counts and pushed the music faster than the dancers could humanly keep pace with. Rambert attempted to keep calm and order, as the flummoxed dancers desperately tried to adjust to the constant chopping and changing. Several naive young English women had just joined the company: one of them was a seventeen-year-old from Essex, born Hilda Munnings – an unprepossessing name unconvincingly Russianised in the cast list as Muningsova before being more flatteringly reinvented as Lydia Sokolova (after the surname of a famous Russian ballerina of the 1880s). Her memoirs offer one of the most reliable insider accounts of the Ballets Russes; she remembered girls during rehearsals 'running round with little bits of paper in their hands, in a panic, quarrelling with each other about whose count was right and whose wrong'.[12]

What made it all the more difficult was Nijinsky's insistence on absolute precision throughout the movement: despite his meltdowns, Fokine had always allowed leeway to individual personality and interpretation, whereas Nijinsky was the military martinet without the necessary ability to explain his commands to the troops. For them, the experience must have been hellish: complementing the backcloths of what Beaumont called 'dreary, half savage, half mystical landscapes',[13] Roerich had designed 'authentic' peasant costumes that made no concessions to balletic prettiness or practicality: the long thick wigs, false beards and smocked blouses in coarse flannel embroidered with arcane symbols were all cruelly uncomfortable and sweatily hot as well as plain hideous. Rambert described Nijinsky's principles: 'Feet very turned in, knees slightly bent, arms held in reverse of the classical position, a primitive, prehistoric posture. The steps were very simple: walking smoothly or stamping, jumps mostly off both feet, landing heavily.'[14] With their heads jerkily cocked to one side and their faces paint-smeared, the dancers were being asked to jettison all their academic training, all their sense of hierarchy and defined gender, for something without narrative or decorum requiring both relentless concentration and fearless abandon.

As with *Faune*, Diaghilev anticipated and to some extent fuelled a scandal by issuing an inflammatory press release that promised 'truly a new sensation which will undoubtedly provoke heated discussion'. It certainly did that: there are said to survive more than a hundred accounts of the furore that the opening performance in May 1913 duly caused. They are wildly at variance and even downright contradictory. Some, it should be said, scarcely dwell on the hubbub: the catcalling and hissing of ground-breaking works was, after all, a fairly commonplace response in Parisian theatres – *L'Après-midi d'un faune* had been given a rough ride only months previously, victim of a dishonourable tradition, often led by idle young blades the worse for alcohol, dating back to Victor Hugo's *Hernani* in 1830 (too left wing, too freewheeling), and including Wagner's *Tannhäuser* in 1861 (no ballet girls in the second act) and Ibsen's *The Wild Duck* in 1891 (greeted with an outbreak of quacking).

Modernist tendencies became an obvious target for pretentious devotees as well as cynical hooligans. At the Théâtre des Champs-Elysées, the audience – toxically composed, as Cocteau noted, of the 'thousand varieties of snobbism, super-snobbism, anti-snobbism'

– presumably came from the same demographic as the folk satirised by Proust in Madame Verdurin's salon or those who had rolled up to the opening of the Italian futurist exhibition a few months previously in 'elegant automobiles, limousines and convertibles . . . to sneer and snicker'.[15] Harry Kessler, one of the few to write in the immediate aftermath of *The Rite*'s première, left what seems an objective report on the audience's behaviour in his diary: 'The public, the most elegant house I have ever seen in Paris . . . was from the beginning restless, laughing, whistling, making jokes.' As volleys of insults and witticisms were lobbed between factions, 'the commotion became general . . . above this crazy din there continued the storm of salvos of laughter and scornful clapping while the music raged and on the stage the dancers, without flinching, danced fervently in a prehistoric fashion.'[16]

Other sources claim that fights broke out and that the police were called in, but there is no solid evidence of this, and one can assume that most of whatever occurred in the auditorium was silly and factitious: as Cocteau cynically put it, 'The audience played the role it had to play.'[17] But the performance was far from a fiasco. 'At the end,' Kessler writes, 'the monde and demimonde went at it until a frenetic applause triumphed so that Stravinsky and Nijinsky had to come on stage and take repeated bows.'[18]

Amid the carnival of mockery that night, some members of the audience were more deeply stirred. Those who watched and listened without prejudice felt a raw nerve being inflamed, as the American Carl van Vechten witnessed:

> A young man occupied the place behind me. He stood up during the course of the ballet to enable himself to see more clearly. The intense excitement under which he was laboring, thanks to the potent force of the music, betrayed itself presently when

he began to beat rhythmically on the top of my head with his fists. My emotion was so great that I did not feel the blows for some time. They were perfectly synchronized with the beat of the music.

This was not merely playful. 'We had both been carried beyond ourselves,' van Vechten concludes.[19]

On the other side of the footlights, it felt dangerously hairy, as the wretched dancers struggled to keep rank and time. Such was the grimness of their facial expressions that wags in the stalls called for doctors and dentists. Lydia Sokolova remembered that

shouting and whistling in the audience began almost as soon as the music, and by the time the curtain went up we were pretty scared. Grigoriev [the ballet master] wrote in his book that . . . 'the dancers . . . were quite unmoved and even amused by this unprecedented commotion'. I can only say that I, for one, was not amused at all.[20]

In the pit, the conductor Pierre Monteux persevered, in Stravinsky's words, 'impervious and apparently nerveless as a crocodile'; in the wings stood Nijinsky, shouting out the complex counts through the fracas (in vain: Stravinsky pointed out that as 'Russian numbers above ten are polysyllabic . . . in fast-tempo movements, neither he nor they could keep pace with the music'[21]). Somehow they kept going without breaking down – and when it was all over, Nijinsky went on to soothe the audience's ruffled feathers with the gentler fantasy of *Le Spectre de la rose*.

'Exactly what I wanted,' Diaghilev commented insouciantly on the hoo-ha, as he led a group of intimates out to dine. Kessler then records that

Diaghilev, Nijinsky, Bakst, Cocteau and I took a taxi and went off on a wild ride through the virtually deserted, moonlit streets of Paris – Bakst with a handkerchief tied to his walking stick, which he waved like a flag, Cocteau and I perched on the roof of the cab, Nijinsky in a dress coat and top hat, quietly contented, smiling to himself.[22]

Cocteau remembered it slightly differently – a drive in silence as far as the Bois de Boulogne, where Diaghilev suddenly began reciting Pushkin and wept, overcome with nostalgia for mother Russia.[23]

What was it about *The Rite of Spring* that so aggravated? An element of the revulsion was rooted in matters extraneous to the ballet itself. The location, for one thing: Diaghilev's favoured Parisian agent Gabriel Astruc paid the Ballets Russes double their usual fee to leave the familiar territory of the Opéra and the Théâtre du Châtelet and instead lend their *éclat* to the Théâtre des Champs-Elysées, the new building he had commissioned on the Avenue Montaigne. This fashionable address put it at a striking distance from the rest of Parisian theatreland, and its architecture, both internal and external, was also unconventional. Constructed in reinforced concrete clad in white marble, its sharply rectangular façade was decorated with nothing but a bas-relief frieze just below the protruding roof. Nowadays it is ranked as a trailblazer for the art deco style, but its austerity was initially found disconcerting.

Although it was designed largely by a Frenchman, Auguste Perret, diehard cultural nationalists considered it suspiciously Teutonic in character: there was a hint of Wagner's Bayreuth in the design of the auditorium, and its more egalitarian hierarchy of seating and sight lines, with *tout confort* at every level. Those of the same right-wing tendency were unabashedly anti-Semitic and therefore sniffy about all Astruc's enterprises: they regarded the vogue for the

Ballets Russes's Slavic primitivism as an affront to the dignity of the French patrimony. All this raised the temperature, as did the violent contrast between *The Rite of Spring*'s scorching aggression and the familiar Gallic romanticism of *Les Sylphides*, which opened the evening's programme.

The critic of *Le Temps*, Pierre Lalo, stated the prosecution's case most forcefully. Of the choreography he wrote, 'Not one line, not one movement of one person offers the appearance of grace, of elegance, of lightness or nobility of expression – everything is ugly – heavily, flatly, uniformly ugly . . . the dancers . . . shake their arms as if they were stumps and their legs as if they were made of wood. They never dance, all they do is jump, paw the ground, stamp and shake convulsively.' Of the score he added, 'the most dissonant music and discordant music yet composed. Never has the cult and practice of the wrong-note technique been practised with such industry, such zeal, or such determination.'[24] The defence came from the likes of Harry Kessler, who sensed a harbinger of a modernism that was making a bonfire of traditions and pieties – 'a thoroughly new vision, something never before seen, enthralling, persuasive . . . a new kind of wildness, both un-art and art at the same time: all forms laid waste and new ones emerging suddenly from the chaos'.[25] Or, as W. B. Yeats put it a few years later when writing about the political chaos of the Irish rebellion: '. . . changed, changed utterly, / A terrible beauty is born'.[26]

Subsequent critics and historians have compared the aesthetic significance of *The Rite of Spring* to the cubism that emerged in Picasso's *Les Demoiselles d'Avignon* (a painting that nobody outside the artist's studio saw until 1916). Lucy Moore, Nijinsky's most recent biographer, sees the ballet as presenting 'the distant past' as 'a metaphor for the tragedy of modern existence'.[27] Some have heard in the thunderous pounding of the music a pre-echo of the bombardments of the western front, only two years in the future; others have seen a foretaste of Soviet collectivism in the focus on a stampede of peasants, moving in without mercy or individuality to fulfil the scapegoat sacrifice of the Chosen Virgin whose self-immolating solo brought the action to its climax.

This may be valid in a longer perspective, but it should be added that while *The Rite of Spring* doubtless caused a sharp initial explosion, the shock it provoked swiftly subsided: further performances in Paris passed without incident, and by the time the ballet moved to London for three performances a few weeks later, the sensation had been downgraded to the status of a curiosity. Before the curtain rose at Drury Lane, the sympathetic critic Edwin Evans gave a brief explanatory talk, as though to render what followed more palatable. The reception was mixed – 'The ayes having it for the most part,' noted the *Standard* – and while some hostile critics trotted out adjectives such as 'ugly' and 'cacophonous', others were respectful: 'I found it very interesting,' *The Lady* admitted primly, while the *Daily Telegraph* found 'much to admire' and *The Times* noted, 'The third and last performance was received with scarcely a sign of opposition . . . London audiences have settled down comfortably to a new development of the ballet after a comparatively short acquaintance with it.'[28] There were also some for whom, like the young man banging his fist on Carl van Vechten's head, it became a defining phenomenon: the young actress Sybil Thorndike told a friend that if her fiancé Lewis Casson 'doesn't go for this, it's the end for us. It's too important to disagree about.'[29] (They didn't.)

Nijinsky then gave an interview to the *Daily Mail* – presumably through an imaginative interpreter and certainly very oddly fluent for someone so inarticulate. 'I cordially say thanks and "bravo!" to the English public for their serious interest and attention in

The *Festival* [sic] *of Spring*,' he says. 'There was no ridicule of the ballet on Friday and there was great applause.' Addressing the criticism that his work lacked grace and charm, he retorted, 'I could compose graceful ballets of my own if I wanted to – by the score. The fact is, I detest conventional "nightingale and rose" poetry; my own inclinations are primitive. I eat my meat without *sauce Béarnaise*.'[30]

And that, after a total of only ten performances, was the end of the theatrical existence of Nijinsky's *The Rite of Spring*. It's an irony that something so vastly and lastingly influential should have survived less than two months. Of course, Stravinsky's score would go on to become a cornerstone of the orchestral repertory and many other choreographers would reinterpret it (including Millicent Hodson's and Kenneth Archer's attempt to reconstruct Nijinsky's original from fragments of evidence). But in June 1913, with money tighter than ever, Diaghilev felt that he had stretched the audience's open-mindedness to its limit, and theatre managers concurred. The time was ripe to pull back, pause and consolidate. Which raised the awkward question of Nijinsky's future.

A crisis in their personal relationship – demonstrating an all-too familiar dynamic between older and younger men romantically involved – would precipitate an answer. Not naturally homosexual, bored and fractious and satisfying himself on the side with Parisian whores, Nijinsky began to lock the door between his and Diaghilev's adjoining hotel rooms. The hostility wasn't kept private either: in society, Nijinsky often behaved like a spoilt brat, openly contemptuous of his patron: '*Histoire longue mais pauvre*,' he drawled at a Parisian dinner table, while Diaghilev was recounting some interminable anecdote. Although infatuated and uncomfortably conscious of Nijinsky's growing disaffection, Diaghilev was also irritated by his egocentric flouncing and sulking.* It can't have helped that to keep him dangling, Diaghilev never treated his protégé as an adult by putting him on a salary with a contract – instead he doled out infantilising pocket money, paid all his expenses and showered him with gifts of unwanted jewellery and the latest gizmos.

What complicated the situation further was that even if audiences regarded Nijinsky's own creations with suspicion, as a dancer in Fokine's works he remained Diaghilev's biggest box-office asset. But Nijinsky and Fokine were at daggers drawn, with Fokine enraged that Diaghilev had allowed Nijinsky to take on *The Rite of Spring* – something that Fokine (with some justification, given nods and hints made after his success with *The Firebird* and *Petrushka*) felt was his by right.

In August 1913, following its fifth London season, the company embarked on its first tour of South America. Because of his neurotic aversion to leaving dry land and a burdensome workload pulling together the programme for 1914, Diaghilev remained in Europe and delegated his financial overseer Baron Günzburg to supervise the operation. This was a bad move with consequences he could not have anticipated. On board the ship was a danseuse without discernible talent called Romola de Pulszky. The wealthy and educated daughter of a celebrated Hungarian actress, she had for some months been stalking Nijinsky, bluffing her way into the back row of the corps de ballet, lingering in the foyers of hotels in which he was staying and feigning a fancy for another dancer, Adolph Bolm,

---

* John Singer Sargent failed in his attempt to paint Nijinsky's portrait. As the Earl of Crawford recorded in his diary, 'The man refused to sit and spent forty minutes blubbing like a child. Sargent was much puzzled at the cause for this demonstration, and ultimately discovered that Nijinsky was bewailing the loss of his pearl necklace.' (David Lindsay, *The Crawford Papers*, p. 304.)

as a smokescreen for her obsession. A three-week Atlantic crossing offered her a golden opportunity to home in on her prey. Nobody thought it was love that motivated her: 'She was so avaricious, she just pounced,' thought Lydia Sokolova, who observed the whole charade.[31]

Booking herself into a first-class cabin near Nijinsky's, she 'accidentally' bumped into him in corridors, on deck and at mealtimes. She befriended his masseur and Marie Rambert, grilling them for inside information. It seems that she was told of the nature of Nijinsky's relationship with Diaghilev, and remained undeterred. One afternoon she slipped into a room in which he was working out ideas to some music by Bach for his next ballet. Although he had asked to be left alone, he allowed her to stay and watch.

Eventually they were formally introduced and held an innocuous conversation in halting French. For a few days subsequently they had only fleeting encounters, until one day Günzburg summoned Romola out of lunch. Expecting to be sacked on account of her inadequate dancing, she was astonished to be told instead that Nijinsky had deputed Günzburg to bring her an offer of marriage. Believing this to be some sort of trick to humiliate her, she rushed to her cabin in a flood of tears.

That evening, according to Romola's (possibly fantasised) version of events, Günzburg sent a note informing her that Nijinsky could wait no longer for an answer. When she emerged from her cabin, there stood Nijinsky pointing at his ring finger: '*Mademoiselle, voulez-vous, vous et moi?*' Yes, she did, and they were married when the ship docked in Buenos Aires. Sokolova described the wedding as 'rather dreary', and nobody who attended the reception considered the marriage a good idea at any level. It was certainly an odd affair: for several weeks, the couple did not sleep together, Nijinsky treating his bride with courtly politesse, and any conversation was severely limited by language barriers. The reason for Günzburg's complicity – his apparent support for something he should have deplored and prevented – has never been satisfactorily explained.

A telegram was sent to Diaghilev. The shock sent him hysterical with rage and grief in high Russian style: however conflicted his feelings had lately become, he was a man of an upper class that held that the lowly born Nijinsky was not only his artistic creation but also his personal property. Losing fealty to a nonentity of a girl whose existence he had barely registered was a terrible blow to his *amour propre*. Revenge had to be taken. The commissions to choreograph were rescinded, and Diaghilev reopened negotiations with Fokine. Grigoriev the ballet master was present as these took place.

> 'But you're on the worst possible terms with him.'
>
> 'What does that matter?' said Diaghilev . . . 'Let's ring him up and see what he says' – on which he went to the telephone and, wiping the receiver with his handkerchief as was his habit, obtained the number . . . There was a to me ominous pause before a conversation started. It lasted no less than five hours . . . As he replaced the receiver, Diaghilev heaved a sigh of relief. 'Well, that's settled, I think,' he said. 'He was a tough nut to crack, though, all the same!'[32]

Fokine had driven a hard bargain that excluded the works of his rival Nijinsky from the repertory and won the rights to choreograph the prestigious score forthcoming from Richard Strauss. In the absence of any legally binding terms of employment, Nijinsky's position was now uncertain. A return to Russia ran the risk of exposing him to a call-up for military service and, in any case, his earning power lay in Europe. He seems to have assumed (or decided to assume) that Diaghilev would be happy about his marriage, because after the company returned to Europe, he sent Diaghilev, then in St Petersburg, a telegram asking when and where he should report for rehearsal. Grigoriev was deputed to send a terse response: 'Your services are no longer required' – the pretext being his grave offence, while perfectly fit, of capriciously refusing to dance one night in Rio.

In a spirit of what could have been either pure disingenuous bafflement or transparent bluff, Nijinsky then attempted to find out what was going on by writing Stravinsky a letter that leaves it unclear whether he understood the reasons for Diaghilev's antipathy, and whether he wanted reconciliation or a clean break.

> I do not believe that Serge can act so meanly to me. Serge owes me a lot of money. I have received nothing for two years, neither for my dancing nor for my staging *Faune*, *Jeux*, and *Sacre du Printemps*. I worked for the Ballet without a contract. If it is true that Serge does not want me – then I have lost everything . . . in all the newspapers . . . they also say I am gathering a company of my own. In truth, I am receiving propositions from every side, and the biggest of these comes from a very rich businessman, who offers one million francs to organise a new Diaghilev Russian Ballet – they wish me to have sole artistic direction and large sums of money to commission decors, music, etc. . . . But I won't give them a definite answer before I have news from you.[33]

Nothing doing, so early in 1914 Nijinsky accepted an offer from the impresario Alfred Butt for an eight-week season at the Palace Theatre looming over Cambridge Circus in London. Built by Richard D'Oyly Carte, the impresario responsible for many of Gilbert and Sullivan's operas, the theatre offered one of the West End's

larger and better-equipped stages, in recent decades home to spectacular musicals such as *Jesus Christ Superstar* and *Les Misérables*.
Yet although Pavlova had regularly danced at the top of the bill
here since 1910, someone of Nijinsky's passionate high-minded
perfectionism would have felt a certain loss of face involved in the
engagement. The Palace was not a majestic opera house of the
sort he was accustomed to command; instead it presented vulgar
variety shows, in which ballet would constitute only one item on
the evening's menu. During his itinerant childhood, Nijinsky had
done little turns alongside his parents in seedier music-hall versions of the Palace, and he had recently given newspaper interviews
expressing abhorrence of them.* Now he was reduced to a slot
between 10.05 p.m. and 10.50 p.m., after a female impersonator
and a Serbo-Croat folk-singer and before a 'Viennese trio' and a
newsreel. Why he accepted Butt's offer is unclear, especially as he
would be required to perform some of the Fokine repertory that
bored him. Still, the fee was a handsome £1,000 a week – well over
£100,000 in today's money – and he knew that London audiences
adored him.

Very soon, however, both parties came to regret their agreement.
Nijinsky was incapable of organising the season on his own. Hir-
ing supporting dancers, commissioning designs, dealing with Butt
and the paperwork – all this was beyond him, not least as time to
rehearse was very short. To assist him he turned to his brilliant
and formidable sister Bronislava, known as Bronia, less than two
years his junior and perhaps the person who understood him better
than anyone. Severely plain yet magnetically compelling, she could
have been his muse: as a junior dancer in Diaghilev's company, she

---

* He was, however, a huge admirer of the London music-hall star Little
Tich, a dwarf who danced on shoes with 70 cm soles.

had created one of the nymphs in *L'Après-midi d'un faune* and until pregnancy disqualified her he had wanted her for the role of the sacrificial maiden in *The Rite of Spring*. Meanwhile she acted as his spokesman. Not short of courage, she had attempted to mediate with Diaghilev when the rift erupted, and even raised the delicate matter of the three years' back salary that Nijinsky believed he was rightly owed. This cut no ice: considering the boy to have been his indentured serf, whose expenses had been readily met and whose caprices lavishly indulged, Diaghilev was unmoved, and indeed unable to pay.

So Nijinska abandoned her contract with the Ballets Russes, much to Diaghilev's displeasure, and joined her brother's London enterprise as principal ballerina and supervisor. What she walked into was chaos. Bakst had refused to provide sets or costumes; Romola, now pregnant, hovered around, under-occupied and irritating everyone; Fokine's choreography for *Les Sylphides* and *Le Spectre de la rose* needed adapting to avoid copyright disputes; and the cramped dimensions of the stage made it impossible for Nijinsky to dance at his magical best.

On the first night Bronia spotted – or imagined she spotted – Diaghilev sprawling nonchalantly in the front row of the stalls with a sardonic smile playing on his lips. Was he there to jinx the event? If so, nobody else noticed his presence. The reception was polite and the reviews enthusiastic, but like some great opera star singing Wagner on a prime-time television show, the combination of Palace Theatre variety and the sublime Nijinsky was not a good fit. A blue-collar audience hoping for fun and games was baffled and, as the box-office receipts began to taper off, Butt had the temerity to suggest that Nijinsky insert some 'authentically Russian' item into the programme to spice things up a bit. Nijinsky was enraged by this presumption, as he was enraged by a back-handed first-night good-luck message from Pavlova, enraged by the fire officer's non-flammable varnish staining the scenery, enraged by the stagehand who made a pass at Romola, enraged at the way that the house lights were turned up between items, enraged by Nijinska's husband spitting at him, and enraged by the smallest details falling minutely out of place. At one point the house manager had to throw a jug of water over him to quell a dressing-room tantrum, and after two weeks, having worked sixteen-hour days, he collapsed with a high fever. Because he then missed three consecutive performances, the contract with Butt became null and void and the remainder of the season was summarily cancelled. Nijinska returned to Russia and Nijinsky was left with the heavy financial liability of paying off his troupe of supporting dancers. He never danced in London again, and the failure of the season left a deep psychic wound.

While all this farce was unfolding, Diaghilev had been back in Russia, patching things up with his querulous old friend Benois. Together they hatched a new sort of experiment just as radical in its way as anything that Nijinsky had attempted. From Paris and London had come calls to complement the ballet with more Russian opera – calls that Diaghilev, whose love of opera preceded (and perhaps covertly exceeded) his love of ballet, was only too keen to answer. To counter the eternal problem of singers' inability to act (Chaliapin aside), he and Benois concocted the original idea of keeping the singers confined to the sides of the stage while the plot was played out by silent dancers in front of them. This might not have been practical for *Le nozze di Figaro* or *La bohème*, but it was an approach aptly suited to two fantasy operas: *Le Rossignol* ('The Nightingale'), a new work by Stravinsky based on a Hans Christian Andersen fairy tale, and *Le Coq d'or* ('The Golden Cockerel'), Rimsky-Korsakov's swansong, a whimsical satire on autocracy first performed conventionally in Moscow in 1909, just months after the composer's death.

Being occupied with *Le Rossignol*, Benois was reluctantly obliged to surrender the larger project of designing the extravaganza of *Le Coq d'or*. That commission passed not to Bakst, as might have been expected (he was temporarily out of Diaghilev's favour), but to Natalia Goncharova, a quiet young woman of noble birth living unmarried in Moscow with another painter, Mikhail Larionov. This earnest bohemian couple represented the furthest reach of the Russian avant-garde, and it is greatly to the credit of the naturally conservative Benois that he recognised their talent and drew Diaghilev's attention to it. Fokine, who was choreographing *Le Coq d'or*, was initially sceptical of her as one of the 'futurists' who 'organised violent lectures on "new art" and "the art of the future"'.[34] But once he visited her studio even he was impressed by her flair and seriousness: yes, she and Larionov were interested in cubism and abstraction and practised a crude form of performance art, which involved painting on to their own flesh and shouting in the street, but as her hugely successful exhibition in a fashionable Moscow gallery had amply demonstrated, her lively sense of colour and graphic vitality were radiant. Diaghilev signed her up and with Karsavina dancing gloriously barefoot as the Queen of Shemakha ('perhaps the most wonderful part I ever had', she remembered[35]), the result was that *Le Coq d'or* enjoyed a huge popular success in Paris and London – a return to the folkloric idiom of *The Firebird*, given fresh edge and vibrancy by Goncharova's modernism – that restored company morale after the Nijinsky debacle and gave Diaghilev fresh confidence in his pursuit of the new. That this version was never performed again was due largely to Rimsky-Korsakov's widow and her excessive demands for royalties.

The big disappointment of the 1914 season – in which Russian opera and the charisma of Chaliapin created more *réclame* than the ballet – was the long-gestated *La Légende de Joseph*, for which expectations ran sky high. But although Richard Strauss was a masterly opera composer, he proved incapable of writing a good ballet score – 'Too turgid, too scientifically constructed, too reminiscent of a difficult exercise in harmony,' thought Cyril Beaumont,[36] while the lavish scenery and costumes, a riot of every shade of gold, overwhelmed both the dance and a plot hampered by Harry Kessler's pretentious scenario. The aesthete Charles Ricketts found the kitsch of the ballet's climax comically abominable:

> The music becomes vulgar beyond belief, a light breaks upon Joseph, the chains fall off, and a golden archangel passes across the upper stage, descends and leads Joseph off to the Savoy Hotel – I believe – to a sort of parody of Wagnerian apotheosis music of the worst type. If the Russians had not been the inspired interpreters of the thing, it would have been intolerable and fatuous.[37]

What interest there was focused on a newcomer, Leonid Myasin, a touchingly fragile figure in the title role envisaged originally for Nijinsky. Wearing only a slip of a white lambskin tunic, in striking contrast to the decadent splendours that surrounded him, he was a near-naked object of both lust and pity as he resisted the wiles of Potiphar's lascivious wife. Any impression his huge black eyes gave of vulnerable innocence was misleading, however: Myasin was an electrically intelligent, fiercely ambitious Russian youth of seventeen, a cool customer who knew the price of everything and would stop at little to get what he wanted. Ballet was not his primary passion: intoxicated by the new Russian dramatic movement led by Stanislavsky, Chekhov and the Moscow Art Theatre, he regarded dancing as a mere stepping-stone to a career as an actor.[38]

But Diaghilev urgently needed a replacement for Nijinsky, both in his bed and on his stage, and sensing the boy's immense potential after spotting him in the corps of the Bolshoi Ballet, he made him offers he could hardly refuse. To Diaghilev's sexual requirements Massine (as he became known) seems to have submitted without hesitation, even though he had absolutely no natural bent towards men. In such a situation, it was common for the ephebe to be obliging, as Nijinsky had been, and Diaghilev's demands do not appear to have been aggressive (later Massine recalled that their coupling was like being in the embrace of 'a nice fat old lady'[39]). In other respects, he was hugely receptive and Diaghilev was delighted by his capacity to absorb the lessons of the Old Masters when they visited galleries and museums together. Massine was clever and thoughtful: he promised to be a source of fresh ideas, and that, for Diaghilev, was as precious a commodity as his body.

Nijinsky's superlative schooling and technique Massine could not match. Given his peculiar skinny physique, he knew he would never be a first-rate dancer, and after exposing his bare limbs as Joseph he would almost always perform in discreetly padded trousers that concealed his slight bow-leggedness. Sokolova also recalled that he had very tight hips and could not pirouette to save his life.[40] The beauty of his face seemed to embarrass him to the point of making himself grotesque. On stage the quality he radiated most powerfully was 'the complete opposite of Nijinsky', wrote Harry Kessler. 'Not a trace of showiness or sensuality; he is all profundity, all mysticism . . . He is Russian to the core (whereas Nijinsky was a Pole), a Russian folk song that moves one to the depths of one's soul.'[41] Diaghilev had picked a winner in what has rightly been called 'one of the most sensational feats of talent-spotting in history'.[42]

Whatever the disappointments of *La Légende de Joseph* and Nijinsky's absence, there was universal agreement among fans of the

Ballets Russes that they had enjoyed a wonderful summer, additionally graced by balmy weather and the enthralling performances of Chaliapin on the operatic front of Diaghilev's enterprise. 'All the smartest and most brilliant people in Society flocked,' recalled Lydia Sokolova, and the dancers became creatures of society-page glamour, offstage as well as on: 'The girls got their clothes from the best dressmakers; the men wore top hats and morning coats, with beige or grey waistcoats and spats. [Pyotr] Vladimirov, our principal male dancer that season, had a little Chinese valet who trotted after him everywhere he went . . . we became a kind of myth.'[43]

For six weeks over June and July 1914 – as the newspaper reports on the situation in the Balkans became more ominous – Drury Lane was packed nightly. Critics and audiences were bewitched by a repertory dominated by Fokine's ballets – *Carnaval*, *The Firebird*, *Les Sylphides*, as well as the novelty of *Le Coq d'or* – starring Karsavina, whose glory had reached its peak. 'Nearly everyone was in love with her,' reported Sokolova. In vain; she was married to a shadowy civil servant in St Petersburg, and not even the persistent attentions of the urbane Aga Khan, educated at Eton and Cambridge, and a patron of the ballet, could tempt her from the path of virtue. One evening when she agreed to have dinner with him, she unfolded her napkin to find that it contained a fabulous emerald. 'Dear Aga, how very kind,' she murmured, gently pushing the lure back across the table. She was not so easily bought, though she needed money. Diaghilev had not paid her for two years, and when he finally persuaded the impresario of Drury Lane to present her with £2,000 of her arrears, Diaghilev immediately asked her for a loan of £400.

As the dancers of the Ballets Russes dispersed for their summer break, Austria-Hungary declared war on Serbia. Within days, Europe's fragile diplomatic house of cards had collapsed as Germany declared war on Russia, dragging France and Britain into its wake. In the words of Diaghilev's biographer Richard Buckle, it was 'the end of *la belle époque*, the end of *art nouveau*, the end of the World of Art (*Mir iskusstva*) movement, the end of empires'.[44]

The basic sources for this chapter are Tamara Karsavina, *Theatre Street*, pp. 223–302; Romola Nijinsky, *Nijinsky*, pp. 99–221; Prince Peter Lieven, *The Birth of Ballets Russes*, pp. 132–213; Cyril Beaumont, *The Diaghilev Ballet in London*, pp. 9–76; Alexandre Benois, *Reminiscences of the Russian Ballet*, pp. 273–366; S. L. Grigoriev, *The Diaghilev Ballet 1910–1929*, pp. 27–102; Michel Fokine, *Memoirs of a Ballet Master*, pp. 140–221; Lydia Sokolova, *Dancing for Diaghilev*, pp. 32–64; Natalia Roslaveva, *Era of the Russian Ballet*, pp. 167–89; Boris Kochno, *Diaghilev and the Ballets Russes*, pp. 60–96; Richard Buckle, *Nijinsky*, pp. 118–325; Nesta Macdonald, *Diaghilev Observed*, pp. 26–134; Richard Buckle, *Diaghilev*, pp. 117–281; Lynn Garafola, *Diaghilev's Ballets Russes*, pp. 3–75; Bronislava Nijinska, *Early Memories*, pp. 317–497; Vicente Garcia-Marquez, *Massine*, pp. 3–42; Sjeng Scheijen, *Diaghilev: A Life*, pp. 206–308; Jennifer Homans, *Apollo's Angels*, pp. 245–89; Jane Pritchard, *Diaghilev and the Golden Age of the Ballets Russes*, pp. 15–70; Davinia Caddy, *The Ballets Russes and Beyond*, pp. 67–159; and Lucy Moore, *Nijinsky*, pp. 52–180.

## 5

# WAR

---

Serge Diaghilev and Leonid Massine, circa 1916

At first there was widespread underestimation of the gravity of the war, the general view being that the fighting would be confined and 'over by Christmas', and anyone would be foolish or craven to panic or change longer-term plans because of it. A Ballets Russes season in Germany had to be cancelled, of course, but after news came of his father's death, Diaghilev appears to have crossed contested borders and made what proved to be his last trip to his motherland, in order to pay his respects.

Back in Europe, there was no great sense of urgency or disruption away from the war zone, and Diaghilev looked westward. He was in receipt of a handsome advance from an American impresario for a tour of the USA in 1916 and there were scores by Stravinsky and the twenty-three-year-old prodigy Sergei Prokofiev in the offing. The rest of the summer and autumn he spent in a leisurely tour of Italy with his new beloved, Massine. In Rome they met up with shouty futurist punks and in Ravenna they absorbed the glories of the Byzantine mosaics. Walking through the Uffizi in Florence, Diaghilev asked the boy whether he thought he could choreograph a ballet. Inspired by contemplation of the luminous colours and sinuous grace of the figures in Simone Martini's gilded painting of the Annunciation, he replied that yes, he thought he could – and 'not only one, but a hundred, I promise you'.[1]

The pair remained in Italy until Easter 1915, when they rented a villa on the tranquil banks of Lake Geneva. Stravinsky lodged a bicycle ride away, and the Swiss conductor Ernest Ansermet became a new collaborator and friend. Bakst, Goncharova and her partner Larionov joined them all. A fresh company of dancers, somewhat low on Russians owing to wartime restrictions on movement, was assembled and billeted in what became a sort of artistic colony, idyllically removed from the horrors of the western front. 'It was a happy time for all of us,' recalled Lydia Sokolova, 'exciting, friendly and expectant'.[2]

Massine was quick to take up his promise, proposing a ballet that drew on the art that he had been newly experiencing. Entitled *Liturgie* and evoking the story of Jesus, it was envisaged, according to Diaghilev, as 'an ecstatic Mass, 6–7 short tableaux. Set in the Byzantine period . . .'[3] Surviving rehearsal photographs show that Massine devised striking tableaux that brought a third dimension to the figures in Cimabue and Giotto altarpieces. With Stravinsky too busy to oblige, several alternative possibilities were considered for the score, among them Gregorian chant, total silence, a futurist cacophony of bells, sirens and spinning tops, and a hollow double floor on which the dancers' feet would resonate like drumbeats. With Goncharova designing costumes that drew on the gilded magnificence of icons and frescoes, the result might have been absolutely dazzling, but as the choice of music became locked in stalemate, Diaghilev pulled the plug on the project, leaving *Liturgie* to stand as the great might-have-been in the history of the Ballets Russes.

Perhaps wary that his protégé had bitten off more than he could chew, Diaghilev then encouraged Massine to make his choreographic debut less ambitiously. *Soleil de Nuit*, a suite of naive folk dances drawn from Rimsky-Korsakov's opera *The Snow Maiden*, received its première just before Christmas 1915 in Geneva, where a newspaper review described it as 'a box of Russian toys brought to life and laughter, shining with gold papers and splashed with colour. Comic costumes for peasants and clowns . . . and Miassine [*sic*], the much applauded choreographer, as a puppet with cymbals and a vermilion face.' Massine was thrilled by the warm reception, but Diaghilev soon deflated him: 'I did not hear them cheering,' he said sardonically. Through such remarks he could keep the boy where he wanted him: Massine still had much to learn, and it was from Diaghilev that he must learn it.[4]

———

On New Year's Day 1916, the Ballets Russes sailed from Bordeaux to New York. It was a rough crossing. Massine stood on deck for hours, mesmerised by the swell and plunge of the waves, but Diaghilev, terrified of sea travel ever since a gypsy had told him he would die on water, rarely left his cabin, emerging only with a life-belt round his neck. When they ran into thick fog and a siren was sounded, he thought his end had come – in fact, the ship was only signalling its passage past the Statue of Liberty.

The company's biggest names were absent. Fokine was trapped behind Russian lines – and, in any case, Diaghilev felt that with Massine's nascent talent to call on, Fokine had outlived his creative usefulness. Karsavina was also detained in Russia. The question of Nijinsky remained complicated. Relations with Diaghilev had undergone *détente* but not *rapprochement* since the fallout from his marriage. Before the outbreak of hostilities, Nijinsky had been hovering about in Paris, slipping surreptitiously into a dress rehearsal of *La Légende de Joseph* in order to inspect his successor Massine. His successor leerily returned the compliment by visiting Nijinsky's ballet class – with Diaghilev's blessing, as he believed Massine needed to know what he was up against.

Nijinsky then returned to his wife Romola's home in Budapest, only to have the Austro-Hungarian authorities declare him an enemy alien after war was declared against Russia. Cut off from ballet under house arrest, he spent the time tenderly playing with his baby daughter Kyra and working on a system of dance notation. But Diaghilev's American impresario had made Nijinsky's presence in the season a condition of the contract, and following the Palace Theatre debacle Nijinsky needed money, so strings began to be pulled in high places with the aim of lifting him out of the enemy zone.

Meanwhile the company opened in New York. It wasn't quite what anyone had hoped for. The audience for ballet, ready to take chances but relatively unsophisticated and prim, responded uneasily to the exotic stereotyping of *Scheherazade* and the climax of *L'Après-midi d'un faune*, now danced by Massine and in deference to delicate sensibilities doctored of any hint of masturbation. Karsavina was replaced by two Russian ballerinas: one was Xenia Makletsova, who proved disastrous and walked out in high dudgeon; the other was the enchanting Lydia Lopokova.[5] A plump little butterball from St Petersburg (where her father was the chief usher in a theatre) with short arms and tiny but propulsive feet, bright as a button, and a chatterbox whose cutely fractured English furnished journalists with amusing copy, Lopokova had danced briefly with the Ballets Russes in 1910 before moving to America to make big money and hurtle through a succession of turbulent love affairs. 'She was sweet to everybody, never jealous and never coveting another dancer's roles,' recalled Lydia Sokolova. 'But she always seemed to be hopping off somewhere . . . she never seemed to belong to the ballet heart and soul.'[6] Artistically, she hadn't flourished, however, and she and Diaghilev needed each other in equal measure: as her name was already familiar, she was a box-office draw, and ballets such as

*The Firebird* afforded her mercurial gifts – a thrilling jump, lightning energy, and playful, slapdash charm among them – a worthy showcase.

After a less than sensational debut in New York, the company embarked on a two-month tour of the eastern states travelling by special train. Their dubious reputation preceded them, and in Boston, the mayor instructed that no bare flesh should be displayed on stage. As far west as Kansas City, reports of the inter-racial goings-on in *Scheherazade* excited the suspicions of the police department. 'I dropped in to see Dogleaf before the curtain went up,' an officer told a local reporter. 'Dogleaf or whatever his name is couldn't understand plain English . . . I told a fellow [interpreter], "This is a strictly moral town, and we won't stand for any of that highbrow immorality."' The performance went ahead, and the threat 'to come right up on the stage and pull down the curtain' if 'the show was too rank' was not enacted.[7] More consequentially, Massine's eye had begun to linger on one of the company's prettiest Russian girls, much to Diaghilev's anxiety. A tyrannical stop was put on the flirtation, but how long could animal instinct be restrained?

Back in New York, diplomacy prevailed: Nijinsky had been released and was en route, but there were still enormous difficulties to be surmounted, mainly relating to his demand for back pay. In front of the gawping press, Diaghilev and Massine met his boat at the dock and presented Romola with roses; Nijinsky handed Diaghilev baby Kyra to dandle. The mood remained frosty, however, with negotiations over lunch made tougher by Romola acting as Nijinsky's hard-headed agent, unmoved by any sentimental appeals to past favours. Finally, an agreement was reached that put paid to Diaghilev's hopes of leaving the USA with any profits: Nijinsky would be paid a percentage of the New York receipts as well as an enormous salary – the same as Caruso's.

It was a truce rather than a settlement, and the money must have been advanced from the American impresario Otto Kahn, rather than paid by Diaghilev, who simply didn't have it. Nijinsky began rehearsing but remained downbeat, and the company soon realised that his two-year absence from the stage had dampened some inner fire. 'He was out of practice and his dancing was by no means what it had been,' thought Grigoriev.[8] 'He had grown heavier and looked sad,' was Sokolova's view. 'He never spoke a word to anyone and picked his fingers more than ever.'[9]

The reviews of his performances in the Fokine ballets were glowingly appreciative, but again a batsqueak note of moral caution could be sensed. Offstage he was described as looking like 'a rough person', but onstage several critics were disconcerted by 'a most unprepossessing effeminacy', while in Fokine's pastoral *Narcisse* his curly golden wig, girlish tunic and brief white 'unmentionables' caused embarrassed titters in the audience. Straight New York did not have Paris's erotic open mind, even if it enjoyed the rubbishy tales of Nijinsky mania in London, as peddled by a ludicrous profile in the *New York Journal* claiming that 'four secretaries were kept busy ten hours a day answering his love letters' and 'ladies of the highest aristocracy had hysterics during his dances'.[10]

After the season came to an end, Diaghilev and the company returned to Europe by a relatively safe route to neutral Spain. The tour hadn't been a particularly happy experience for anyone involved. Always prone to high-handedness, Diaghilev made it clear he rather despised what he saw of Yankee culture, and Americans bridled at his old-school hoity-toity European manners. On one occasion he hit a recalcitrant stage manager with his walking stick and nearly started a brawl; a few hours later, some unidentified person dropped a heavy metal object down from the flies and hit him on the head – he was lucky it didn't kill him.

However, Otto Kahn felt confident that an appetite for Nijin-sky and the Ballets Russes had been whetted and the brand could be exploited further. So a new contract was negotiated in which Diaghilev essentially rented the company out for a further American tour on a profit-share basis, allowing him to remain in Europe with Massine and a small group of dancers developing new work. The fly in the ointment was Kahn's insistence that Nijinsky, as the star attraction, should be put in overall control of the American operation. Diaghilev knew that this was lunatic, but his hands were tied, and he needed the almighty dollar if the company was to survive as a going concern.

The Atlantic was as calm as a mill pond but infested with U-boats, and when the company landed in Cadiz, hydrophobic Diaghilev fell on his knees in relief and kissed dry land. In Madrid, performances were given under royal patronage. 'What exactly is it you do?' a baffled King Alfonso asked Diaghilev at a reception. 'Your Majesty, I am like you,' he replied smartly. 'I don't work, I do nothing. But I am indispensable.'[11] Everything and everybody Spanish charmed him. He commissioned a short ballet from Massine inspired by Velázquez's painting *Las Meninas*, as well as exploring Hispanic musical traditions with the composer Manuel de Falla, and making a lightning trip to Paris, where he visited a studio in Montparnasse and encountered a stocky and bullish young artist from Barcelona with fierce eyes and a thick flop of black hair; Pablo Picasso was already celebrated among the initiated for his wistful rose pastorals, primitivist aggressions and cubist experiments.

It was pesky Jean Cocteau who effected the introduction. In his continuing quest to fulfil the injunction of '*Étonne-moi, Jean*', he had been badgering Diaghilev for years with an idea for a sur-real circus ballet and this was a sharp nudge. Initially, it all seemed to fall into place: Cocteau would write the scenario for *Parade*, in which a series of circus acts advertise their talents on the streets in a vain attempt to lure an audience into a fairground; Picasso, passing out of his cubist phase and ready to take a new direction, would design scenery and costumes; the maverick composer Erik Satie would produce a collage of a score incorporating random sounds of everyday life; Massine would choreograph – and Diaghilev's patron Misia Sert (the remarried Misia Edwards) would pay for it all. On paper, at least, it looked like a dream collaboration between some of the finest avant-garde talent of the age.[12]

More pressingly Diaghilev had to deal with the company's return to America, where for the first time in the Ballets Russes's history, he would cede direct and daily 'indispensable' control. Nobody felt confident that Nijinsky had the personal or managerial skills to lead the company through an arduous four-month fifty-city coast-to-coast tour, but that was the devil's bargain made with Kahn. What made Nijinsky even more of a liability was that he had blackballed the invaluably steady and competent company manager and ballet master Sergei Grigoriev, whom he considered interfering. A highly strung Russian member of the company, Nicolas Kremnev, was the substitute, but even his infatuated girlfriend Lydia Sokolova admitted that he was 'too much one of the boys' and all too similar to Nijinsky in having 'absolutely no sense of proportion and no tact' – in sum, 'the last person who should have been given a position of such responsibility'.[13]

Nijinsky had remained in America with his wife and daughter during the summer, pondering new ballets while holed up at a seaside hotel in Maine. The one that came to some sort of fruition was a treatment of the mythical exploits of the German prankster Till Eulenspiegel, using Richard Strauss's tone-poem of that name as the score. Accounts of the ballet are even sketchier than they are for *Jeux* or *The Rite of Spring*, but its young American designer Robert

Edmond Jones left a vivid account of its bumpy gestation and the nightmare of working on the sets and costumes.[14]

Compulsively picking the side of his thumbs until they bled, Nijinsky seemed 'tired, bored, excited, troubled', his inexhaustible perfectionism married to an 'extraordinary nervous energy' that left a sense of 'something too eager, too brilliant, a quickening of the nerves, a nature racked to dislocation by a merciless creative urge'.[15] Ideas flowed thick and fast, only to be capriciously dropped and peremptorily replaced or reversed; heedless of schedules, bedtime or sober reason, he appeared or disappeared at all hours, constantly distracted by tiny details at the expense of the bigger picture. When he saw Jones's sets on stage for the first time and realised that they didn't fit the proscenium in the way he had envisaged, he screamed with incoherent rage and then fell over and sprained his ankle, causing the scheduled opening to be postponed by a week.

Yet at its première in New York, *Till Eulenspiegel* was, briefly, a success. As sumptuously colourful as anything by Bakst, Jones's fabulous designs presented a grotesque vision of a medieval Gothic city in which ladies wearing six-foot-high steeple headdresses and trailing yards of brocade were teased and seduced by Nijinsky himself in the title role – a mercurial Puck playfully intent on puncturing pomposity and pretension until the law catches up and sends him to the gallows. 'One of the most impressive exhibitions to be seen on our stage today,' proclaimed the *New York Times*.[16] Despite the applause of public and critics, however, the dancers knew that they were covering up a mess: like *Jeux* but more so, *Till Eulenspiegel* was unfinished – Sokolova, who played an apple-seller, remembered how 'we laughed at the applause . . . when we [had] improvised nearly half the ballet'.[17] The solipsism of genius meant that Nijinsky had worked out his own part meticulously, but never integrated it with the rest of the action.

On tour, everything fell apart. From his failure to welcome the dancers at the port when their ship docked, the worst forebodings about Nijinsky came to pass. Not merely hopelessly disorganised and indecisive, he was, as Sokolova put it, evidently 'not quite right in the head',[18] his sanity further impaired by the influence of two ardent Tolstoyans among the male ranks. This pair of fanatics, the epileptic Dmitri Kostrovsky and Nikolai Zverev (why were they working for the hedonistic Ballets Russes?), monopolised his attention on the endless train journeys between cities with sermons and homilies. Romola, excluded, called them 'leeches' and issued an ultimatum: them or me. It was them, and she stomped off to New York. But Nijinsky was susceptible: born a Catholic, he had once dreamed of becoming a monk and he now signed up to vegetarianism, pacifism, hair shirts and marital chastity, as well as egalitarian principles that led him to make unwise last-minute casting changes, propelling callow young dancers into leading roles for which they were ill prepared and pushing seasoned principals into the back row.

As curtains rose late, intervals were protracted, programmes changed from those advertised and Zverev frequently stood in for Nijinsky, word of disappointment got round and receipts plummeted. Journalists in outlying places such as Omaha and Tacoma couldn't make sense of the Russian names and garbled their reports; the PR people put out a tabloid fake news sheet full of inane titbits (Nijinsky's views on American football and so forth). The dancers split into feuding factions and even went hungry for lack of money. Desperate telegrams were sent to Grigoriev, describing 'an incredible state of chaos'[19] and begging him to come over and sort things out, to no avail. It was too late to salvage.

At Christmas, the company's caravan of fifteen carriages crossed the Rockies and arrived via Salt Lake City in Los Angeles. Here Nijinsky flew in an aeroplane for the first time and met Charlie Chaplin, his exact contemporary, similarly catapulted to global fame from a humble background and possessed of a genius for physical expression. Whether or not they realised that they were both working in the vanguard of art forms for which they were creating the vocabulary, they were fascinated by each other: 'a god of passionate sadness' is how Chaplin described Nijinsky.[20] What a pity it is that Hollywood's cameras never rolled to record the Ballets Russes on so much as a newsreel – Diaghilev distrusted the idea of film, and refused several offers from studios.*

From California, the company wended its way back east, sailing for Europe just a few weeks before the USA entered the war in April 1917. The tour had flopped financially overall, and been a very mixed success artistically. 'Not only did this season saddle our accounts with a large deficit,' wrote Grigoriev. 'It also compromised our reputation so gravely that the Diaghilev Ballet was never able to appear in America again.'[21]

———

While this fiasco was unfolding, Diaghilev had been based in Rome, commissioning old and new collaborators and consorting with the noisy futurists. Massine was being kept very busy, with three ballets on the stocks: not only *Parade*, but also a selection of miniature fairy tales, *Contes Russes*, and *Les Femmes de bonne humeur*, his first truly considered and personal creation, drawing on a comedy of manners

* Although with the arrival of the talkies he finally seems to have relented: in 1929 some filming was being negotiated as an element of a tour of the USA that never took place.

by Carlo Goldoni using dance manuals of the seventeenth and eighteenth centuries and designed by Bakst in a parody of Venetian galant style.

In this highly stylised and exquisitely composed frolic relished by the dancers, Massine began to experiment with a new aesthetic that matched classically smooth movement of the legs to jerky, almost marionette-like movement of the upper body and arms – the ideal of curvaceous fluidity giving way to curtailed angularity, making an effect that owed something to the flickering, abrupt rhythms of the silent cinema as well as the mechanistic obsessions of the futurists. King Alfonso was one of its ardent admirers: forgetting its name, he quaintly described it as 'the ballet where they move all the time'.[22] Diaghilev himself began to dabble hereabouts: always fascinated by the techniques of stage lighting and frequently taking charge of them himself, he created a short kaleidoscopic spectacle called *Fireworks*, with music by Stravinsky and designs by the futurist Giacomo Balla. Programmed as an interlude, with no dancers or dancing involved, its flickering mutating images suggested an abstract cinema and adumbrated theatrical trends of the 1920s, but it baffled those expecting ballet to contain a human element. An Italian critic described it as running through 'disturbing crystalline forms, beams of coloured light, coral formations, symbols of the infinite (spirals and running light-waves), emblems of light (obelisk, pyramids, rays of sunlight and sickle moons), aerodynamic symbols (flights of swifts and firebirds) . . . all projected onto a black backdrop, illuminated from behind with red rays'.[23] Grigoriev dismissed it with barely disguised scorn: Diaghilev 'maintained that it interpreted the music; and this cubist [*sic*] fantasy proved much to the taste of his advanced artistic friends'.[24]

By hopping between countries that were either neutral or noncombatant, the Ballets Russes had to date found the war more an inconvenience than a threat, displacing them from London and Paris while opening other horizons in their place. But the violent turmoil that erupted in Russia in 1917 had a profound impact: March brought the country riots followed by a first wave of revolution in the course of which the tsar abdicated. This was the brief moment at which Diaghilev's 'liberal' generation and friends took the reins, and he duly received a telegram from what was now called Petrograd asking him to return to his enfranchised motherland as minister for culture. This had been Benois's suggestion: the offer was turned down, but it was a difficult decision. Mildly progressive in his political outlook, Diaghilev was pleased at the turn of events and at the end of one performance of *The Firebird* in Paris, he instructed that as a gesture of solidarity the crown and sceptre that the tsarevich receives at his wedding should be replaced by the Phrygian cap of liberty and a red flag waved by a peasant. After a spate of hate mail, however, this classic instance of virtue-signalling was abandoned and the homage to monarchy and tradition restored.

Diaghilev came to love Russia all the more intensely because of his exile – originally self-imposed but now enforced – and despite his cosmopolitan veneer, he remained nostalgic for his roots there. Somewhere he still nursed a desire to take his ballet home and show those who had thwarted or underrated him what he had done for Russia in the eyes of the world. But *Parade* would show how far from his roots his aesthetics had travelled. Its first performance in Paris in May 1917 'has gone down in history as the moment when the avant-garde elbowed its way into mainstream European élite culture', according to Sjeng Scheijen, 'and its reputation is therefore perhaps greater than it might otherwise deserve'.[25] Why?

Lacking the high seriousness of Nijinsky's pre-war experiments, its tone was merrily surreal, anticipating the screwball zaniness that became such a characteristic of Western culture in the hectic post-war decade. Although Cocteau had devised the original concept, his ideas were increasingly sidelined and Picasso had come to dominate the way in which the show developed over some scratchy, squabbling months in Italy. Satie's music was, in the words of Arthur Gold and Robert Fizdale, 'fresh, jazzy, unpretentious . . . clearing away both the Wagnerian underbrush and the Debussyan haze'.[26] Satie's music was deliberately banal and the parameters of Massine's choreography – with its music-hall wit, panache and jerkiness – were dictated by the costumes. It was an animated cartoon, clearly not to be taken seriously and free of any deeper purpose beyond smug delight in its own modernist irony and ingenuity.[27]

Cocteau explained Picasso's genius as a stage designer very simply: 'Before his advent the decor had played no part in the piece; it had merely looked on.' Picasso made tableaux that were truly *vivants*.[28] His gently whimsical drop curtain, painted in the style of the *saltimbanque* paintings of his 'rose' period, showed harlequins, a priest, a toreador, a sailor and others sitting round a table and gazing at a winged ballerina on the back of a winged white horse. It rose to reveal an urban landscape in a skewed cubistic perspective crowded with high-rise buildings that could be interpreted as either the skyscrapers of Chicago or the slums of Naples. At the centre was the entrance to a fairground, out of which emerged grotesque figures. Only their legs were visible because they wore over their heads and trunks ten-foot-high papier-mâché boxes on which were modelled images of the USA and France – an Uncle Sam hat and megaphone for the American, a Parisian chestnut tree and pipe and stick for the Frenchman – as well as a prancing two-man pantomime horse with an African-style mask. 'The dancers detested these costumes, which were a torture to move about in,' wrote Grigoriev, not least because the poor souls were simultaneously required 'to do a lot of stamping, which was intended to suggest conversations between them'.[29] The premise was that the boxed figures represented rival fairground managers advertising their rather hopeless attractions – a pair of tightrope-walking acrobats, a fire-breathing Chinese conjuror, a jazz-dancing Mary Pickford type taking snaps with a Kodak camera. The climax was a general farcical collapse of all parties, as the crowd fails to roll up.

As news filtered through of French troops falling like flies in the pointless carnage of the Nivelle offensive, Parisian audiences were presented with something that cockily straddled popular and highbrow culture, unsure whether it wanted to annoy or charm. The first performance took place at a matinée in aid of the Red Cross and the audience was a bizarre mix of wounded Allied soldiers, the *gratin* of Proustian Paris, and the younger avant-garde such as the poets Guillaume Apollinaire and e. e. cummings as well as the *vieille-garde* of Pierre-Auguste Renoir and Claude Debussy. A baffled Matisse asked Massine: '"What does it mean when the girl [i.e. the Mary Pickford impersonator] jumps over the rope, rolls over on the ground and kicks her feet up in the air?" That, replied Massine, is very simple: "The catastrophe of the *Titanic*."'[30]

As anticipated, and indeed hoped for, the spectacle provoked booing, whistling and cheering in equal measure. 'Real bedlam' was the teenage Poulenc's memory; 'I have heard the cries of a bayonet charge in Flanders, but it was nothing compared to what happened that night,' bragged Cocteau, who insensitively described it as 'the greatest battle of the war'.[31] Some of those worried by what was happening in Russia suspected *Parade* of being infected with a dangerous revolutionary tendency and the conservative press had a field day (Satie was sentenced to gaol for a week after sending libellously abusive postcards to a hostile reviewer). Perhaps the most telling verdict on the première was that of a grand lady overheard by Cocteau: 'If I had known it would be like this I should have brought the children.'[32] Whereas the savagery of *The Rite of Spring* had posed an aggressive full-frontal assault on a society still in some sort of order, *Parade* merely played insouciantly with the frivolous novelties of cubism, futurism and the slapstick of Chaplin and the Keystone Cops. Stern critics might complain that it ignored the tragedy of a meaningless war in which the past was devastating itself, in order to surrender to the absurdity of a morally vacuous world in which nothing made sense or really mattered. Such iconoclasm would give *Parade* a certain limited popularity among the young, but its jokiness swiftly wore thin.

Yet *Parade* was a significant portent of the broad post-war movement, led by Cocteau and his coterie, towards what Lynn Garafola has called the 'sophisticated commonplace'.[33] Writers, artists and composers felt licensed to engage with ordinary life and popular culture in an exuberant spirit of ironic parody and knockabout fun; no more dissolving into the Wagnerian sublime, no more staring into misty impressionist horizons or what Keats described as 'huge cloudy symbols of a high romance'– the light was bright and electric now, the mood upbeat. In the wake of this tendency, another more eclectic phase in the story of the Ballets Russes was inaugurated – one that rejected Russian and orientalist inspiration, questioned classically schooled dancing, looked beyond traditional theatrecraft, and gave young painters who rejected realism and romanticism a billboard for their experimental art at a time when the war had destroyed the market. As Jane Stevenson puts it, 'A ballet commission from Diaghilev was a way of establishing commercial value, because it put specimen work in front of a large audience of wealthy opinion-makers with an interest in the arts, and because his reputation as a talent-spotter was so strong.'[34] In sum: 1917 saw Diaghilev well ahead of the game, with Picasso's genius featured prominently.

Meanwhile the last eighteen months of the war took their toll. After the Paris season, the company returned to the safe haven of Spain, where it had become very popular. In Madrid Nijinsky returned to the company. He was bubbling with plans to open a dance school and choreographic laboratory. 'He behaved quite amiably at first,' thought Grigoriev, 'and we hoped that his relations with Diaghilev would improve.'[35] But in the wake of the *Sturm und Drang* of the previous three years, Diaghilev had lost interest and moved on – his survival instinct to the fore. Nijinsky might have remained the company's essential box-office draw, but he was no longer as necessary to the future as he had been and no longer ranked as the choreographer who would lead ballet forward. Massine was now in the creative ascendancy: he had developed a close personal bond with Picasso and was hatching ideas for a distinctively Spanish ballet, abetted by the flamenco virtuoso Félix Fernández García.

His is one of the most sorry tales in this chronicle.[36] A scrawny little fellow with a sallow complexion, ominously nicknamed by his acquaintance *El loco*, 'the crazy guy', Félix had been spotted and befriended by Diaghilev and Massine in a cabaret in Seville. His sheer physical abandon was stunning: Sokolova remembered how 'he danced on his knees and leaped into the air and crashed his body down on the side of his thighs, turned over and jumped up with such speed that it was unbelievable that the human body could stand such a strain without injury'.[37] Sensing his star potential, Diaghilev swiftly signed him up. From the beginning, linguistic barriers and misplaced expectations of financial reward and global fame caused tensions, but Félix's intense enthusiasm and incandescent dancing (and singing) were irresistibly exciting to Massine. Félix initiated him into the strutting, preening and stomping that gave Spanish dance its spirit of *duende*, and its vocabulary of *jota, fandango, farrucca, cachucha, bolero* inspired him, not least because its customary male costume of black trousers allowed him to hide his bow legs. Together with Diaghilev and the composer Manuel de Falla, they embarked on an enthralling research trip round the Spanish provinces and countryside: Félix knew all the best dancers as well as the cellars and tabernas in which they let rip. In Seville, Massine used a 16-millimetre camera he had acquired in Italy to record the flamenco stars Antonio López Ramírez and Juana la Macarrona; in Córdoba, they found 'cobblers, barbers and pastry cooks' dancing in joyous competition with each other, fuelled by *jamón* and *jerez*. Here was a fresh source of energy, the raw real thing.[38]

Nijinsky was stuck dancing the old Fokine stuff. He had expressed generous admiration for what he saw of Massine's work, but he could only be discombobulated when he realised the extent to which he had been supplanted. Egged on by his wife Romola, who was fanatically protective of his status and ready to suspect conspiracy against him at every whisper, he allowed what had started as justified hurt to slip into truculent sulking and curdle into deeper mental disturbance. Further sermons from the Tolstoyan evangelists Kostrovsky and Zverev did nothing to steady him. After he attempted to bunk off from an advertised performance without excuse and the police were called in to restrain him, he was no longer on speaking terms with Diaghilev. But at least the problem could temporarily be shelved, as the company was now contracted to return to South America with Nijinsky heading the bill: he had agreed to go on Romola's condition that he would be paid in gold before every performance. Once again Diaghilev stayed behind: far too afraid of the Atlantic crossing to travel himself, he appointed the broad-shouldered Grigoriev as his deputy and left him to handle the troubled and troublesome genius.

The tour was unhappy. The ship carrying the company docked in Montevideo, not Rio as planned, causing delays and ructions. In São Paolo poor Lydia Sokolova gave premature birth (the father being the drunken and violent dancer Nicolas Kremnev, whom she had married with dubious legality) and was told that the baby girl was likely to die. A fire in a train destroyed all the scenery for two of the ballets, and the Argentine impresario was a swindler.

Most poignantly, the fortnight in Buenos Aires found Nijinsky sliding inexorably into psychotic paranoia. With his wife busily stirring the toxic brew, he hired a bodyguard and interpreted everything as personal affront or physical attack. On stage he could not be relied on. Obsessed with the horrors of war, he spent hours manically repeating classroom dance exercises and screaming futile obscenities at his innocent colleagues. On 26 September 1917, Vaslav Nijinsky danced the title roles in *Le Spectre de la rose* and *Petrushka*: it was his last appearance with the Ballets Russes.

––––––

The ensuing months were the bleakest in the company's twenty-year history, if not altogether unproductive ones. The disintegration of Europe in the last exhausted phase of the war permeated everything and closed off opportunities. The Bolshevik phase of the Russian revolution and the Peace of Brest-Litovsk that Lenin disgracefully signed with Germany left Diaghilev's hopes of returning to his homeland ever more distant, as his friends were toppled from their precarious positions of power. In the longer term, this had a beneficial result as, over the next decade, a new wave of exiles would recharge the creativity of the Ballets Russes. But, in 1917, the situation looked irredeemable.

Back in Europe, bedraggled and exhausted by the South American tour, the Ballets Russes played hand-to-mouth seasons in Lisbon, Barcelona and Madrid that just about kept the enterprise going throughout the winter. But then what? To Falla, Diaghilev despaired: 'I am lost. What is going to become of me? My only solution is to go into a monastery.' 'Give it up,' advised Misia Sert bluntly.[39] In the spring came a last-ditch two-month tour of the Spanish provinces covering over 3,000 miles. Often travelling in bumpy horse-drawn convoys and performing with improvised sets and partial costumes in primitively equipped venues, the dancers went underpaid and sometimes hungry and threadbare. The first wave of Spanish flu also took its toll. But being dancers – members of a profession endemically resilient in adversity and ready to see the funny side – they 'all accepted this quite cheerfully', Grigoriev recalled, 'finding life in Spain most interesting and the people delightful'.[40]

As it is always darkest before dawn, there came a moment when Sokolova's sickly baby was in mortal danger. When she went to Diaghilev to beg money for medicine,

> he took me to his bedroom, opened a wardrobe trunk and brought out a little leather bag. He undid the string and emptied on the bed a heap of copper and silver coins from various countries. This, I suppose, was all the money he had left . . . I was always glad that I had seen the gentler side of Diaghilev's character and had known how kind he could be in the days of deepest despair.[41]

The baby recovered, and a lifeline was finally thrown in the form of a contract with the impresario Oswald Stoll to appear at the flashy London Coliseum as part of a variety bill. Stoll was a genuine fan, and several Russian stars, including Karsavina and Ida

Rubinstein, had appeared there as guests before the war. They had merely done brief turns, however, without complex scenery or subtle lighting. The Ballets Russes had previously been presented for entire evenings in the grandest theatres without competition from acrobats, prestidigitators or infant prodigies, so this was a humiliation – and Nijinsky's experience of a fifty-minute slot at the Palace was not a good omen – but there was no other option if the company was to be kept together. The further hurdle was finding a way to transport the scenery and costumes from Spain to England: in the light of the surrender to Germany, none of the Allies was keen to put itself out for anything Russian, while a journey by sea ran the risk of U-boats. Only after King Alfonso intervened at the highest diplomatic level did the laissez-passer across France come through. When the crucial assent came from London in a cryptic overnight telegram, Diaghilev woke Sokolova in her bedroom; he needed to be sure he had understood the import of the English text correctly. Yes, he had, and they both burst into tears of relief.

But the tension of the previous months had taken a toll on Massine's relationship with Diaghilev. The entirely heterosexual Massine was cerebral, ruthlessly self-interested and totally absorbed in his work: he might have been able to cope routinely with Diaghilev's undemanding physical needs, but he bridled at a cloying, clinging, wheedling need for affection and intimacy that intensified whenever Massine showed any sign of wanting a little fresh air. Diaghilev would have done anything to help Massine advance and succeed but, to be blunt, he also wanted gratitude in the form of a cuddle. When things had looked terminal in Spain and he had cried out for some sympathy or support, he had written reproachfully to Massine that he had 'received not one word of tenderness, not one word of joy in return for my warmth . . . Some day you will understand and some day a ray of light will illuminate your heart of glass.'[42] But

145

such pathetic appeals weren't going to wash: Massine had a mind that was elsewhere and a hard heart.

———

Passing through Paris as the German 'Big Bertha' howitzers pummelled the city, Diaghilev and his company were shocked to witness the extent of the destruction that the war was wreaking – it was their first exposure to bomb craters, wounded soldiers, food coupons and boarded-up shops. Subject to a blackout and swarming with men in uniform, London wasn't in a much better state, and the Coliseum was unappealing. Now the contract had been signed and he was safely in situ, Diaghilev was no longer cap in hand. Instead, on the assumption that he was doing this proletarian variety hall a great favour, he regained his hauteur. The theatre's vulgar drop curtain covered in spangles and sequins would have to go, and the crude lighting rig would have to be improved in order to render the requisite poetical atmosphere. Through the persuasive skills of which Diaghilev was master, this was managed but, as Sokolova explains, there was nothing that could be done about the deathtrap stage:

> It sloped down slightly towards the middle, and the apron sloped down towards the orchestra. The brass studs, as big as tea plates, scattered all over the stage, were also dangerous. There was a gap about an inch and a half wide between the part that revolved and the part that stayed still. With all the machinery underneath, it was a very hard stage to dance on and had no spring in it whatsoever.[43]

As well as negotiating this minefield, there were other anxieties, and a sceptic might have thought the odds were stacked against them. It was four years since the Ballets Russes had appeared in

London and the world was now a very different place in terms of taste and sensibility. Diaghilev's great aristocratic friend and door-opening money-raising patron Lady Ripon had died. Did the pre-war social élite that had idolised the company at fashionable Covent Garden and Drury Lane still exist, and would it be prepared to make the passage to see a single one-act ballet – performed twice daily, matinée and evening – in a West End variety theatre where the public was often less than elegant? There was no superstar Nijinsky or Karsavina on the bill. New dancers had been recruited at very short notice to fill gaps left by those who had dropped out over the lean months in Spain. Swiftly put through their paces in a rough rehearsal room improvised in Shaftesbury Avenue, could they emerge as adequate? Massine was an unknown quantity as a choreographer, and scarcely remembered for his scantily clad appearance in *La Légende de Joseph*. Almost all the scenery had to be repainted, and in some cases redesigned. And Spanish flu had begun its decimation.

They were lucky in one thing – the tide of the war had begun to turn decisively in the Allies' favour, with encouraging news filtering through daily. The Ballets Russes could catch this swelling tide of optimism and the unprejudiced Coliseum audience could open up to the novel comedy radiated by Massine's witty and teasing *Les Femmes de bonne humeur* and his fairy-tale *Contes Russes*. 'Not only a brilliant work of art, but the most exhilarating entertainment,' applauded the *Observer*.[44]

The puckish personalities and mercurial techniques of two Polish male dancers, Leon Woizikowski and Stanislas Idzikowski, earned applause, and Massine's interpretations of some of Nijinsky's former roles had a power and character of their own that won him favourable comparisons. But the sensation was Lydia Lopokova. She had none of Karsavina's regal elegance and lyricism – the aura of tsarist St Petersburg now destroyed by Bolshevism – but she bubbled. Plump, capricious and merry, without self-importance or reserve, she could be seen as a herald for post-war 'liberated' femininity and the Bright Young Things of the 1920s – a free spirit who could airily fling her drawers into the wings when they slid down her legs during a performance of *Les Sylphides* and carry on unblushingly regardless. Here was a ballerina who young chaps and their girlfriends in the gallery could take to their hearts; they christened her 'Loppy' and mobbed her outside the stage door. The fans didn't know the half of it: a habitual bolter, married at this point to Diaghilev's smarmy business manager Randolfo Barocchi (at least a bigamist, rumoured to be a quintigamist[45]), she became an obsession of the gossip pages and was taken up by London hostesses, amusing drawing-rooms with her idiosyncratic but voluble English. Never a conformist, however, she had a few surprises to spring.

Performing twice a day six times a week for six months gave the company a stability it badly needed after four years dominated by one-night stands. The relocation to the Coliseum also had the beneficial effect of putting ballet on the right side of cultural progress: a new audience for serious modern work came not only from the fashionable Chelsea set led by the siblings Osbert, Sacheverell and Edith Sitwell (who became besotted camp-followers), but also from those of less privileged social status who came to watch the stand-up comedians and stayed to watch Massine, despite previously thinking of ballet only in terms of Pavlova's dainty flutterings. There is also an even broader cultural perspective to what one might call the democratisation of the ballet audience.* As the troops came home and the lights came on again in the aftermath of war, dancing became a national obsession.

* See pp. 217–24.

Such was the success of the Coliseum season that at the end of March 1919 Oswald Stoll would not let Diaghilev go. He moved the company to one of his theatres in Manchester for ten days and then returned it immediately to London, where it played for fifteen sold-out weeks as the sole attraction in the Alhambra Theatre in Leicester Square. Here, within a fortnight in July, Massine gave the first performances of two of his masterpieces, *La Boutique fantasque* and *Le Tricorne*.

In rehearsal Massine worked phenomenally fast and hard, with a forensic focus that was in stark contrast to Nijinsky's hesitant inarticulacy and backtracking. Massine left nothing to chance and, unlike Fokine, he tended to treat dancers as machines rather than collaborators. Very few people ever said they liked him, but he didn't waste their time – he knew exactly what he wanted. 'Something insuperably impersonal let itself be felt behind his fine artistry,' reflected Karsavina, who never felt comfortable with him. 'He never got angry, nor did he give any praise.'[46] Behind this impenetrable façade was a keen mind and a watchful eye. Out in Trafalgar Square on Armistice night, he showed no hankering to join the jubilation; instead he stared transfixed at the way that the crowds jigged and jostled, storing up the scene for future use.

Both his new ballets had been simmering for some time. The germ of *La Boutique fantasque* – a ballet on *Toy Story* lines, in which mechanical dolls in a shop magically come to life and defend their maker and themselves from predatory customers – had in fact been seeded three decades earlier when Diaghilev had visited Vienna and seen his first ballet, *Puppenfee* ('The Fairy Doll'). Presumably he shared his memories of it with Massine, who took up a concept that might have looked exhausted (*Petrushka* was only one of many ballets that had played on the theme) and gave it a fresh Mediterranean flavour, using a score assembled from some scintillating tunes by Rossini and choreography full of emphatic footwork and bold flourishes that suggest the influence of his Spanish sojourn. Bakst had sketched some designs, but Diaghilev sensed that they weren't what a new era of taste required and rather shabbily passed the commission behind Bakst's back to a handsome young Frenchman, André Derain. Such ruthlessness between the old friends caused a rift, but it proved to be the right decision for *La Boutique fantasque*. Derain breathed the modern spirit of sunny fauvism into the mid-nineteenth-century setting.

Massine might have been a dark horse and a control freak, but he also had a vivid sense of the ludicrous and the show he served up was a deliciously wacky confection that seamlessly integrated narrative mime with pure dance. Focused on a pair of dolls – originally impersonated by Lopokova and Massine – so infatuated with each other that they refuse to be parted when they are sold off to different buyers, the witty scenario also featured, among much else, a pair of poodles sniffing each other's behinds, some furious Cossacks, and a British upper-class twit. Lopokova's and Massine's dazzling cancan* and a romp of a grand finale invariably brought the house down. 'I can do nothing but rhapsodise,' wrote the critic of the *Sunday Times*. 'It makes me feel a child again.'[47] 'So tremendously alive, so exhilarating that we catch our breath at the sheer exuberance of it all,' gasped *The Nation*.[48] The ovations were ecstatic: in the words of Massine's biographer Vicente Garcia-Marquez, 'London's reception of *La Boutique fantasque* was one of the greatest outpourings of love and acceptance accorded any theatrical event during the years immediately after the war, if not *the* greatest.'[49]

* After Lopokova married John Maynard Keynes in 1925, they were known at parties to dance a version of this they called the Keynes-Keynes (Richard Buckle Collection, Banker's Box 8).

1  Diaghilev with his nanny, by Léon Bakst.

2  A page of Russian folk art from *Mir iskusstva*.

3  Alexandre Benois and Igor Stravinsky, 1911.

4 Vaslav Nijinsky suggesting a sunnier side to his normally
withdrawn and sullen personality.
5 Nijinsky's beautiful classical schooling is evident in this
image from Michel Fokine's *Le Pavillon d'Armide*.

6  Nijinsky in *Prélude à l'après-midi d'un faune*.

7 Ida Rubinstein in *Le Martyre de Saint Sébastien*.
8 A typically sumptuous backdrop design by Bakst for *Thamar*.

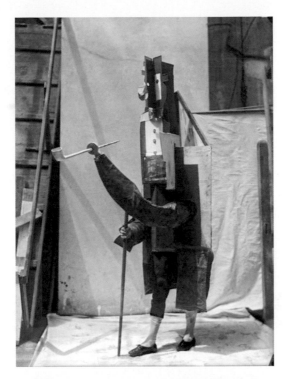

9 A figure in Leonid Massine's *Parade*.
10 The formidable Bronislava Nijinska.

11 (*left*) Lydia Sokolova in Nijinska's *Le Train bleu*.
12 (*right*) Lydia Lopokova.

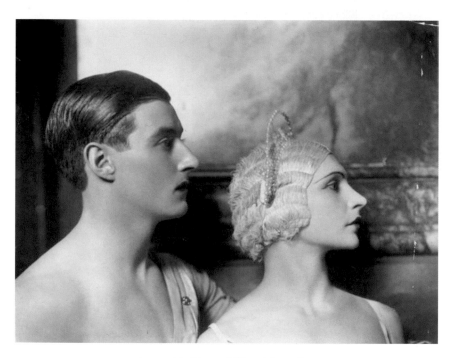

13 Anton Dolin and Vera Nemchinova.

14  The Russian émigrée teacher Serafina Astafieva (*right*)
arranging a tableau in her Chelsea studio.
15  Leonid Massine and Margot Fonteyn in *Le Tricorne*,
Sadler's Wells Ballet, 1947.

16  One of Bakst's costume designs for an attendant courtier
in *The Sleeping Princess*.

*Le Tricorne* ('The Three-cornered Hat'), enjoyed similar success. A comedy of mistaken identities in which a corrupt magistrate attempts to seduce the wife of an honest miller, it was built on a thrilling score by Falla that drew on the rhythms and ululations of Andalucian *cante jondo* and embodied all the Spanish culture Massine had imbibed before it became mere touristic cliché. Picasso was the designer: no longer the rough-edged Left-Bank *flâneur* of the days when he had signed up for *Parade*, he came to London for rehearsals behaving like an international celebrity. Flush with Diaghilev's fee of 10,000 francs (not far short of £150,000 today), he booked into the Savoy with his new wife Olga Khokhlova (formerly a junior dancer with the Ballets Russes whom he had encountered while working on *Parade*), socialised with the Bloomsbury crowd and had a Savile Row tailor run him up a smart suit. But his vision of *Le Tricorne* was something of stark simplicity – the whitewashed walls of a typical Spanish village linked by a great pink and ochre arch, behind which was a backcloth of white mountains and a pale blue sky. Before the war, *Scheherazade* had stimulated a kitschy vogue for jewelled turbans, leather pouffes and harem pants; *Le Tricorne* would bring on a rash of fringed shawls, beribboned guitars and outsize ear-rings, but it originally represented a more authentic response to the realities of Spanish dance than anything peddled by Bizet's *Carmen* or the *olés* of La Belle Otero at the Folies Bergère. In old age, Massine told Richard Buckle that this was the ballet of which he was most proud and Picasso's designs were 'acclaimed by painters as a masterpiece'.[50]

Where was Massine's mentor, the phenomenal Félix, in all this? Alas, nowhere. Although he had been brought to London in the hope that he could take the leading role of the miller in *Le Tricorne*, it became clear in formal rehearsal that he was a fish out of water. Explosive in temper and incapable of subduing his instincts, he could not accept that in ballet one had to follow a preordained series of steps and stop at a fixed point: his flamenco was a thing of passionate improvisation, never responding to the music in the same way twice or finishing when it needed to finish. The harder Massine tried to rein him in, the jumpier Félix became. In an attempt to instil the principle of keeping regular time, Massine gave him a metronome. It had only an unintended effect: Félix became obsessively attached to the thing, walking along the street listening to it as if hypnotised and making his footsteps coincide with its inexorable *tick-tick*. The idea of pairing him with Sokolova for a tarantella in *La Boutique fantasque* also proved a dead duck, and his only stage appearance with the Ballets Russes would be as a pedlar with a tray of ribbons in the background of the fairground scenes of *Petrushka* – where, as Sokolova compassionately put it, 'he could play about and improvise to his heart's content'.[51]

Massine now felt sufficiently proficient in the Hispanic style to replace Félix in *Le Tricorne* and by all accounts (including his own) he made something utterly magnificent out of it. Dancing the miller's *farruca*, he felt that

> the mental image of an enraged bull going into the attack
> unleashed some inner force which generated power within
> me. I felt an almost electrical interaction between myself and
> the spectators. Their mounting excitement had the effect of
> heightening my physical strength until I was dancing with a
> sustained force that seemed far beyond my reach at other times.[52]

Poor Félix would sit and watch rehearsals, occasionally being asked to demonstrate matters of style or inflection: the humiliation must have been devastating, the last straw. Sokolova was humiliated too, as Karsavina had returned unexpectedly to the company and was immediately cast in the role of the miller's wife that was up to that moment being created on her. This was bad casting, and several critics remarked how ill at ease the innately regal Russian Karsavina looked as a Spanish peasant ('a racehorse being set to take a coster's cart to the Derby', quipped the *Observer*[53]). It was hardly surprising that she was on less than sparkling form. Since her return to Russia in 1914, her life had been in turmoil – an embarrassing divorce from her banker husband Vasili Mukhin; the birth of her son, following which she had danced very little; a second marriage to the boy's father, British diplomat Henry James Bruce; and finally the trauma of a desperate escape from the Bolsheviks that had led her and her husband and baby to a close shave with death. Moreover she had entirely missed out on both the evolution of Massine's angular choreographic style and the company's enriching immersion in Spain and the idioms of Spanish dance. One night after she had dined with Diaghilev at the Savoy, Félix was brought in to demonstrate. In the deserted ballroom, she recalled,

he needed no begging and gave us dance after dance. In between, he sang the guttural songs of his country, accompanying himself on the guitar . . . it was very, very late. The . . . performance must cease or [the waiters] would be compelled to put the lights out. They went over to Félix too, but he took not the slightest notice, he was far away . . . The lights went out. Félix continued like one possessed. The rhythm of his steps – now staccato, now languorous, now almost a whisper, and then again seeming to fill the large room with thunder – made this unseen performance all the more dramatic. We listened [*sic*] to the dancing enthralled.[54]

But even if his art was unimpaired, Félix was turning ever more mentally unstable, eating his meals to the *tick-tick* of his pet

metronome and distracting the dancers during rehearsals by pop-
ping up wearing funny hats and making silly faces. Up to a point
this was tolerated – the Ballets Russes was accustomed to eccentricity. Then one evening he was spotted backstage plastering his
face with barbaric smears of greasepaint, and the next thing anyone
knew of him was that he had been arrested after breaking into St
Martin-in-the-Fields at night, screaming that it was a brothel and
dancing naked on the altar. Certified insane, he was incarcerated
for the rest of his life in an asylum in Epsom.[55] The whole affair was
hushed up, and Félix died forgotten in 1941.

Only a few months previously Nijinsky had performed his own
mad last dance. It took place in St Moritz, where he had been
in retreat since returning to Europe in the wake of the South
American fiasco. At first, he seemed calmer. Settled in a moun-
tain chalet, he had enjoyed periods of tranquil domesticity with
Romola as he worked on his system of dance notation and skated
and sledged with their daughter. But through 1918 his moods
became more extreme and even violent. He contemplated creating a ballet set in a brothel, in which a withered old crone sold
'youth to age, woman to woman, man to man'.[56] On long silent
walks through the pine forests, he hallucinated trails of blood in
the snow; at home, he spent hours obsessively drawing dark circles and elaborate abstract patterns; to the villagers, he presented
himself as a priest-like figure, wearing a large crucifix round his
neck, distributing gifts and accosting strangers with rambling
religiose exhortations. Paranoid schizophrenia is a name often
given to such behaviour.

On 19 January 1919, the noticeboard of the Suvretta House,
a palatial ski-resort hotel outside the village, advertised a Sunday
afternoon recital by the world's most celebrated dancer. Some
twenty curious guests assembled, among them the young Swiss

writer Maurice Sandoz, who left an account of what ensued. It differs in several details from that of Romola Nijinsky.

Playing the smiling host, Nijinsky ushered everyone in affably before solemnly announcing 'This is my marriage with God.' Wearing only practice clothes and sandals, he then sat on a chair and stared fixedly at his audience for some minutes. Finally he stood up and after issuing conflicting instructions to the wretched pianist, he began by improvising to the melancholy of a Chopin prelude, making a precise gesture to correspond to each chord – an attitude of defence, a sweeping welcome, hands raised in prayer and then falling as though his joints had snapped. When this ritual had finished, he rolled out two strips of black and white velvet over the floor to form a cross. 'Now I will dance you the war.' What ensued was the evocation of an apocalyptic battlefield, its terror and chaos, its destruction and deathliness – 'his face ravaged . . . striding over a rotting corpse, avoiding a shell, defending a shallow trench that was soaked in blood'. So graphically intense was his tragic satire that the audience was too stunned to applaud. A couple of shorter outbursts followed, perhaps intended as ironic encores: one merely incoherent, as though 'imitating the movements of a medium trying to raise a table in the air', the other something of 'delicious grace'.[57]

Thus closed Nijinsky's unparalleled career: in the evening he returned home to continue the terrifying diary, written over three months, that records in poorly spelt Russian his paranoid delusions and psychotic babble. Berating Diaghilev and spouting garbled Tolstoyan philosophy, he lurches over hundreds of pages between all-consuming love, megalomaniac egoism and petty vindictive hate. Flashes of piercing lucidity alternate with delirious gobbledegook, like the gasps of a drowning man momentarily surfacing for air. After scribbling a series of lunatic letters to Diaghilev, Cocteau, his mother, the President of the Council of the Allied Forces and Jesus among others, he fell silent. For the next thirty years of his curtailed life, Nijinsky was locked in and locked up with Romola holding the keys, as memories of his dancing became a legend of divinity.

———

No sooner had Félix collapsed than the ranks were further depleted when the Ballets Russes's newest star, Lydia Lopokova, went AWOL. At the height of her success in London but embroiled in the breakdown of her marriage and a troublesome love affair with a White Russian officer – and perhaps also piqued by Karsavina's return to queenly precedence – she bolted again. Without any warning, she sent Diaghilev and Grigoriev cursory notes claiming to be suffering a nervous breakdown and for the next six months remained invisible. The press naturally loved the mystery but the trail went nowhere until she re-emerged six months later, apparently without the officer, in a musical comedy on Broadway. It would be over a year before she returned to London.

Top-tier ballerinas were in short supply, as Karsavina was henceforth less available than she had been, taken up with a husband on foreign postings and freelance appearances. Two younger Russians, the sparky Vera Nemchinova (long-suffering girlfriend to the Tolstoyan proselytiser Nikolai Zverev) and elegant Lubov Tchernicheva (usefully married to Grigoriev) stepped up: both of them were highly accomplished, but neither ever quite caught the imagination of a wider public. As for Lydia Sokolova, she had neither the Mariinsky technique nor the facial beauty for glamour roles, nor the girlish personality to suggest simpering prettiness; she was a tough one, excelling in sheer physical stamina and as an interpreter of strongly defined characters. This endeared her to Massine, who cast her as the Chosen Virgin when Diaghilev commissioned him to re-choreograph *The Rite of Spring* in 1920.

This was one of several projects that became possible only after a furious and extensive rift between Diaghilev and Stravinsky had been healed. Money was its root cause – Stravinsky grasping it, Diaghilev lacking it. Flashpoints included the extent to which royalties were owed on scores such as *The Firebird* and *Petrushka* that had originated in Russia (a nation then outside the Berne copyright convention); Diaghilev's lordly assumption that he had first call on Stravinsky's new work; and Stravinsky's consequent resentment at being treated as though he was one of Diaghilev's serfs. But feuds between Russians are chiefly opportunities for the renewal of love and loyalty, and once the bad blood had been spilled and some sort of mollifying resolution achieved, both parties surrendered to bear hugs and vodka toasts. Stravinsky would go on to provide the Ballets Russes with a series of scores that opened up new horizons.

First came a misfire: a balletic reduction of his pre-war opera *Le Rossignol*, in unhappy collaboration with Henri Matisse (who was out of his element in the theatre and found Diaghilev impossible), awkwardly intricate choreography from Massine and insufficient orchestral rehearsal. But then followed the enchanting *Pulcinella*, with music drawn from manuscripts of Pergolesi and other eighteenth-century composers and transformed by Stravinsky's spikily inflected arrangements into something with breathtaking kick and wit – a watershed in the development of a modernist neoclassicism that the composer regarded as his 'discovery of the past . . . a backward look, of course . . . but it was a look in the mirror, too'.[58] For subject matter, Massine returned to his fascination with the *commedia dell'arte* and the street puppet theatres of Naples, devising the simplest of plots round the stock figure of crafty Pulcinella and his amorous escapades. Picasso at first got the wrong end of the stick and presented sketches for something in fancy Second Empire style that so enraged Diaghilev that he threw them on the floor and stamped on them. After the inevitable huffing, Picasso went back to the drawing board and came up with something suggesting a nocturnal piazza with a miraculous simplicity that, as Sokolova put it, 'showed triumphantly what cubism could be and could do'.[59] A white floor-cloth and an absence of footlights created what Richard Buckle described as 'one of the most beautiful stage settings ever made'.[60] After the première at the Paris Opéra in May 1920, there was a wild party, hosted by a Persian prince in a chateau in the suburbs (an event commemorated in *Le Bal du Comte d'Orgel*, a novel by the teenage prodigy Raymond Radiguet, the love of Cocteau's life). It ended at 3 a.m. with bedrooms being raided and a riotous pillow fight instigated by a very drunk Stravinsky.

Next came a return to *The Rite of Spring*. The necessity of a huge orchestra requiring extensive rehearsal made this a very expensive project, but Roerich's scenery and costumes, kept in storage since 1913, could be recycled, and the brilliant young couturière Coco Chanel, newly embarked on a tempestuous affair with Stravinsky, generously guaranteed the production against loss (rather to the chagrin of Misia Sert, her friend and rival for Diaghilev's female affections, who liked to think she was the primary bankroller). Stravinsky hadn't greatly approved of Nijinsky's attempt to imitate the score's complex rhythms literally in the choreography; he was marginally happier with Massine's version,* which, in Massine's words,

* Stravinsky would admit during an interview with the BBC's Third Programme forty years later that Massine's 'Dalcrozian gymnastics' dismayed him, and he preferred the piece left as a concert work, open to the listener's imagination.

'did not account each bar as an individual thing to choreograph'.[61] Instead it followed its own contrapuntal passage through the score, sidestepping the title's ethnographic implications and the pathos that had imbued Nijinsky's treatment. But the abstraction made it more 'mechanical', according to Grigoriev, and it 'failed to be moving'.[62]

Sokolova, aged twenty-four, was given her big break when she was cast to dance the Chosen Virgin whose sacrifice forms the climax of the work. The challenge could hardly have come at a worse time for her, with a three-year-old daughter in frail health, the breakdown of her marriage to the drunken Kremnev and a burgeoning clandestine romance with another dancer, Leon Woizikowski, who was otherwise involved. But her capacity for hard work was boundless and in gruelling sessions with the relentless and dictatorial Massine, she forced the steps for the seven-minute solo into her muscle memory, often without reference to the music. The idiom bore 'little relation to any kind of dancing that had been done before', giving the impression of 'a creature galvanised by an electric current'. 'Whatever it did to the audience, it nearly killed me,' she recalled. 'I had to keep thinking, acting, and counting all at once'[63] – helped only at some points by one of the corps surreptitiously calling out the numbers. And to make it all the more nerve-racking, she had to stand stock still for twelve minutes before the solo, staring out into the auditorium brandishing a clenched fist, commanded to not so much as blink.

She was rewarded with a personal triumph, but the ballet itself earned a mixed reception and many of the critics agreed with Grigoriev. In London, *The Times* called it 'passionless';[64] 'mere plastic exercises, denuded of all expression . . . an apotheosis of exhibition gymnastics'[65] was the verdict in Paris of the revered Franco-Russian critic André Levinson. Many choreographers have grappled with *The Rite of Spring* since then, and none of them has

decisively mastered it: perhaps the music is too graphically vivid
and rhythmically complex for dance to add anything to the visceral
impact it has in the concert hall.

Massine's relationship with Diaghilev was now fast coming
unstuck on all fronts and those in the inner circle held their breath
for the inevitable schism. It wasn't just that Diaghilev was unusually
irritable and edgy; a more fatal sign was that in the past Massine
had always deferred to Diaghilev's judgement – now he could afford
to ignore or defy it, and sometimes to win his point. The toast of
the town, irresistibly attractive to women, garlanded with acclaim
and inundated with offers, he no longer needed Diaghilev, and he
wanted his freedom – sexual as well as artistic. To put Diaghilev off
the scent, Massine feigned interest in Sokolova and made an ill-
considered joke in his speech at *The Rite of Spring*'s opening-night
party to the effect that he was about to run off with her. Through
his spies Diaghilev was all too aware of Sokolova's romantic situation and would have realised that this was only bravado. So what
was the game? When he put private detectives on Massine's trail,
it emerged that his attentions were in fact focused on a pretty and
talented English girl in the company's lower ranks with a stage
name of Vera Savina, née Clark. 'As innocent as a new-born lamb,'
thought the more worldly Sokolova.[66]

In Rome in January 1921, there were ugly scenes. According
to some accounts, Diaghilev summoned a trembling Savina to his
hotel suite and got her drunk as he tried to persuade her to desist.
When she refused, he stripped her naked and flung her into Massine's room through the adjoining door screeching, '*Voilà*, there is
the whore you are going to leave me for.'[67] Less luridly, Grigoriev recalls Diaghilev 'in great agitation' asking him one morning
to inform Massine that his contract had expired and there would
be no further call on his services.[68] The message was delivered as

Massine was starting a rehearsal – he turned deathly pale as if he had not expected it, but quietly left the room and wasn't seen again. Savina left the company the same day. They married a few months later, only to divorce in 1925.

After a few days of the tearful hysteria obligatory to Russians at such moments, Diaghilev recovered some composure. 'I shall find someone else,' he said.[69]

The basic sources for this chapter are Tamara Karsavina, *Theatre Street*, pp. 298–354; Romola Nijinsky, *Nijinsky*, pp. 205–326; Cyril Beaumont, *The Diaghilev Ballet in London*, pp. 9–76; S. L. Grigoriev, *The Diaghilev Ballet 1909–1929*, pp. 92–182; Lydia Sokolova, *Dancing for Diaghilev*, pp. 65–184; Boris Kochno, *Diaghilev and the Ballets Russes*, pp. 95–152; Nesta Macdonald, *Diaghilev Observed*, pp. 125–266; Richard Buckle, *Diaghilev*, pp. 283–372; Lynn Garafola, 'The Ballets Russes in America', pp. 122–40 and *Diaghilev's Ballets Russes*, pp. 76–97 and 330–44; Bronislava Nijinska, *Early Memories*, pp. 494–508; Leslie Norton, *Massine and the Twentieth-Century Ballet*, passim; Vicente Garcia-Marquez, *Massine*, pp. 43–163; Sjeng Scheijen, *Diaghilev: A Life*, pp. 294–374; Jennifer Homans, *Apollo's Angels*, pp. 245–89; Jane Pritchard, *Diaghilev and the Golden Age of the Ballets Russes*, passim; and Lucy Moore, *Nijinsky*, pp. 180–215.

# 6
## NOVELTIES

———

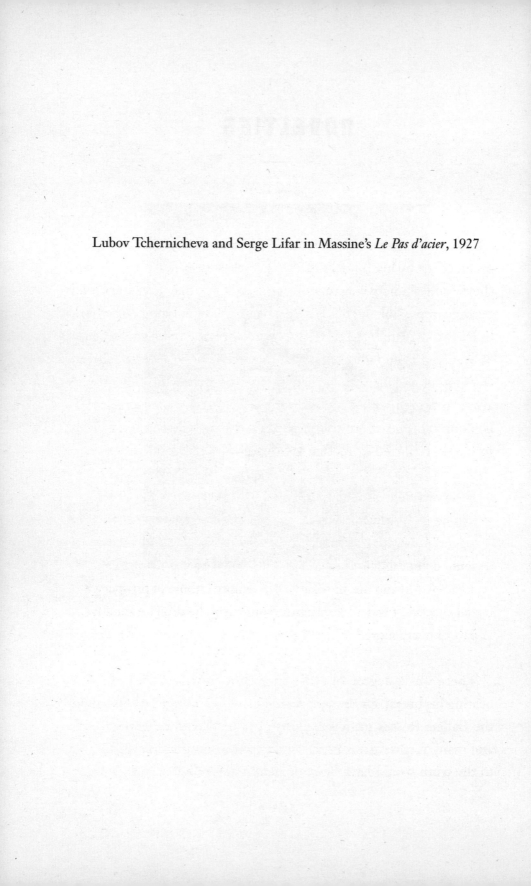
Lubov Tchernicheva and Serge Lifar in Massine's *Le Pas d'acier*, 1927

Through the war years and their aftermath, Diaghilev had been excluded from his homeland. As the revolution had turned Bolshevik and vindictive against his class, a sense that his return had become impossible fuelled his nostalgia: 'Oh how I long to be back in Russia,' he lamented to Grigoriev, 'to breathe in its air and gain new energy from its soil. But shall I ever be able to?'[1] His beloved stepmother had died and he had no news of his half-brothers in the army. Although such anxieties were seldom mentioned to anyone, he poured his heart out to the conductor Ernest Ansermet, who in July 1919 reported in a letter to Stravinsky,

> He is very depressed and exhausted and cried a great deal. He told me it was time to shut up shop because he felt he was at loggerheads with everyone . . . He loved Russia, he said, but he could do nothing for her . . . he complained he was living in a dream world and not in reality, in an empty bubble of prosperity and success. It was all just masturbation. And he didn't want any part of it any more.[2]

There was a degree of self-dramatising in this: even as he was beating his breast, *La Boutique fantasque* and *Le Tricorne* had brought the Ballets Russes to new heights of popular and critical success, and many further irons in the fire were warming up nicely. Closer to the truth would have been the admission that a certain Russian romanticism had played itself out. Continuous chronological narrative of a sort purveyed by Fokine fell from favour, to be replaced by the plotless, the episodic, the disjointed, the abstract – disconnection rather than connection, suites of dances rather than stories. Bakst's exotic palette had become *vieux jeu* in an age of cubism; the company's personnel had become increasingly international; and, depending on your perspective, its aesthetic culture had been transformed, enriched or diluted by its encounters with Spain and Italian *commedia dell'arte*. Massine's innovations were challenging and shaking the absolutist classical traditions of the St Petersburg school: in an interview with the *Observer*, he laid out with crystalline clarity his manifesto for an 'emancipation' from classicism: 'There are many possibilities in the movements of the body that have never been taken into account. The classic school concerned itself almost solely with the feet, the leg, the knee and the arms . . . And yet our bodies have an orchestra of thirty different instrumentalists, each of which is duplicated and each of which is capable of being brought into play.'[3] Conservatives were sceptical and would become more so, their position encapsulated by André Levinson who deplored 'the growing tendency towards a burlesque exaggeration of movement, a style that was angular and labored . . . it was no longer that indefinable soaring sprit that pleased but the heavy stroke'.[4]

A stream of White Russian émigrés was on its way west, however, to reinvigorate the company's roots. One of its number was the *wunderkind* composer Sergei Prokofiev, commissioned by Diaghilev in 1914 when he was only twenty-three and now ready to produce; another was his old Nevsky Pickwickian friend the emollient and efficient Walter Nouvel, eagerly signed up by Diaghilev as his business manager and who remained a loyal functionary for the rest of his life. Even closer would be Diaghilev's professional relationship with another, unexpected arrival – a cadaverously beautiful seventeen-year-old called Boris Evgenievich Kochno.[5]

Born in 1904, the son of a colonel in the Hussars under the tsar, Kochno and his mother had left Moscow in the turmoil of 1917, making their way down through Ukraine, where at one point they encountered the Polish composer Karol Szymanowski, who became violently infatuated with the youth. Moving on to Paris in 1920, Kochno fell in with the alluring bohemian couple Sergei and Vera Sudeikin. She was an actress who eventually became Stravinsky's second wife; he was a minor artist and a friend of Diaghilev's from *Mir iskusstva* days who had designed an unsuccessful *Salome* ballet in 1913. An unabashed bisexual, he took Boris under his wing and then decided that he could do all parties a favour by passing him on to Diaghilev. It was a smart move.

Wildly ambitious and precociously cultured, with poetic aspirations, Kochno was ready for anything. Sudeikin carefully plotted the introduction, grooming Kochno in what to say and what not to say and impersonating the impresario in an imaginary interview. Such preparations were hardly necessary: Kochno had read up on the Ballets Russes and had even seen Sokolova in *The Rite of Spring* during the 1920 Paris season. He knew exactly how to make himself agreeable as well as homosexually available. The moment Kochno appeared on Sudeikin's fabricated errand, Diaghilev was enchanted and impressed to the point of offering the boy a job as his personal secretary.

Kochno asked what his duties would be: 'A secretary must know how to make himself indispensable' was the gnomic reply, and Kochno unfailingly heeded it.[6] Nobody altogether liked him, but there he invariably was, fastidiously polite, evasively epicene, slipping around and standing back, fitting in and picking up, a foxy shape-shifter and gate-keeper with a disconcerting habit of talking with his eyes half closed, not only indispensable but also ubiquitous.

Diaghilev gave him no salary, but paid his expenses, bought him smart clothes and allowed him a ration of six cigarettes a day. Whatever physical relationship they had soon dwindled – perhaps it was merely ephemeral. One story that circulated is that during their first meeting Diaghilev had told Kochno to take off his clothes. 'Too hairy!' he announced dismissively when he saw him naked, and took no further bodily interest in him;* perhaps, as Richard Buckle shrewdly suggested, the fact that both men came from the same social class may have been 'a little off-putting' too.[7] But they became profoundly and unshakably intimate, addressing each other coyly in letters as 'darling' and 'little kitten'.[8] Massine had fired Diaghilev up with his energy and creativity, his mercurial intellect and osmotic receptivity; Kochno, on the other hand, a reflective intellectual who kept his counsel, smoothed him down and reassured him.

Despite these new assets, the void left by Massine's departure remained, and the new works of 1921 were mounted without any overall choreographic vision.

For *Cuadro Flamenco* Diaghilev cannily exploited the Hispanic habit of improvisation that had been Félix's downfall by recruiting a group of peasants, gypsies and low life and allowing them to go their own way and let rip with guitars and castanets, framed by a set designed by Picasso, who recycled some ideas discarded from *Pulcinella*. Selected through hilariously chaotic auditions in Seville,

---

* An alternative version of this anecdote is told by Jean Babilée, who presumably heard it from Kochno himself: 'Kochno once asked Diaghilev, "Do you think I am handsome?" Diaghilev replied without a moment's thought, "You will be handsome when you shave your head." He gradually lost his hair and was great!' (Michael Meylac, *Behind the Scenes at the Ballets Russes*, p. 279.)

the ensemble included the ravishingly beautiful María Dalbaicín, a mercurial dwarf called Gabrielita, and the legless Mateo el sin Pies ('the without feet'), who appeared on a trolley and then danced on the stumps of thighs encased in leather sheaths. The concept of the show sounds so simple, yet it proved a constant headache backstage. The dancers could be neither tamed nor disciplined and their expectations of fame and fortune were deluded. Illiteracy also made them suspicious of anything approaching a written contract; instead they made ever-inflating financial demands and insisted that their sisters, cousins and aunts came along for the ride too. They weren't united among themselves either: hypersensitive to every passing rumour and furiously competitive, they would attack each other in alcoholic rages as they flounced, bridled and threatened. The authenticity of their raw bravado in performance was irresistible, however, with primmer elements in the stalls left blushing in consternation at the women's habit of acknowledging applause by cupping their breasts and shaking them at the audience.

The other novelty was *Chout*, with a scenario adapted from a folk tale characterised by what the young Diaghilev fanatic Cyril Beaumont described as 'tortuous Russian humour' involving the high jinks of devious 'buffoons'. Better categorised as a farce in dumbshow rather than a ballet, it was cobbled together by Goncharova's partner Larionov and others. The action, replete with cartoon violence, was deemed infantile and not very funny, but Larionov's aggressively cubist setting ('So vivid and so dazzling that it was almost painful to look at the stage,' thought Beaumont[9]) and young Prokofiev's electric score won stunned admiration from many – one exception being the influential and venerable critic Ernest Newman of the *Sunday Times*, whose persistent sniping at the new Russian school of composers finally goaded Diaghilev into a barbed letter of riposte:

In my fairly wide travels, I have never read such *démodé* articles with such 'provincial' ideas as those of Newman. What a pity for such an amiable man. This year, he has a few white hairs. Why make those white hairs blush at the laughter of young people all over the world? Poor old friend, act with the dignity of your advancing years and do not align yourself with the fools who boo the première of *Carmen* or the paintings of Manet or the poetry of Mallarmé.[10]

What happened next seems to negate this claim to be cheerleader of the new, pointing to a curious dialectic in the last phase of Diaghilev's Ballets Russes: a pursuit of the modish and the contemporary that bounced off a regressive fixation on the courtly culture of Louis Quatorze.

Diaghilev was greatly struck by the success of a spectacular orientalist musical comedy, *Chu Chin Chow*, which had been drawing nightly full houses in London's West End since the latter part of the war. Why should he not compete by producing a ballet blockbuster, fun for all the family, that would run and run and make everyone a lot of money? Thus he alighted on the idea of re-staging *The Sleeping Princess* (so called to distinguish it from the pantomime *The Sleeping Beauty*, and sometimes referred to as *La Belle au bois dormant*), the fairy-tale ballet with a score by Tchaikovsky and choreography by Petipa that had so enchanted Alexandre Benois and the Nevsky Pickwickians when it was first staged in St Petersburg in 1890.

But since then revolutions of culture and fashion had left this pageant of monarchist grandeur identified with everything from which Diaghilev had been attempting to liberate ballet. Interviewed by *The Times* in 1911, Diaghilev had specifically dismissed it as 'interminable' and too baroquely Frenchified to be of relevance to his enterprise. Slow and stately, it was encrusted with imperial rituals and traditions of homage that the twentieth century had rendered meaningless: parades of dainty fairies in tutus waving magic wands at bewigged monarchs could mean little to sophisticated adults in an age of Picasso's cubism, Stravinsky's primitivism and Massine's angularity. Even before the war, truncated versions of the more dramatically coherent nineteenth-century ballets such as *Giselle* and *Swan Lake* had been written off as dusty relics, and a gilded production of scenes from *The Sleeping Beauty* with Pavlova had flopped in New York in 1916. Diaghilev was now proposing an uncut version spread over an entire evening, something quite unheard of in London, where no single ballet ever lasted for more than forty minutes. So this new project represented a gamble with public taste and habit, as well as a reversal of aesthetic principles.

To some extent Diaghilev's calculations were mercenary, and circumscribed by the failure to find a successor to Massine. Yet, at a more personal level, the project must also have assuaged his longing to return to his roots and the lost world of his youthful experiences. Although he had no sentimentality about tsarist absolutism, the moral certainties implied by Petipa's symmetries and formalities had an atavistic appeal to him, evoking emotions of awe and reverence that modernism suppressed. In 1926, Jean Cocteau would publish a book promoting the idea of *un rappel à l'ordre*, a 'call to order' aimed at slowing the frenetic pace of artistic change. 'The speed of a runaway horse counts for nothing,' he sagely remarks. Style was moving too fast in too many directions away from what he called '*solide élégance*' and '*formes authentiques*' that respected clarity, handicraft and draughtsmanship. *The Sleeping Princess* anticipated that position and pushed it a stage further into radical conservatism. Sjeng Scheijen's view that it was also 'an act of political defiance . . . an ambitious celebration of pre-revolutionary tsarist art, performed by decidedly unproletarian political refugees, presented in the capital of the anti-Bolshevist coalition's main ally' is perhaps excessively contentious.[11]

To an unusual extent, Diaghilev was hands on throughout. He 'entered into every detail of the production', according to Grigoriev, and 'took an active part in the *mise en scène*, directing much of it himself'.[12] Stravinsky was engaged to edit Tchaikovsky's score, providing some new orchestration and inserting numbers from other Tchaikovsky ballets. The choreography was largely taken from Petipa, transmitted via Nikolai Sergeyev, a ballet master who had escaped from Russia with documents notating the steps, and the dancers were groomed by the venerable Enrico Cecchetti, who had participated in the 1890 production.

To fill in the gaps and add some new numbers, Nijinsky's sister Bronislava was brought back into the fold: she had fallen out with Diaghilev when she had sided with her brother during the rift of 1913, but now that Nijinsky had lost his sanity the question of her loyalty was no longer an issue and reports of ballets she had created in Kyiv suggested she had great potential. Her aesthetic was influenced by constructivism, her brother's experiments and a fascination with what would one day be called 'gender bending' (she herself dressed mannishly and often danced male roles). Privately, she thought the *Sleeping Princess* project so retrograde as to be 'an absurdity', but she needed work and had no options.[13]

To fill the large cast Diaghilev recruited at all levels. London's beloved 'Loppy', Lydia Lopokova, returned after dalliances and a miscarriage to dance the gracious Lilac Fairy; Stravinsky's lover Vera Sudeikina played the non-dancing role of the Queen; the flamenco seductress María Dalbaicín made a stylish appearance as Scheherazade among the wedding guests in the final scene; and in a tremendous coup the Italian Carlotta Brianza, who had created the role of Aurora in St Petersburg thirty years previously, was persuaded to reincarnate herself as the hideous crone of a wicked fairy, Carabosse.

Three stellar émigrée Russian ballerinas were found to dance the demanding central role of Aurora. If the 'call to order' was also a reassertion of the classical Mariinsky style of dancing that Nijinsky and Massine had subverted, then they epitomised it. With Karsavina out of the running as she had chosen to accompany her husband on a diplomatic posting to Bulgaria, in for the première came Olga Spessivtseva (simplified for Londoners to Spessiva), a spindle-slender birdlike creature of raven-haired beauty who had been holed up destitute and tubercular in a garret in Riga until an agent tracked her down. One of those dancers who seemed almost pathologically self-involved (in her case sometimes to the point of ignoring the music altogether), she was revered for the serene fluency of her technique and marvelled at for her favourite tipple – hot champagne. Her two deputies, older, more worldly and scintillating, were Lubov Egorova and Vera Trefilova, both based in Paris.* Fans and critics had great fun assessing their relative merits.

Yet it was the spectacle more than the dancing that stunned audiences and sold the show. Commissioning the designs from Benois – an expert in the Louis Quatorze period of the ballet's setting and guardian of vivid memories of the original 1890 production – would have been the first and obvious choice, but he was ensconced in St Petersburg as curator of Old Masters at the Hermitage and refused to leave Russia. Derain wasn't interested, and Picasso, Goncharova

---

* As back-ups, Vera Nemchinova and Lydia Lopokova also stepped in for a few performances. According to Lydia Sokolova, the latter was no good: 'She lacked the necessary poetry . . . I felt that at any moment . . . she would burst out laughing or lose her drawers.' (*Dancing for Diaghilev*, pp. 194–5.)

or Larionov would have been unsuitable. So Diaghilev went cap in hand to Bakst, who had been licking his wounds in Paris since *La Boutique fantasque* had been stolen from him and given to Derain.

At first Bakst baulked. He had already designed the piece for Pavlova's dead-duck New York staging and the scale of the project was daunting – over 300 costumes, to be produced on a timetable that allowed barely three months for preparation. His arm was twisted as only Diaghilev knew how, and he set to, drawing on engravings of baroque palaces designed for the stage by the eighteenth-century Bibiena dynasty, with barley-sugar columns, marbled pilasters, exotic statuary, domes, colonnades, and vast flights of stairs on a dizzyingly angled perspective that increased the illusion of vast depth and height.

To execute these magnificent backcloths four different scene-painting studios were engaged, including that of Elizabeth and Vladimir Polunin, who had also expanded Picasso's sketches on the floor of their atelier. Bakst sent out his instructions from Paris 'like a field marshal', Polunin recalled, but 'it was often difficult to fathom his meaning'[14] and more problems were caused by the poor quality of the crudely fire-proofed canvas purchased. Some of the costume designs were recycled from Pavlova's version, but they all required such impeccable and elaborate tailoring that the seamstresses were still delivering the finished articles to the stage door only minutes before the first performance. Bakst had a bipolar temperament and according to his biographer Charles Spencer, 'the physical effort' and 'nervous exhaustion' that the project required, alongside 'the effect of his advanced sense of isolation and depression, must have shortened his life'.[15]

So hair-raisingly complex was the rehearsal schedule that the première had to be postponed for two days at the last minute. Diaghilev was in the theatre at all hours, adjusting, finessing, inspecting. With the Ballets Russes's reputation in London at a new peak, the stakes could not have been higher, not least because a fortune had been invested in the show – the impresario Oswald Stoll had stumped up a massive £10,000 for the scenery and costumes, to be recouped from the box-office takings. A punt was being taken that anything opening with a splash in November in the West End's popular Alhambra Theatre could hope to catch the market for a Christmas family treat. But production costs had doubled to the tipping point at which even the sale of every ticket couldn't have balanced the books.

And naturally the opening night was a disappointment, albeit one that also drew the usual storms of applause for the dancers. The stage was simply too small and primitively equipped for the challenges the production posed. Glitches in the flying machinery meant that two of the special effects collapsed into bathos, as the timber frame lifting the magically ascending thickets of foliage broke 'with a great cracking noise' and some descending gauzes snagged on a piece of scenery and ended up looking like 'a monster bale of muslin in a draper's shop'.[16] These clunks reduced Diaghilev to sobbing rage and hysterical shrieks to the effect that the whole thing was a catastrophe.

It absolutely wasn't, but the burden of the reviews was twofold: Bakst might have surpassed himself: 'All the colours of all jewels, of all sunsets, of all flames, are in the stage pictures . . . such orange, saffron and moss-green of the court ladies. Such glistening azure and ermine of the royalties' robes', swooned the *Daily Mail*;[17] 'Spectacle has never reached such an artistic height as M. Bakst attains in this old ballet,' decided *The Times* – but didn't it all lack 'intimacy and directness of feeling'?[18] And wasn't it ultimately, as *Vogue* insisted, 'a long-winded, cumbrous, mechanical' affair, 'constructed on the formal mid-Victorian lines' and replete with 'abysmal commonplaces'?[19]

The surviving photographic record, unanimated by the subtle atmospherics of Diaghilev's lighting, certainly makes the spectacle appear merely pompous – an overdressed Edwardian pageant, played out against flat painted boards and canvases. Nor can the images begin to suggest the magical effect that the muted grey and black palette of the scenery had when set against the gorgeous scarlets, purples and yellows of the costumes. Some commentators worried that the clean line of the dancing was encumbered and muddied by so much splendour, all tasselled and wigged in brocades and velvets, while those signed up to modernism considered the heavy realism in Bakst's concept as retrograde to the Ballets Russes's innovative spirit. Bloomsbury's sophisticates were revolted (Lytton Strachey told Sacheverell Sitwell that 'it made him feel sick'[20]) and perhaps those without a sweet tooth found it just too much of a good thing.

After that knife-edge first night and the subsequent mixed reviews, however, things settled down: the king and queen visited, the town flocked and over the Christmas period all seemed to be well. But come the new year, the West End sunk into one of its periodic and inexplicable slumps and the expense of sustaining this enormous cash-hungry creature became unsustainable. Every tactic was tried or considered to boost sales. Cuts were made to the running time and more matinées scheduled. There was talk of filming the show, in 'natural colours' with synchronised music[21] and thoughts of pepping it up by introducing live animals; or a child who could act as a once-upon-a-time narrator; or a comic episode to be enacted in front of the curtain; or a witty ironic speech to be written by George Bernard Shaw. To no avail. The bills mounted, the receipts dropped; it would just have to close.

Yet it ranks as the most glorious of failures and served its higher purpose – Grigoriev remembered Diaghilev watching it from the wings and proudly sighing, 'This is the last relic of the great days of St Petersburg'[22] (even if, superstitious as he was, he gloomily decided that its problems constituted 'an occult warning' that it was not his 'business to revive the glories of a bygone age'[23]). The production played over a hundred performances. A late upswing was not enough to turn the financial tide, but the last week a sell-out, so at least the show went out in triumph before passing into legend.

Its legacy ran deep: of all Diaghilev's productions, this was the one recalled by posterity with the most hushed awe, as a totally immersive experience of another world, another era. In some it inspired a fanatical response: Cyril Beaumont 'went almost every evening . . . for the whole of its run' and remarked that the Alhambra had become 'a kind of ballet club' of kindred devotees.[24] But to see it once could be enough, especially for the young: the cartoonist, stage designer and architectural historian Osbert Lancaster was only eleven when he was exposed to its magic and it changed his life:

> Nothing I had ever seen had in any way prepared me for the magnificence that was disclosed on the rise of the curtain of the Alhambra, and for weeks afterwards my drawing books were packed with hopeful but pathetic attempts to recapture something of the glory of that matinée, and then and there I formed an ambition that was not destined to be fulfilled for more than thirty years.[25]

*The Sleeping Princess* cost Diaghilev dear. He had banked on a six-month run and then a transfer to Paris, but such was the shortfall on the deal that the impresario Stoll took the scenery and costumes hostage. Sequestered for decades under the stage of the Coliseum, many of these gorgeous artefacts tragically rotted before being bought up by a private collector. Owing Stoll £11,000 he simply did not have, Diaghilev was reduced to selling prized personal possessions – down to a black-pearl collar stud given to him by Lady Ripon. To make matters worse, his long-serving and -suffering Italian valet had absconded, taking booty with him. Having cadged the considerable amount of £300 from the wealthy mother of Hilda Bewicke, one of his junior English dancers, Diaghilev then slunk off to Paris where he and Kochno took attic rooms and ate their meals in a seedy *guinguette* alongside the cab drivers.

The Ballets Russes's future in Britain was now in jeopardy, inasmuch as the law forbade Diaghilev to enter any new contract until the debt was paid off – thus preventing any further seasons in London, his primary power-base since 1918. The workforce was left high and dry with salaries in arrears, and even steadfast old-timers such as Lydia Sokolova were obliged to seek out alternative employment in the froth of the dance-based musical shows that were all the rage – a market that Massine was busily serving. Yet, as Benois put it, 'Diaghilev's real nature was that of a fighter.'[26] He was down but not out; if *The Sleeping Princess* was a cul-de-sac, it was not the end of the road. The question was only how and where the project could be rebooted. For a moment, he contemplated establishing a joint-stock company raising money through shareholders. But this would have tied Diaghilev's hands to all sorts of regulatory surveillance by men in suits: ever the loner and chancer, he preferred to rely on the patronage of susceptible wealthy ladies who could be charmed to sign cheques over a bibulous lunch.

Deals with theatres in the straitened post-war era had become ever tighter, but somehow enough was scratched together three months later to mount a brief season in Paris. Extracts from *The Sleeping Princess* were performed, using costumes recycled from storage, alongside two new short works with scores by Stravinsky, both with roots deep in Russian culture.

*Mavra* was a farcical one-act opera based on a poem by Pushkin with music by Stravinsky and a libretto by Kochno. This flopped, and in the process brought one of Diaghilev's most important relationships to a sorry conclusion. One rider that Bakst had insisted on in accepting the Herculean challenge of designing *The Sleeping Princess* was that he was also allotted the more chic assignment of *Mavra*, conceived originally as a curtain-raiser. Diaghilev agreed, but when it became clear that staging *Mavra* before *The Sleeping Princess* would result in a performance running for well over four hours, the opera was postponed. When it re-emerged eighteen months later, Diaghilev again did the dirty on Bakst by assigning it to another designer. There was another furious quarrel, exacerbated by Diaghilev's failure to pay Bakst fully for his labours on *The Sleeping Princess*, and Bakst died unreconciled and wretched in 1924. *Renard* was an animal fable, choreographed with liberal use of circus acrobatics by Nijinska and narrated by singers in the orchestra pit. This was considered much more likeable, but proved short-lived. After its première, the *branché* literary English couple Sydney and Violet Schiff threw a lavish party at the Hôtel Majestic, at which Diaghilev, Picasso and Stravinsky rubbed shoulders with Marcel Proust and James Joyce. The evening wasn't much fun; none of these geniuses got on particularly well with each other. But the show was back on the road.

Going where? The question of a return to Russia festered. The new regime had made overtures, offering Diaghilev a visa to the Soviet Union and dangling the possibility of a tour. Some part of him might have been fulfilled by that homecoming, but he was too sceptical of Bolshevik treachery to accept, particularly because the indispensable Kochno and others in the company would have been arrested as liable for military service once they crossed the border. The solution came via the sewing-machine heiress and salon hostess Winnaretta Singer, widow of the Prince de Polignac, a force for good in Parisian musical life who had commissioned *Renard* from Stravinsky. Her husband's nephew was married to Charlotte, heiress of the Grimaldi dynasty that governed the principality of Monaco. Through Winnaretta's intercession and Charlotte's complaisance, a plan was hatched that would save the Ballets Russes from a precarious hand-to-mouth existence and give the company for the first time a permanent base that would allow it to function year round.

Monaco had ranked as the poorest state in Europe until its rulers decided in the 1850s to invent the city of Monte Carlo and make its fortune, Las Vegas style, out of low-regulation, high-stakes gambling and tourism *de luxe*.[27] It became a place, Osbert Lancaster would put it, 'where leisure was taken seriously'.[28] Amid the fast set, decadent royals and gold-digging courtesans who soon swarmed the place, Russian plutocracy was also numerous, swelled after the Revolution by émigrés with trunks crammed with jewels and cash. Money may have been uppermost in everyone's mind, but to provide momentary relief from the tribulations of roulette and *chemin de fer* at the roaringly successful casino (formally known as the Société des bains de mer de Monaco), the architect of the Paris Opéra Charles Garnier was commissioned to build alongside it a bijou concert hall of similar gilded lavishness, later expanded to accommodate theatrical performance too. It was this building that the Ballets Russes would inhabit, to the benefit of all.

The deal was simple: the company would be generously subsidised to be resident here from autumn to spring, spending the weeks up to Christmas rehearsing, followed by a ballet season that would segue into the existing opera season. The summer months would be spent touring or on leave. The town was a known quantity, as the company had appeared there regularly if intermittently since 1911 and capacity audiences were virtually guaranteed. Diaghilev was excited by the possibilities. He could dabble in opera production again, and he hatched plans to establish an annual arts festival, a museum of 'living [i.e. modern] art' involving Picasso and an avant-garde variety theatre called Plastic Hall that would combine dance with film and other genres – Cocteau's bright idea. The staging of a handful of small-scale little-known French operas, smartly made over by young composers and painters, was all that transpired – the public was not interested; nothing, sadly, came of either the arts festival or the Plastic Hall.

The finest fruit of this new phase in the story was *Les Noces* – a stylised depiction of the celebrations surrounding a Russian peasant wedding. It had been a long time coming. Stravinsky had been working up the music on and off for a decade, and it had passed through several transformations before reaching its final shape – scored for four pianos and percussion, with voices chanting and shouting a Joycean collage of toasts, blessings and jokes, old wives' tales and pious exhortations.

Diaghilev now felt sufficiently confident of Nijinska to commission her for the choreography. Her brother and then Massine had previously been pencilled in for this assignment, and the impersonality and angularity of what she produced suggest the stylistic influence of both of them. But nothing should detract from her own genius in exploiting a vocabulary that included episodes of stabbing downward-thrusting feet, deep bends from the waist, hands firmly clenched in defiance rather than gracefully extended in languor, and the formation of what Stephanie Jordan calls 'the hard geometry of phalanxes, wedges, pyramids and walls'[29] shaped in flat horizontal lines, with the women hovering on pointe to resemble the elongated figures in mosaics and icons. The bride and groom dance very little, their parents not at all: the energy in the movement all radiates from the community of wedding guests, their steps and movements often undifferentiated by gender. The classical corps de ballet owes something to the straight lines of the military parade ground; Nijinska reinvents that unity here in terms of the constructivist fascination with the machine and the Bolshevik emphasis on the mass rather than the individual. As much proletarians as peasants, the dancers are implacable and heedless, drained of personality, subsumed into the collective. Neither Bride nor Groom shows any enthusiasm for this mating, as they are being brought together by custom rather than emotion: they seem to be only robots, impelled by Stravinsky's complex rhythmic commands.

There is another dimension to the project that has been insufficiently noticed: it represents the result of a collaboration between two creative women. Although female choreographers ('ballet mistresses') of little repute had long been arranging dances in the variety theatres, and women had won more recognition as painters since impressionism, new ground was being broken here on the front line of the avant-garde. So unquestionable were the talents involved that nobody felt special pleading was at work. Natalia Goncharova initially designed *Les Noces* in the richly coloured, naive picture-book idiom she had used for *Le Coq d'or*, but she and Nijinska eventually agreed to eliminate any hint of sentimental pageantry and substitute instead a concept of stark, almost penitential simplicity. The dancers wore dark brown and white costumes based on their rehearsal clothes; the scenery gave only the most minimal indications of bare cell-like interiors. Yet the spectacle was in its way every bit as memorable as that of Bakst's *Sleeping Princess*, and *Les Noces* stands as the first indisputably great work of theatrical art predominantly created by women. Diaghilev could be dismissively rude about the female physique, professing himself repulsed by Rubensesque breasts and buttocks, but it is to his credit that, in this case at least, talent not gender was his criterion.

*Les Noces* had its première in Paris in June 1923 and reached London three years later: its radicalism shocked and bewildered some, but enthralled many others and today, when the impact of so many other Ballets Russes sensations has faded, it continues to exert its unique power. In a box at that first performance sat the spectral figure of Nijinsky, next to his wife Romola. Locked in his madness, he sat in impassive silence throughout a performance that also included 'his' *Petrushka*: at what level could he have registered that *Les Noces* was music once destined for him to choreograph and that it had passed instead to his sister? Lydia Lopokova (whose relationship with Diaghilev had soured since his failure to pay her for *The Sleeping Princess*) wrote to her future husband Maynard Keynes, 'I went into the box and there I saw indeed Nijinsky but he did not know me, nor anybody, he does not recognise anyone, but being in a quiet state the doctors want to give him a thrill, so as to move him, and then perhaps he might be cured.'[30] But he was unmoved and uncured.

Not to be outgunned by the Schiffs and their swish do at the Majestic after *Renard*, Gerald and Sara Murphy – the wealthy American couple at the epicentre of Riviera chic who served as models for Dick and Nicole Diver in Scott Fitzgerald's *Tender is the Night* – threw an even more lavish soirée to celebrate *Les Noces*. Keen amateur artists, the Murphys had become Ballets Russes hangers-on, working for nothing as scene-painters in Goncharova's and Larionov's studio, but their value was more about the almighty dollar than their artistic abilities. For the party they rented a barge on the Seine and assembled a guest list led by the usual suspects. The gimmick was the replacement of fresh flowers (this being Sunday, and all the florists closed) with pyramids of old toys bought up from a Montparnasse flea market and arranged by Picasso into a massive improvised sculpture crowned by a stuffed cow perched on top of a ladder. Cocteau showed off as usual, dressing up in naval gear and shouting out that the barge was sinking when it wasn't. At another point in the proceedings, Stravinsky ran the length of the cabin and leapt cleanly through the central hoop in a huge laurel wreath hung from the ceiling in homage to his score.

But for sheer éclat nothing could surpass the *'fête merveilleuse'* held a week later at the Palace of Versailles, organised in aid of its restoration by Diaghilev's pre-war Parisian colleague Gabriel Astruc. Juan Gris designed a cubistic installation that played off the dazzling baroque reflections of the Galerie des Glaces, where a translucent staircase leading to a platform was erected, and Louis XIV's bedchamber was commandeered as the dressing room (after the late-running dress rehearsal, Diaghilev and Kochno ended up locked in and obliged to hunker down for the night on the enormous royal couch). Actors of the Comédie-Française in costumes of Molière's era declaimed verse, mingling with opera singers and dancers who performed excerpts from *The Sleeping Princess*. As a climactic apotheosis, a figure impersonating *le Roi Soleil* slowly ascended the staircase in fabulous blue and gold robes, hailed by trumpeting heralds (one of them Kochno in Roman armour) and accompanied by ladies in vast panniered skirts and blackface pages who spread out a magnificent train embroidered with golden fleurs-de-lys. Later, while a banquet illuminated by flaming torches was served in the Galerie des Batailles, fireworks exploded in the gardens and on the terraces. 'It was something I could expect to see only once in a lifetime,' recalled Sokolova,[31] and a consummation of Diaghilev's penchant for the *ancien régime*.

———

Now that Diaghilev was established on a firmer footing in Monte Carlo, dancers such as Sokolova and Woizikowski were only too happy to abandon the mediocrity of the commercial scene and flock back to him. A brisk, clever, Anglo-Irish girl who had pretentiously changed her name from Edris Stannus to Nina Devalois (*sic*) joined up too, as did five new boys from Kyiv, former pupils of Nijinska. Four of these latter were mediocrities, but the fifth stood out, not for his prowess but for his determination, and Diaghilev's susceptible eye was immediately caught by him. Manipulative, self-seeking and self-dramatising, without being notably intelligent, Serge Lifar was never considered a pleasant human being – there was something reptilian about his sleek tawny beauty and over-ingratiating manner. Aged barely eighteen, he immediately excited suspicion within the company, but he worked furiously hard to improve his feeble technique and by dint of shameless, wide-eyed sucking up to Diaghilev, he shimmied up the greasy pole.[32]

Just ahead of him, however, was another eager young beaver, full of beans and rather too pleased with himself. Born in West Sussex, the Catholic son of a county cricketer and master of hounds, Patrick Healey-Kay had appeared in the back row of *The Sleeping Princess*, billed as Patrickieff. The idea of a healthy middle-class British lad becoming a Russian ballet dancer may have been astounding to the point of scandal, but he was unstoppable, a proper Footlights Fanny. Signed up by Diaghilev after an audition in the classroom of one of the St Petersburg teachers now based in London, he changed his name to Anton Dolin and made his way to Monte Carlo where Diaghilev took him under his wing and into his bed.[33] Dolin cheerfully complied – having been initiated in the confessional as an altar boy, he was sexually uninhibited and late in life he told an interviewer that the older man's requirements were 'straightforward, rather adolescent, and did not involve any form of penetrative intercourse'.[34]

Extrovert and earthy with butch beach-boy physiques, Dolin and Lifar lacked classically academic St Petersburg training and the hauteur that went with it. Their talents were attuned to the anything-goes hedonism of the 1920s – a phenomenon that life in fast and wicked Monte Carlo encouraged the Ballets Russes to embrace. Fun was the keynote now and, for the first time, an engagement with contemporary culture and the physical freedom that had come after the Great War with looser, lighter dress, the worship of the outdoors, the craze for sunbathing, sport and sex. Jazz was the soundtrack of the era and although it was a music that Diaghilev professed to abhor, he was not immune to its spirit and the Ballets Russes's two hits of 1924 are both imbued with its exuberance.

Les Biches translates not as 'the bitches' but as 'the does' or more liberally as 'the little darlings' – a title intended to indicate a certain frisky innocence (in England, the ballet was also more flatly presented as The House Party). Designed in pastel shades by the whimsical French painter Marie Laurencin and choreographed by Nijinska to a scintillating score with choral interpolations by Poulenc, it's a dry subtle satire of the sophisticated flapper lifestyle, set in the pink salon of a fashionable villa presided over by a pretentious hostess – shades of Ottoline Morrell? – toying with ropes of pearls and brandishing a cigarette holder (Nijinska danced this herself, to great effect). Among her guests are three bicep-flexing male athletes in singlets and shorts who move in absurd unison; two silly little girls in grey, presumably the titular does, who snatch an ambiguous surreptitious kiss; and the androgynous garçonne, an icily chic woman with short hair in a navy-blue jerkin barely covering her buttocks who yields to one of the athletes without pleasure or desire.

A work that hinted without solemnity at lesbianism and toyed with categories of gender, *Les Biches* provoked blushes and raised eyebrows in the audience: the balletomane Cyril Beaumont described it primly as 'a genuine cross-section of a phase of contemporary life, a presentation rendered the more piquant by the very delicacy of its considerable imputations'.[35] Nijinska seems to observe the inexplicable goings-on with the unjudging eye of an anthropologist recording the rituals of an alien tribe, but recent critics such as Lynn Garafola have interpreted *Les Biches* trenchantly as 'a critique of the narcissism and voyeurism that make up the business of sex',[36] at a time when women were busily laying claim to the fashions of masculinity (trousers, sportswear, smoking and the Eton crop or bob). But the ballet's genius surely lies in its evasiveness: who are these people, and what exactly is going on here? Poulenc summed the conundrum up neatly: 'In this ballet, as in certain of Watteau's pictures, there is an atmosphere of wantonness which you sense if you are corrupted but which an innocent-minded girl would not be conscious of . . . a ballet in which you may see nothing at all or into which you may read the worst.'[37]

Six months later came something both similar and different – *Le Train bleu*, named after the first-class express that during the 1920s ran during the summer season from Calais via Paris to the Riviera. This was straightforward farce, a balletic trip into the world of the P. G. Wodehouse musical comedies, superficial verging on empty-headed and lacking the subtlety of *Les Biches*. With choreography by Nijinska based on characters and situations proposed by Cocteau, it took place *sur la plage*, where *poseurs*, gigolos, *cocottes* and flappers – a woman representing the tennis champion Suzanne Lenglen, a golfer in plus fours, Bright Young Things frolicking in swimwear, tourists snapping with the latest Kodak cameras – had come out to

flirt and party and flaunt their bodies.* No consequences or implications arise; it's just a romp.

Up to the last chaotic minutes of rehearsal, the enterprise
looked doomed. A feud between Cocteau and Nijinska had left
the dancers bewildered by conflicting sets of instructions. Darius
Milhaud's music was tinkling and trivial, the dancers felt uncomfortable in product-placement costumes by Coco Chanel (now
among Diaghilev's female intimates), and the perfunctory designs
by Henri Laurens left Grigoriev amazed that 'Diaghilev should
ever have accepted . . . so poor a decor'.[38] But triumph was snatched
from the jaws of disaster, thanks mainly to the sensational success
of Dolin as *le beau gosse*, 'the handsome lad', strutting and preening in his bathing drawers to impress the girls. Inspired by cabaret
turns such as Divina and Charles, a pair of elegant gymnasts all
the rage at London's Kit Kat Club, Dolin insouciantly combined
pirouettes and *jetés* with one-armed handstands, double backflips
and cartwheel stunts in a style that married athletic precision to
balletic grace. If *Les Biches* reiterated the Ballets Russes's tendency
to subvert sexual stereotypes, *Le Train bleu* played them straight.
Dolin's persona was one of unabashedly exhibitionist virility – 'I
have never been noted for my modesty,' he admitted in his autobiography[39] – and his performance made him an instant matinée
idol.

*Le Train bleu*'s charm was sensational but ephemeral, and a

---

* Cocteau was obsessed at the time by the American aerialist Barbette,
the stripteasing transvestite star of all the floor shows in Pigalle. 'No
mere acrobat in women's clothes, nor just a graceful daredevil, but one
of the most beautiful things in the theatre,' he wrote. 'Stravinsky, Auric,
poets, painters, and I myself have seen no comparable display of artistry
on the stage since Nijinsky.' (Lydia Crowson, 'Cocteau and "Le Numéro
Barbette"'.)

couple of modern attempts at revival have failed dismally. Its durable legacy is Picasso's final contribution to the Ballets Russes – a magnificent drop curtain depicting two robust women running ecstatically along a beach. This was based on a gouache created two years before the ballet: Diaghilev had seen the canvas in Picasso's studio and asked his permission to use it as a model. The scene painters did such a fine job of expanding its dimensions that the artist signed the result in approval, and it now constitutes one of the greatest treasures of the Victoria and Albert Museum.

The revolving doors continued to turn. First Nijinska stomped off to start her own short-lived company. Although she had enjoyed a brilliant run and might have been considered irreplaceable, Diaghilev made little attempt to keep her. He was exhausted by what Kochno called her 'stubborn, authoritarian character' and felt that he had enjoyed the best of her. After the fracas with Cocteau, she too had had enough. A woman of furious passions and implacable enmities, she read the writing on the wall and responded to her disengagement with paranoid rage. Lifar, whom she despised, she rightly identified as the next big thing in Diaghilev's life; and she looked warily at a young dancer with choreographic aspirations called George Balanchine (originally Balanchivadze, of Georgian ancestry), another Soviet exile who had joined the company along with his wife Tamara Geva and the dazzling young ballerina Alexandra Danilova.[40] This group had been wandering round Europe looking for opportunities and ended up destitute in Paris until Diaghilev held an audition in Misia Sert's drawing room and signed them up. He had immediately registered Balanchine's intelligence and pumped him for news of what the Soviet Union now called Leningrad. Balanchine told him about the experiments with physically extreme movements being conducted by Kasyan Goleyzovsky, a choreographer who had picked up where Fokine left off, pushing classical balletic vocabulary to sculptural extremes.

But neither of these protégés was ready for the oven yet, and when it came to choreography for two new ballets of 1925 *Zéphire et Flore* and *Les Matelots*, there was no alternative but to re-engage Massine. His financial terms were extortionate – he had just acquired a group of deserted islets off the Amalfi coast, and their development would consume vast amounts of his earnings for the next forty years – but Diaghilev paid up, held his nose and kept his former lover at arm's length: '*Comment vas-tu?*' said Massine at the first encounter; '*Comment allez-vous?*' Diaghilev icily responded. Massine had 'no soul, no heart and no taste and was only interested in money', he told others.[41] All negotiations were conducted via Kochno, who wrote the scenarios and sat in on rehearsals. Just to complicate matters further, back in the ranks was Massine's first wife Vera Savina, recently dumped.*

The situation was thoroughly awkward. Massine was clearly ill at ease, speaking only to issue instructions and ignoring poor Savina. The moment his work was done, he returned to the even more lucrative West End, choreographing a Cochran revue written by Noel Coward. Neither of the ballets he had created was among his best. The frothy *Les Matelots* (sailors cheating on their girlfriends) caught on in London when Diaghilev spotted a one-legged busker playing the spoons outside the Coliseum and gave him a turn in the show; *Zéphire et Flore* (a mythological pastorale) was a damp squib despite Georges Braque's arrestingly fanciful designs and a cast of young lovelies including both Lifar and Dolin.

Two personalities as strong as theirs – both barely out of their

---

* 'Pity we cannot tell her story of visits to her solicitor re the divorce when he said why do you want to divorce him [*sic*] She replied well you see he will insist on the three of us being in bed at the same time.' (Lydia Sokolova, undated letter to Richard Buckle, Richard Buckle Collection. Doc. Box 19.)

teens and blessed with equally massive egos – could not coexist for long. In the wake of Dolin's triumph as *le beau gosse*, Lifar had to up his game. Feigning despair, he melodramatically sought an audience with Diaghilev and announced that he was leaving the company to join a monastery. This did the trick: Diaghilev wept, made the sign of the cross and promised him the earth if he stayed. Lifar duly dropped his monastic whim, and was taken to Venice to be initiated. 'Your number's up, chum,' Sokolova advised Dolin, when she spotted Lifar shortly afterwards wearing a new pair of plus fours – a giveaway sign of Diaghilev's special favour.[42] Fortunately, Dolin didn't much care. His market value was riding high and he was ready to hoof it back to the West End and its big fees. It had been easy enough for Lifar to nudge Dolin out of the picture. However, Diaghilev's deeper bond with the indispensable Kochno – discreet, efficient, emollient, cultured and *sortable* – would prove impossible to unravel and became the ultimate barrier to Lifar's advancement even after Diaghilev's death.

To outsiders all this amorous intrigue was the stuff of gossip, whispered but scarcely clandestine: Diaghilev made no bones about his proclivities and must have felt that his 'rootless cosmopolitan' status and public reputation afforded him some invisible protection against paltry national laws. People in the business talked of his 'abnormal psychology', a 'regrettable' aspect of his nature or a deplorable personal habit, sometimes shaking their heads wryly or chuckling about it, but it appears to have inspired little animosity or abuse. Half a century later, Stravinsky reflected that it was 'almost impossible to describe the perversity of Diaghilev's entourage – a kind of homosexual Swiss guard',[43] but whatever the commonplace prejudice behind this, their complex and emotional friendship was unaffected. Whether Diaghilev's erotic fancies clouded his judgement is another matter. He certainly can't be accused of favouring or promoting pretty boys of mediocre talent, and it could be argued that his relationships with Nijinsky and Massine ran a course that would have been no different had he not been sexually involved with them.

In his sharply amusing memoir *Passport to Paris*, Vladimir Dukelsky – a young Russian composer who wrote the music for *Zéphire et Flore* – gives the most vivid and candid evidence of Diaghilev's camp conversational manner. As they were introduced, the great man

> dropped his monocle, adjusted another in its place . . . examining me minutely. 'Ah, a good-looking boy,' he drawled. 'That in itself is most unusual. Composers are seldom good-looking. Neither Stravinsky nor Prokofiev ever won any beauty prizes. How old are you?' I told him I was twenty. 'That's encouraging, too. I don't like young men over twenty-five; they lose their adolescent charm and sleep with any woman who gives them the nod.'

Diaghilev was barking up the wrong tree here, since Dukelsky was entirely heterosexual. This was accepted without demur, but

> Diaghilev wanted me to keep away from women, whom he professed to abhor, not merely as useless (to him) sexually but because of their colossal stupidity and greed. Sergei Pavlovitch was, I'm afraid, over-fond of such generalisations; along with women, his pet peeves were homosexuals and balletomanes. This intelligence might appear startling in view of his being both things himself. However, he explained the paradox by insisting that he only liked manly and virile youths . . . simpering and mincing *tantes* he detested . . . 'Don't get mixed up with women, Dima . . . not now anyway, when you're working for me. All they are good

for is gold-digging or venereal disease – ghastly things both.' I assured him that women had played no part in my life and to give weight to this statement, reluctantly admitted my still virginal status.

'A virgin at twenty – most interesting,' drawled Diaghilev, dropping his monocle. 'That reminds me of an uncommonly beautiful young man who was in the Horse Guards; about your age he was, too. I wined and dined him nightly without the slightest success.'[44]

And so forth.

Dukelsky was one of Diaghilev's white hopes, but he was one who got away. Before he met Diaghilev in 1924, he had spent a couple of years in New York, where George Gershwin befriended him and he caught the jazz bug that was all the rage. Sceptical of all things American after the scarring tours of 1916–17, Diaghilev was immune to the infection. He listened to Gershwin playing *Rhapsody in Blue* in silence and deplored the 'idiotic . . . negro' night club that Cole Porter improvised on a barge in Venice.*[45] Diaghilev's dream was that Dukelsky should prove to be next in line to Stravinsky and Prokofiev, but it was not to be – the amiable score for *Zéphire et Flore* enjoyed only moderate acclaim and Dukelsky soon succumbed to Broadway where he won easy fame and fortune as a song writer under the Americanised name of Vernon Duke.

Having paid off the bulk of the debt incurred by the failure of *The Sleeping Princess*, the Ballets Russes had returned to London late in 1924, after an absence of nearly three years. Over the ensuing months, it played three long and happy seasons at the Coliseum,

---

* Porter did, however, enjoy a brief and intense love affair with Kochno, much to Diaghilev's dog in-the-manger irritation.

once again consolidating its hold on the English public's affection, sharing the bill with all manner of inferior entertainment. 'It became a question which would last the longer, the roaring cheers of the audience or the raising and lowering of the curtain,' the *Observer* recorded after one performance. 'The management wanted to get on with their programme. They had "Sporting Life" to show on the screen, but the audience did not want it. "Extra Ballet!" they cried. When the management persisted with the pictures they booed and protested. It was "More Ballet!" they wanted, not the pictures'[46] – a theme taken up by *Vogue*, whose pages suggested that 'those who pretend that the best contemporary painting makes no appeal to the Man in the Street should hear the roar of applause with which the decors of Picasso and Pruna are greeted by the Man in the Gallery'[47] – even if that man might well have been 'one of the four Oxford undergraduates' described in the *Morning Post*, 'who had been gated for the rest of term for arriving on more than one occasion at their college after one o'clock in the morning. Their reason (which they did not tell the dons) was that they had paid lightning visits to the Russian ballet at the Coliseum "motoring up afterwards quite drunk with beauty, as one of them described it".'[48]

First nights continued to be madly fashionable. The *Daily Mirror* gawped at the turnout of artists and writers, aristocrats and socialites for the opening of the June 1926 season:

Lord Balfour, Mr H. G. Wells, Miss Poppy Baring, Mr Noel Coward, the Hon. Stephen Tennant, Mr Augustus John, Lady Waterhouse and the Duke of Lenorado . . . One beautiful fair-haired woman wore what looked like a Guard's crimson cloak with a black velvet collar and a silver brocade waistcoat. Lady Diana Cooper was in a pale gold sequin dress matching her golden hair, which she now wears waved and bobbed. The Duchess of Rutland, who was with her, brought her umbrella into the stalls . . .[49]

A more humbly born Londoner became the company's next star. In the same studio run by Serafina Astafieva in the King's Road from which Dolin had emerged, Diaghilev spotted a stick-thin thirteen-year-old named Alicia Marks.[50] A Jewish girl from Finsbury Park, she had been lined up to appear as an attendant fairy in *The Sleeping Princess* until diphtheria intervened. Now that her father had died, her family was in desperate circumstances and she was left the breadwinner. Meek and biddable, she displayed a preternatural ease of technique and there was something fascinating about her china-doll serenity. Diaghilev sensed her potential and was persuaded to take her on, renaming her Alicia Markova. Although the child continued sickly – she 'looked as though a tight squeeze would kill her', thought Sokolova[51] – there was something imperturbably steely and determined about her too, and the old lags had to suppress a certain irritation at her sang-froid.* In her first role in *Le Chant du rossignol*, costumed only in white silk pyjamas and diamantine bangles, Sokolova found her 'little neck . . . so thin that when during the performance, the time came for me to twist the necklace of skulls round it, I felt an overwhelming desire to strangle her in earnest'.[52]

Markova's repertory was obviously limited by her age and frailty, and her appeal was primarily that of a charming novelty. Diaghilev otherwise remained short of new stars who could reach beyond the coterie of hardened fans and sell to a wider public. In London, the defection of matinée idol Anton Dolin was keenly felt, while

---

* Massine later found her so stubborn to work with that he nicknamed her 'The Chinese Torture'. (Julian Braunsweg, *Braunsweg's Ballet Scandals*, p. 118.)

older favourites such as Karsavina and Lopokova were past their
best and would commit only to short contracts. Both of them had
married into the English establishment – Karsavina to the banker
and diplomat Henry Bruce, Lopokova to the economist Maynard
Keynes. But Karsavina was restricted by her devotion to her roles
as wife and mother, while Lopokova was as disdainful of Diaghilev
the 'born wicked prima donna with intrigues' as she was of Massine the 'dirty insect'.[53] Vera Nemchinova was highly efficient and
versatile, but too cool to be loved and too easily seduced by the big
bucks of West End revue, despite her nominal adherence to the
Tolstoyan philosophy of her partner Nikolai Zverev. The one big
draw was Lifar, whose exotic allure, 'both childish and diabolic',[54]
inspired many unspeakable infatuations. One votary of the Ballets
Russes cult, the writer Ethel Mannin, recalled 'a young man in the
amphitheatre . . . leaning over the rail with his long hair falling over
his face and crying hoarsely, "Serge! Serge!" . . . finally, when he
could clap and cheer no longer the young man sank back into his
seat, huddled there in a state of collapse.'[55]

Of the younger generation, Alexandra Danilova was by far the
most talented. Graduating as she had from the toughest class of
the Mariinsky school, where a more orderly and courtly regime
had persisted through the Revolution, she was shocked by the Ballets Russes's low technical standards and a slapdash make-do spirit
that never allowed enough rehearsal: 'We were pretty much left
to our own devices,' she recalled in her autobiography.[56] Certainly
the pressure to make money by performing as often as possible left
everyone dancing far harder than was good for their bodies. Nor
could Diaghilev pay them enough, and in 1925 a disgruntled workforce presented a petition and threatened to strike. It got nowhere,
because there was nothing to give, nothing in reserve, and two
leaders of the protest ended up ruthlessly fired. Whatever came in

instantly went out, and often the cupboard was left bare: after an inexplicably disastrous week in Berlin in 1925, there wasn't even enough money to transport the company back to base in Monte Carlo. Beyond the plain truth that there was no secret stash, Diaghilev's finances were never transparent or rigorously accounted, and his personal expenditure was inextricably entangled with that of the company. He was not honourable: vast bills run up at smart hotels were left unpaid and royalties weren't passed on to composers until the very last minute (the source of much of his bickering with Stravinsky). His furious outbursts of temper and air of entitled hauteur often led him to bite the hand that fed him: a vicious row over the supply of dancers for Ravel's opera *L'Enfant et les sortilèges* led to Monte Carlo cutting its initially generous subsidy and various impresarios retired from the fray of negotiating with him sighing 'never again'. Even poor Mrs Bewicke, widowed mother of the lowly dancer Hilda, from whom Diaghilev had cadged a loan of £300 after the flop of *The Sleeping Princess*, was forced to take recourse to the law to get him to keep up his repayments.

Throughout the 1920s, Diaghilev became increasingly reliant on the volatile patronage of the super-rich. The newspaper magnate Lord Rothermere, owner of a palatial villa on Cap Martin conveniently close to Monte Carlo, coughed up for a couple of years. But he was infatuated with his ballerina mistress Alice Nikitina and Diaghilev had to keep him sweet by promoting her beyond her just deserts. When he lost interest in 1928, he was thrown back on Lady Juliet Duff, daughter of his pre-war patron Lady Ripon. Although not notably wealthy herself, Lady Juliet proved a tireless and selfless fundraiser, soliciting contributions for the cause from other *grandes dames* around town. She faced the eternal problem that although her circle was generally happy to shell out for reassuringly familiar fare, few were prepared to sponsor eccentric or incomprehensible modernism. The idea that something beautiful had turned ugly crops up repeatedly. A letter to Diaghilev from Lady Cunard dropped a heavy hint that programming rebarbative quantities such as *Les Noces* for George V's visit might not be tactful: 'I hope you will change the performance and [do] the Boutique, Sylphides and the Carnaval. Otherwise I fear His Majesty will not really love the ballet as we all feel he would if he *first* saw the classical ballets of some years ago.'[57] Such remarks were typical, and at one point Diaghilev was forced to make up the shortfall by cutting up some of Picasso's scenery and selling the squares as a job lot to his dealer.* Even more disgracefully in his eyes, he considered grasping the last straw of signing up to an American tour.

Yet through all this final phase of his endeavour, Diaghilev's nerve never failed him. He continued to take long risks on young talent and to experiment with music and design, all the while shuffling the cards and playing his hand with a mixture of cunning and judgement. In 1926, the Ballets Russes finally left the variety bill at the Coliseum and gave stand-alone seasons at Her Majesty's and Lyceum theatres instead. Almost as a gift to his loyal London public, Diaghilev began for the first time to take an interest in British music and subject matter. He rejected a proposal from Ralph Vaughan Williams and the surgeon-scholar Geoffrey Keynes for a ballet based on Blake's engravings of Job; the idea of a Tudor ballet foundered, and he wasn't much taken by the wunderkind composer William Walton. But he did commission Walton's twenty-year-old chum Constant Lambert to write a score based on *Romeo and Juliet*. Alas, it sounded 'much like any other example of second-rate

* 'To the remarkable list of Diaghilev's achievements, perhaps another should be added: his assistance at the birth of the market for twentieth-century art.' (Garafola, *Diaghilev's Ballets Russes*, p. 261.)

modern music and made no impression on the public whatsoever', as Grigoriev sniffed,[58] and it went down as a fiasco. Shakespeare was only an indirect source, as the setting was a rehearsal studio where two dancers – an ill-matched Karsavina and Lifar – played out their love affair with only vague reference to the play's plot. 'The whole conception of the ballet indeed seemed to be based on a desire to shock,' Grigoriev explains. 'Thus it was in two parts, between which, though the curtain was lowered, its bottom was kept some feet above the stage, so that the audience could see the dancers' legs as they moved across it; and at the end Lifar, as Romeo, appeared dressed as an airman, ready for elopement with Juliet by aeroplane. These "modern" touches were apparently to Diaghilev's taste.'[59]

Established British painters such as Augustus John and Wyndham Lewis had been passed over as designers, and Diaghilev took Picasso's recommendation in plumping for the gifted but erratic twenty-five-year-old Christopher Wood. But Wood soon stomped off in protest against Diaghilev's tendency to 'poke his nose into everything',[60] and Diaghilev ended up staging the work on a bare stage, using front cloths painted by the fashionable surrealists Max Ernst and Joan Miró. More purist and leftist members of this brotherhood, including André Breton and Louis Aragon, were appalled at what they considered a sell-out to the mainstream and organised a terrific protest for the first night in Paris. Leaflets were scattered around the auditorium, catcalls, howls and whistles erupted and the police were summoned to quell the furore. It was the last great scandal of the Ballets Russes. But after a handful of performances in London (where it was considered merely 'a soufflé'[61]) the ballet was forgotten.

Nijinska had returned briefly as its choreographer, but from now on it would be young George Balanchine who held pride of place. Since arriving in the company in 1924, he had been cutting his teeth by arranging ballet interludes for grand opera in Monte Carlo, and now he was ready for anything that was thrown at him. Unlike his predecessors in this position, he did not suffer from an outsized or psychotic ego: mild-mannered, good-humoured, modest and resourceful, he worked fast and without fuss or tantrum. Away from ballet, he was enigmatic – 'absent as a tangible personality', as his future patron Lincoln Kirstein would put it.[62] But it helped that he was without ambivalence a ladies' man, immune to the homoerotic intrigues of Diaghilev's court.

His first major success was one of those supremely stylish crowd-pleasing entertainments, like *La Boutique fantasque* or *Le Train bleu*, in which Diaghilev the savvy showman emerged to trump Diaghilev the visionary innovator. With a scenario and music by two great English eccentrics Sacheverell Sitwell and Lord Berners, *The Triumph of Neptune* was a mint humbug of a patriotic romp, with designs inspired by the tuppence-coloured sheets depicting the scenes and figures of Victorian fairy pantomimes, as printed and published by Benjamin Pollock in his toy-theatre shop in Hoxton. Balanchine knocked it off without any trouble, incorporating jigs, hornpipes and reels into his choreography. The scenery transformed every few minutes, the costumes glittered with tinsel and sequins, and two-headed giants vied with flying fairies. Even the grouchiest critics were entranced, and its success served as a reminder that Britain had a great dance tradition of its own – and perhaps it was time for natives to reclaim it.

But other premières did nothing to mollify the prevalent view that despite all the glories in his back catalogue, Diaghilev was selling out to the affectations of modish modernism, pursuing the *outré* and arcane for its own shocking, baffling sake. Soured by his experience with *Romeo and Juliet*, Constant Lambert later wrote in his brilliant polemic *Music Ho!* that whereas 'before the war Diaghilev created a vogue for Russian ballet, after the war he created merely a vogue for vogue'.[63] This became a familiar position, shared even by those who understood it more from the inside: Lydia Lopokova, for instance, turned critic and snapped at *Les Noces* as 'a way to stir up a highbrow' and suggested 'that the ballet seems to have lost some of its tenderness, some of its soul'.[64] In his memoirs, Benois would sound a more emphatically apocalyptic note, mourning that 'spiritual and physical affectation in the pursuit of *le dernier cri* never achieved such grotesque absurdity as it did in the first years of the twentieth century . . . What a number of sects, formulas and theories have appeared! What clever specialists in doctrine, what brilliant and tortuous sophists, what professionals of paradox! Diaghilev was always inclined towards this creative saturnalia; it is not surprising therefore that he was drawn into the abyss.'[65]

Diaghilev was galled but undeterred by this attitude, and occasionally hit back – one persistent tormentor, Ernest Newman of the *Sunday Times*, was denied a press pass after he wrote off Balanchine's *La Pastorale* as 'silly'. Newman may have been right. It was a skit on the silent cinema, in which a risqué film is being shot in a field. 'An opportunity for one more display of the new gymnastic method,' sniffed one critic.[66]

Three ballets premièred in 1927–8 provoked just such responses. *La Chatte* was very chic – *étrange* and extravagant. Drawn from Aesop's fable of a young man whose prayer that his beloved cat could become human is answered with disastrous consequences, it could have been presented in a Beatrix Potter manner. Instead the Russian constructivist sculptors Naum Gabo and his brother Anton Pevsner created costumes encrusted with glittering mica and a 'heroic, interplanetary' set[67] that offered kinetic effects, framed by black oilcloth and furnished with abstractly geometric constructions in translucent celluloid. Balanchine's choreography suggested the human–feline divide in a role that exploited the unearthly qualities of ballerinas such as Spessivtseva, Nikitina and Markova, and Gabo's minimal tunic exposed Lifar's alluring physique (further graced by his newly reduced nose, as recommended by Diaghilev). 'There have been few ballets in which the beauty of young people's bodies [have been] shown to better effect,' thought Sokolova.[68]

Two even more brazenly audacious works choreographed by Massine made no concessions to conventional beauty. Fired by the pumping energy of Prokofiev's hard-edged score, *Le Pas d'acier* ('The Dance of Steel') has often been compared to Fritz Lang's 1929 epic film *Metropolis* for its depiction of society reduced to an industrial machine, fed by cogs and pistons, in which boilers steam and pistons hammer amid what Cyril Beaumont called a 'mighty whirlpool of rhythm'. The dancers were shown as proles, taken from countryside to factory and assigned repetitive tasks that they executed with massed production-line efficiency. The Bolshevism implicit in this caused surprisingly little protest, perhaps because of the absence of any plot: 'a great deal of activity accompanied by considerable noise, but it all appeared rather meaningless', Beaumont added.[69]

Weirdest of all, and a world away from the materialism of *Le Pas d'acier*, was *Ode*. Since the mid-1920s, Diaghilev had been allowing Kochno increasing artistic scope, calling him his 'young oak',[70] treating him as dauphin and encouraging him to collaborate with choreographers by providing them with plot lines and concepts. Drawing on a lengthy florid poem addressed by the eighteenth-century poet Mikhail Lomonosov to the Empress Elizabeth dauntingly entitled 'An evening meditation on the Majesty of God on observing the Aurora Borealis', *Ode* reflected both Kochno's literary ambitions and Diaghilev's costly new passion, shared and inspired by Kochno, for collecting rare editions and manuscripts of the great Russian writers of the past.

*Ode* soon transcended its roots in Diaghilev's persistent nostalgia for baroque splendour to become a benchmark in the theatrical avant-garde. According to Kochno's synopsis, a statue of Nature (in a fluted white costume resembling a Doric pillar) comes to life and shows a student (dressed in black like an *abbé*) the wonders of creation, from flowers to bacteria to constellations. Dancers rendered faceless by fencing masks wore black gloves and nude-effect white body-suits; above them hung two inexplicable rows of gibbeted dolls, strung out on pulleys. What it meant, who could tell? The critic of the *Morning Post* was not alone in being able to make 'neither head nor tail' of it.[71]

Neither the score by young Nicolas Nabokov, cousin to the novelist Vladimir, nor Massine's choreography, was of much consequence. As with *Parade* a decade previously, nobody in the creative team was on good terms with anyone else and the rehearsal period was misery, but in the end it was the designer who dominated. He was the surrealist-symbolist painter Pavel Tchelitchev, a tortured and obsessive homosexual aristocrat with a penchant for celestial esoterica, and what he and his brilliant technical assistant Pierre Charbonnier created was a dazzlingly original lighting plot, incorporating the new technologies of cinematic projection and neon. Great washes of coloured illumination alternated with slow-motion film of images both cosmic and microcosmic; behind misty gauzes, ectoplasmic forms and solid figures were indistinct from each other; luminous cords formed Euclidean patterns. The dancers struggled inside their phosphorescent body-stockings. Nowadays such things may be commonplace, but in 1928 they seemed supernatural. Diaghilev thought the whole thing insane. He had left Kochno in charge, but could not resist storming into the final rehearsals to pull it all together, which he just about did.

None of these works have left any trace beyond the history books, but two subsequent works by Balanchine have continued to thrive for a century. *Apollon musagète* ('Apollo, leader of the Muses', today known simply as *Apollo*) was a ballet for string orchestra by Stravinsky, commissioned by an American patron and given its première in 1928 in the Library of Congress in Washington DC, with unsuccessful choreography by Adolph Bolm, first of several early Ballets Russes stars to emigrate west. When it passed to Balanchine in the summer, he found the perfect idiom through which to embody the score's temperate classical lucidity. It offers a simple allegory: the boy Apollo appears as a beautiful but untutored youth, seeded with power, energy and ambition but lacking in discipline, grace or sensibility. His fertilising and purifying encounters with three aspects of the feminine – Calliope the Muse of poetry, Polyhymnia the Muse of mime and Terpsichore the Muse of dance – in turn empower him with their enriching gifts (at one point, the supine Apollo is touched by the tip of Terpsichore's finger, like Adam granted life by God on Michelangelo's Sistine Chapel ceiling). As a result, he becomes an artist and leader, both creative and commanding. Perhaps Balanchine was thinking of himself.

A corrective to the wilful sensationalism and visual extravagance underlying so much art of the 1920s, *Apollon musagète* was 'a call to order' that made little initial impression: critics misjudged its modesty and serenity, calling it 'solemn', 'meandering' and 'tenuous', even as they admired Lifar in the title role. Over the next forty years, Balanchine would simplify the designs and refine the text; posterity now acknowledges the ballet as one of the supreme masterpieces of the form.

Sadly, this calmly beautiful work contributed to the many bones of contention that dogged the last years of Diaghilev's long but bumpy friendship with Stravinsky. Diaghilev had to accept second pickings on *Apollon musagète*, but he was furious when Stravinsky assigned *Le Baiser de la fée*, an hour-long score in the style of Tchaikovsky, to glamour girl Ida Rubinstein, who was using her wealth to return to the stage with an operation that would sit in direct competition to the Ballets Russes.* Stravinsky retaliated by becoming enraged by Diaghilev's wanton (but not uncharacteristic) decision to introduce pointless cuts into *Apollon musagète* and threatened to withdraw his permission to perform it. The pair had come through such spats before, but this one was never resolved: they bumped into each other at the Gare du Nord en route to London and made a vague arrangement to meet there. But despite lodging round the corner from each other, they never communicated again.

Balanchine's next commission was constructed out of a scenario by Kochno and a score by Prokofiev. For the first time since Fokine's unhappy *La Légende de Joseph* and Massine's aborted *Liturgie*, the Ballets Russes returned to the Bible for source material, and struck third time lucky. *The Prodigal Son* followed a simplified version of the New Testament parable, stripped of the envious brothers and the killing of the fatted calf. Naturally inclined to create dances rather than plots or characters, Balanchine was not normally drawn to work with strong narratives, but here he was given a frame on which he could create something that was both clearly legible and ingeniously inventive – the choreography for the serpentine siren seductress and her crew of grotesque debauched companions is as witty as it is expressive.

When Matisse turned down an offer to design the work – his experience on *Le Chant du rossignol* had been unhappy – the

* See pp. 239–40.

commission passed to the eccentric religious painter Georges Rouault: his richly dark and boldly archaic designs, devoid of whimsy or frippery, are a perfect match for the fierce graphic primitivism in Prokofiev's music and the mime and dance forged by Balanchine. Lifar played the title role: it was perhaps his finest achievement, and certainly one that reflected his own outsized personality. Rattled by the return to the company of Dolin (renewing his search for artistic laurels, a far more accomplished dancer than he was, and someone almost as cockily bumptious) and restless for new horizons, Lifar had rehearsed the ballet listlessly and without enthusiasm. Come the first night, however, he found the key within:

> The hero I was personifying was myself, tortured by a presentiment that this was the end of something, the end of a dying world . . . it was I . . . with my need to renounce a protection that threatened to become restrictive, oppressive . . . It was I that was harrowed . . . what I was acting was my own life.[72]

Yet something that transcended ego emerged from Lifar's interpretation: nothing else that the Ballets Russes had produced can match the unaffected intensity of emotion generated by this work's climax, as the exhausted prodigal, robbed, humiliated and in rags, crawls back to his father, who lifts him into his arms, enfolds him in his cloak and cradles him like a baby.

———

The tragedy of another prodigal son finished without any such uplifting, forgiving reconciliation. Diaghilev took Lifar to meet Nijinsky. Impenetrably mad, largely locked into sullen silence, he was living in Paris with his sister-in-law (his wife Romola having decamped to America to raise money). The calves and thighs that once powered his preternatural jump had now turned monstrously flabby, exposed as he sat inert in a dressing-gown, mumbling and fiddling and occasionally bursting into meaningless laughter. In the evening, Diaghilev took him to the Opéra to see *Petrushka* once again – one of his greatest achievements, in which his former part- ner Karsavina was still dancing the role of the ballerina doll. Before the performance, he was led onto the stage. Harry Kessler, also present, was struck by 'his big eyes, like a sick animal' and a 'look that was uncomprehending and yet deeply moving'.[73] He seemed to recognise nobody, but when Karsavina lent forward to kiss him, he 'turned his head like a child that wants to hide tears'.[74]

One final infatuation lit up what was to be the last year of Diaghilev's life. Even though he kept faith with his potential, he had become sceptical of Lifar, whom he had unmasked, accord- ing to Grigoriev, as 'sly and scheming, too ambitious and too fond of self-advertisement'.[75] But now he fell for the innocence of a sixteen-year-old émigré composer named Igor Markevitch, who was studying musical composition in Paris with the celebrated ped- agogue Nadia Boulanger.[76] Wide-eyed and dazzled by a great man's attentions, Markevitch surrendered quickly. Although heterosexual (he would eventually marry Njinsky's daughter Kyra), he found it easy to satisfy Diaghilev's uncomplicated sexual urges, and later confessed to colluding with them through a commendable candour that involved no recrimination or sense that he had been abused or even exploited.*

---

* In a memoir published in 1980, Markevitch made an early plea for gay marriage: *'J'estime qu'un grand mouvement d'opinion devrait être entrepris pour encourager et faciliter les mariages d'hommes ou de femmes.'* ('I feel that a major shift in opinion should be made to encourage and facilitate marriage between men or women.') (*Être et avoir été*, p. 191.)

Diaghilev was entranced by the boy and determined to promote what he regarded as his precocious genius. There was genuine ardour here too, as for a son: as Markevitch touchingly put it in his memoir, '*Il s'attachait à mon avenir comme si c'était le sien*' ('He committed himself to my future as though it was his own').[77] Although performances of Markevitch's piano concerto excited no enthusiasm whatsoever, Diaghilev was undeterred; here, he believed, was the successor to the venal and perfidious Stravinsky. Giving the lie to those who felt that his enthusiasm for ballet was ebbing,* he proposed that Markevitch should compose a ballet based on Hans Christian Andersen's fable 'The Emperor's New Clothes', for which Lifar would be given his chance as a choreographer and Picasso would be the designer.

But Diaghilev was now dying from a diabetes the gravity of which he refused to acknowledge. Refusing to follow doctors' orders or moderate his diet beyond substituting saccharine for sugar, he suffered terribly from sores and abscesses. The indispensable Kochno had the unenviable daily task of draining out the pus.

In London in July he saw the company for the last time, performing a programme that fittingly bookended the Ballets Russes's endeavour, including *Petrushka* with Karsavina and Lifar as *Le Fils prodigue*; the company went on give its final performance in Vichy on 4 August 1929. Accompanied by the enraptured Markevitch,

---

* Half a century later, Balanchine confided in Robert Craft: 'Nobody will believe me of course, but Diaghilev did not know anything about dancing. His real interest in ballet was sexual. He could not bear the sight of Danilova and would say to me, "Her tits make me want to vomit." Once when I was standing next to him at a rehearsal for *Apollo*, he said, "How beautiful!" I agreed, thinking that he was referring to the music, but he quickly corrected me: "No, no, I mean Lifar's ass; it is like a rose."' (Quoted in Charles M. Joseph, 'Diaghilev and Stravinsky', p. 201.)

Diaghilev was taking a peripatetic vacation at the time, embracing visits to the opera in Munich and Salzburg. Markevitch then returned to his mother in Switzerland and Diaghilev wearily made his way to the Grand Hotel des Bains on the Venice Lido. His condition rapidly worsened: he had swallowed a rotten tooth, he had violent pains in his back, and his fatigue became feverish weakness. Lifar and Kochno were summoned as he faded. Misia Sert and Coco Chanel visited his bedside too.

At dawn on 19 August 1929, Diaghilev breathed his last, aged only fifty-seven. Raw with grief, panic, exhaustion and a long-suppressed mutual dislike, Lifar and Kochno, two young men in their mid-twenties who owed Diaghilev everything, sunk to violent fisticuffs over his corpse, 'tearing at each other's clothes, biting one another like wild animals', according to Misia Sert. Lifar considered himself Diaghilev's official lover and 'spiritual heir'; Kochno had the brains and had done the service. They would both make grabs for Diaghilev's treasures and possessions. The stakes were high: what next, who should inherit, how much was there to inherit? There was no money to speak of and, without Diaghilev himself, no solid basis to the organisation either.

Nobody had realised quite how ill Diaghilev had been, and the first terse reports of his death shocked the world. Grigoriev fainted when he received the telegram from Kochno; feeling 'orphaned' and with his world 'suddenly left empty',[78] Markevitch came close to drowning himself in Lake Geneva. The dancers read or heard the news on their various summer holidays. Old enmities evanesced: Walter Nouvel, his staunch friend from Nevsky Pickwickian days and a constant backroom presence in the Ballets Russes, wrote to a devastated Stravinsky: 'Now when he is in the grave, all is forgotten, all is forgiven, and I understand that one can't apply the normal measure of human relationships to this exceptional man.'[79] Another

Nevsky Pickwickian, Alexandre Benois, whose influence had been formative but who had seen almost nothing of his friend in the last decade, lamented that 'a part of me has been cut off and I feel I've become a cripple'.[80]

Misia Sert paid off all the expenses. As Lifar theatrically attempted to throw himself into the grave, Diaghilev was buried in the cemetery of San Michele. A month later, his half-brother Valentin, a Red Army officer arrested without charge, appears to have been executed in a Soviet prison camp.[81]

The basic sources for this chapter are Cyril Beaumont, *The Diaghilev Ballet in London*, pp. 183–300; S. L. Grigoriev, *The Diaghilev Ballet 1909–1929*, pp. 152–261; Lydia Sokolova, *Dancing for Diaghilev*, pp. 172–280; Boris Kochno, *Diaghilev and the Ballets Russes*, pp. 150–279; Nesta Macdonald, *Diaghilev Observed*, pp. 224–381; Richard Buckle, *Diaghilev*, pp. 345–541; Lynn Garafola, *Diaghilev's Ballets Russes*, pp. 76–97, 330–44; Leslie Norton, *Massine and the Twentieth-Century Ballet*, passim; Vicente Garcia-Marquez, *Massine*, pp. 43–163; Sjeng Scheijen, *Diaghilev: A Life*, pp. 374–541; Jennifer Homans, *Apollo's Angels*, pp. 245–89; Jane Pritchard, *Diaghilev and the Golden Age of the Ballets Russes 1909–1929*, passim.

# 7

# RIVALS

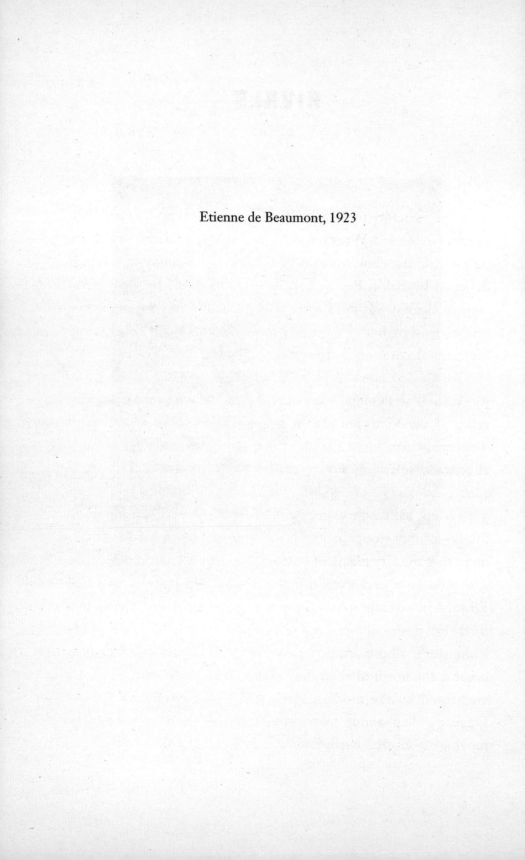

Etienne de Beaumont, 1923

In the years before the Great War, Diaghilev had pretty much had the field to himself. What he packaged in Russia and sold in Europe (in essence, the choreography of Fokine and Nijinsky in stagings designed by Bakst, Benois and Roerich, to music by Stravinsky) embodied what was in effect a new art form – the one-act dance drama, growing out of venerable courtly tradition but also feeding off recent innovations in theatre and the visual arts.

There wasn't much else of substance around, let alone originality. At the Paris Opéra, you could see anodyne pastorales, quaint relics of the Victorian era; at London's Alhambra and Empire Theatres, there were themed floor shows, devoid of emotional content, featuring dainty excursions by charming china dolls such as Adeline Genée and Phyllis Bedells; on the bills of the bigger variety halls, star ballerinas and their partners were granted fifteen-minute slots like circus acts – it was in such an environment that the airy magic of Pavlova flourished. Gentlemen in the audience were perhaps more aroused by that popular trope of Edwardian pornography – Salome removing her seven veils in a titillating flesh-coloured mime, performed by ladies such as Ida Rubinstein, whose studied gestures and rapturous expressions became the norm of silent film acting. The higher-minded were enchanted by the modern classicism glowing through Isadora Duncan's diaphanous free-form inspirations and the barefoot moving-to-music eurhythmics emanating from Dalcroze's temple at Hellerau. Those with more overtly proletarian tastes in the music-halls were mesmerised by displays of sexually abusive 'Apache dancing', in which a cloth-capped street-corner rough (or pimp) would fling his girl (or whore) around as they engaged in a dismayingly violent altercation of slaps, punches, kicks and black-eyed submission.

But for ballet as something serious and sustained, something that could rival opera in its artistic ambition and emotional impact, Diaghilev was your only man and Russian the only flavour.

After the Great War, it was a different story, as society had changed radically and others, usually with pockets deeper than Diaghilev's and sometimes with bright ideas too, muscled in on the act. Diaghilev always kept an eye out for anyone treading on his coat-tails. He was shrewd enough to bend with the wind – he could follow public taste as well as lead it – but he was also extremely competitive and sometimes irrationally sensitive in response to threats. Before this aspect of the history is explored, a largely unanswerable question should be asked: where was the audience for this phenomenon coming from?

Because nobody at this time thought to record marketing trends, anecdotal evidence surviving from diaries and letters is our only solid source of information. In pre-war London, it is fair to assume that the boxes and stalls at Covent Garden would have been filled with the high society of royalty, the lords, the diplomats, the landed, and the plutocratic *arrivistes*, inasmuch as they were subscribers who would have attended whatever was on the bill. A hard core of wealthy Belgravia ladies, familiar to readers of Henry James's novels, invited stars including Karsavina to their soirées and wrote Diaghilev substantial cheques.

At the other end of the scale, there are indications that bohemia and the intelligentsia – vorticists, Wagnerites, art students

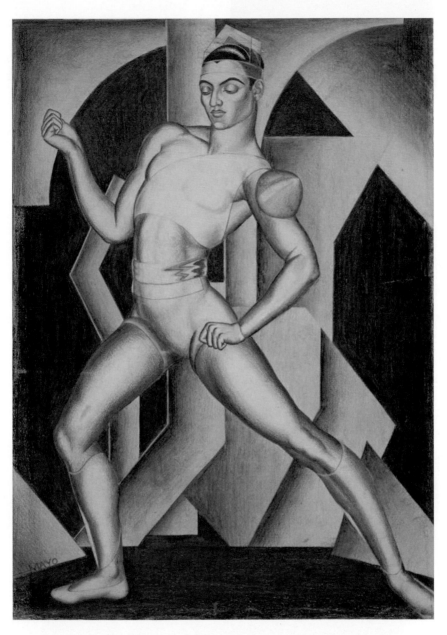

17  A highly sexualised Serge Lifar, as seen by Eileen Mayo.

18 *Les Noces*, Royal Ballet, 2012.
19 Alexandra Danilova and Leonid Massine as the cancan dancers
in Massine's *La Boutique fantasque*.

20 *La Création du monde*, Ballets Suédois.

21 Apparently the only preserved image of the baby ballerinas
posing as a trio: (*left to right*) Tatiana Riabouchinska,
Tamara Toumanova, Irina Baronova, circa 1933–4.
22 Massine's *Les Présages*, Original Ballet Russe, 1947.

23 An image that can easily be misinterpreted today: Arnold Haskell and Irina Baronova, circa 1935, photographed by Baronova's father.

24  Vaslav and Romola Nijinsky, 1947.
25  Tamara Karsavina at the opening of the
Diaghilev exhibition, 1954.

26 The Marquis de Cuevas en route to his costume ball, 1953.
27 The ludicrous duel between Serge Lifar and the Marquis de Cuevas.
Sporting an eye patch, the future leader of France's Front National
Jean-Marie Le Pen stands as de Cuevas's second.

28  Jean Babilée and Nathalie Philippart in Roland Petit's
*Le Jeune Homme et la mort*.

29  A balletomane's dream: Monty Morris (*left*) up close to
Alicia Markova and Frederick Ashton.
30  The Trocks in their slapstick parody of *Les Sylphides*.

– patronised the cheaper seats. Up in the gallery, according to a columnist for the *English Review*, could be spotted 'the Egyptian coiffure of the ladies, the waistcoats of poets, the side-whiskers à la Café Royal, the shawls and kissing curls, the nightly kaleidoscopic assembly'.[1] On a young architect from suburban Beckenham called Austen Harrison, the Ballets Russes fell 'as a thunderclap';[2] the beauteous poet Rupert Brooke decided that ballet 'can redeem our civilisation' and saw the Russians fifteen times over the summer of 1911, *Scheherazade* being his particular favourite. 'And now, I'm going once more,' he wrote to his girlfriend Ka Cox. 'On Monday with Margery, and probably Noel. We feed at 7.15, Eustace Miles [vegetarian restaurant]. James'll be there, have tickets.'[3] Like punk some sixty years later, an enthusiasm for Diaghilev's productions marked out one's allegiance in the culture wars – and indicated a readiness to loosen the restrictive corset of Victorian and Edwardian values.

Most members of Bloomsbury's intellectual élite were fans too, though by no means discriminating connoisseurs. Virginia Woolf referred to the Ballets Russes simply as 'the dancers', as if there were no others. Disappointingly, despite fairly regular attendance, she left no specific opinions of what she saw; no more did another habitué, E. M. Forster. Lytton Strachey had a crush on the idea of Nijinsky and bought himself a new suit 'of darkest purple' when the aesthete hostess Ottoline Morrell invited him to meet his idol. No sparks were struck during the encounter: Strachey reported to his friend Henry Lamb that although Nijinsky was 'very nice' and 'certainly not a eunuch', communication was limited as 'the poor fellow cannot speak more than 2 words of any human language'. Strachey's infatuation did not extend to admiration of *The Rite of Spring*, which he described as 'one of the most painful experiences of my life . . . I couldn't have imagined that boredom and sheer anguish could have been combined together at such a pitch.'[4] Strachey's best friend Dora Carrington referred to Diaghilev as 'Djaggers' and wrote breathlessly to the painter Mark Gertler, 'I did love that new ballet Tales for Children [Massine's *Children's Tales*] the conception of the mad girl in the bed is excellent and the outspread cloak with the females underneath';[5] Ottoline persevered with Nijinsky, and her kindly and motherly attentions seem to have touched him. 'Lady Morrell is so tall, so beautiful, like giraffe,' he was heard to say, and he gave her a treasured photograph of himself as Petrushka.[6]

The Ballets Russes quickly became a common inspiration for outfits at fancy-dress balls, perhaps among those who knew about the original only by hearsay. In *Tenterhooks*, a silver-fork novel by Oscar Wilde's friend Ada Leverson, 'a very young man' called Mr Cricker is said to dance at parties in imitation of Nijinsky, though the effect is reminiscent of the comedian George Grossmith. Leverson was quick off the mark here: *Tenterhooks* was published in 1912, only months after the Ballets Russes had made their London debut.[7] Civil servant Oliver Strachey and psychoanalyst Karin Costelloe went to a soirée in 1913 dressed as Karsavina and Nijinsky, enacting 'Spectre de la rose with great success'; and in 1914 Lady Ottoline Morrell allowed students from the Slade School of Art to borrow from her exotic wardrobe in order to prance through *Scheherazade* to the accompaniment of a pianola in her drawing room.[8] Did D. H. Lawrence draw on this occasion for *Women in Love*? In one episode of this novel (published in 1920, but written some years earlier), Gudrun and Ursula Brangwen decide to entertain their fellow guests at a house party hosted by the Contessa, a figure not unlike Lady Ottoline, with 'a little ballet on an Old Testament theme, in the style of the Russian ballet of Pavlova and Nijinsky'. Lawrence's imagination, however, conceived this as something that Dalcroze rather than Fokine would have choreographed:

> It was finally decided to do Naomi and Ruth and Orpah . . . Ursula was Naomi, Gudrun was Ruth, the Contessa was Orpah.
>
> The Contessa was ready first. Alexander went to the piano, a space was cleared. Orpah, in beautiful Oriental clothes, began slowly to dance the death of her husband. Then Ruth came, and they wept together, and lamented, then Naomi came to comfort them. It was all done in dumb show, the women danced their emotion in gesture and motion. The little drama went on for a quarter of an hour.[9]

After the Great War, a distinct change in the constitution of London's audience for the Ballets Russes can be detected: it became broader, less weighted towards the upper crust. The hardcore bohemians were still filling the gallery – 'gaunt, angular women with lank, untidy, bobbed hair and shapeless clothes, and red-bearded ballet maniacs who would think nothing of waiting ten to fifteen hours in the rain for a seat in the gods', as a faintly repulsed Cecil Beaton later recalled[10] – but the move to variety theatres such as the Coliseum and the Alhambra, away from the more expensive and exclusive opera houses of Covent Garden and Drury Lane, brought the magic within reach of a more middle-class and even proletarian clientele.

Diaghilev, an unapologetic snob, had no evangelical ambition to feed the masses, but confections such as Massine's effervescent *La Boutique fantasque* and Nijinska's Riviera frolic *Le Train bleu* were dishes perfectly calculated to satisfy a sweet-toothed need for cheerful, colourful entertainment offering an innocently escapist vision of the world. And Diaghilev was not such a fool as to look the gift horse of a popular hit in the mouth.

One of Beaton's 'gaunt, angular women' might have been Ethel Mannin, a fiercely determined twenty-something girl of left-wing views who later became a popular novelist and travel writer. Her devotion to Diaghilev's work in the 1920s was boundless: 'All that was silly, trivial, regrettable and just plain bad in the decade is redeemed by the fact that it was the decade of the Russian ballet,' she wrote.

There was nothing like [it] for making one feel that one had grown wings and soared amongst the stars . . . Last nights were as exciting as premières. The emotional fervour, the wild hysteria of those Russian ballet farewells, the flowers, the wreaths, the exhausting applause, the relentless calling of the gods – to the gods. It was something unique.[11]

Obsessed with *La Boutique fantasque*, the artist David Bomberg started standing in the theatre foyers selling his own programmes for the ballets at two shillings and sixpence each. He was doing a roaring trade until Diaghilev got wind of what was going on. Leighton Lucas, a British dancer in the corps, remembered the craze as 'a religion':

A friend of mine, a queer little balletomane, he used to have a little photograph of Lopokova, and built a little shrine to it, and burnt candles in front of it every day. This was the intensity of his devotion to this art. And I saw a girl at Charing Cross Road fall down on her knees and try to kiss Idzikowski's hand as he [a principal dancer] went down the road towards the Coliseum.[12]

Note that dangerous word 'queer', its meaning discreetly on the cusp here between odd and homosexual, and increasingly present in accounts of the cult of the Ballets Russes. Ethel Mannin's memoir uses a less ambiguous term:

> The Russian Ballet was the urnings' outing – for both sexes. Those pale slender young men who called each other 'my dear' and raved about Serge Lifar, and who during the intervals stood about in pairs or groups of their kind and discussed the music of George[s] Auric and Prokofieff, the painting of Pedro Pruna and Marie Laurencin, the choreography of Balanchin[e] and Massine . . . And those Eton-cropped young women with collars and ties and tailor-made suits . . . talking in murmurous ecstasy of Tchernicheva and Danilova, of Nikitina in *Les Biches*, quarrelling a little over thin, colourless little Alice Markova and Vera Savina, growing a little jealous of each other's enthusiasms . . . charming little urnings, so 'interesting', so much alive . . . a good deal of pose to it all, but why not?[13]

A good deal of pose indeed. A teenage Cecil Beaton recalled how 'the Russian ballet burst like a miraculous flower into my life', sighing in the antique manner of the Aesthetic Movement, 'One does not go to the ballet to get rid of emotion, but to gain consciousness of emotion, consciousness of living.'[14] Two precocious Etonians, Harold Acton and Brian Howard, caught the same infection: with the help of a wind-up gramophone, they pranced around their rooms in their own versions of *Petrushka* and *Scheherazade*. In the vacation they were spotted by a fellow pupil sashaying into the stalls at Covent Garden

> in full evening dress, with long white gloves draped over one arm, and carrying silver-topped canes and top hats, looking perhaps like

a couple of Oscar Wildes. My stepmother was astonished at the sight of them, and thought they must be foreigners.[15]

This pair embodied 'the beautiful burgeoning boys', noted by Herbert Farjeon in *Vogue* (a magazine that went through a phase of feverish balletomania), 'who seemed to recline on art like Madame Récamier on her couch and to regard the dancer and the décor as a kind of personal adornment. Indeed, they might almost be said to wear the Russian Ballet like a carnation in their button holes.'[16] Posses of Bright Young Things such as Beaton, Diana Cooper, Oliver Messel and Evelyn Waugh were all in on it too, at least as far as parading for the first nights.

There must also have been thousands of people in the ballet audience beyond such coteries: married couples from the suburbs, spinster secretaries, foreign tourists, clerks, and drones like Leonard Bast in E. M. Forster's *Howards End*, hungry to elevate themselves through culture. But of these we know nothing.

The broader context to this exultation was a phenomenon sweeping through society as virulently as the Spanish flu epidemic (and must have contributed to the transmission of the virus). In 1919, the *Daily Mail* called it 'the mania of the moment' and the *Daily Express* decided that Britain had gone 'Dancing mad!'[17] This wasn't just a nine-day tabloid wonder. 'The twenties scene was dominated by the dancing craze,' Ethel Mannin recalled in her memoir. 'You danced whenever and wherever you could.'[18] Something similar, as James Laver noted, 'always takes place after great disasters. There was such a craze after the Black Death and also . . . after the French Revolution.'[19]

Social dancing had of course been popular since time immemorial, and before the Great War it had received a fillip from the ballrooms that are such a feature of grand Edwardian hotels. But its pace remained staid and its mood was inhibited, not least by the tight long skirts that were de rigueur for women. Come 1919, everything relaxed and the pace quickened. More feminine flesh was exposed to daily outdoor life, as hemlines rose to mid-calf and sleeveless dresses became respectable. Restrictive layers of densely laced underwear were discarded; girls swam, sunbathed, played tennis; they could cut their hair short and it was smart to look flat-chested and boyish. Thus liberated in their physical mobility, females of all classes and ages took with gay abandon to the floors of the palais de danse that sprang up all over Europe and the USA in the early 1920s. Feeding an insatiable appetite, the turkeytrot succeeded the foxtrot and the shimmy gave way to the all-conquering Charleston. Nobody may now remember how to do the buzzard lope or the chicken scratch, but they too among so many others had their moment. It was the Jazz Age, and jazz is music that gets people moving.

What this meant was a new receptivity. Ballet could no longer be seen either as the domain of the aesthetically enlightened and privileged, or as a mere novelty act. Instead it became part of a wider culture, developing a discourse that went beyond the burning of ecstatic incense or the snap verdicts of the music critics. The young T. S. Eliot related Massine's 'completely inhuman, impersonal, abstract' style to his aesthetics of masked detachment;[20] art critics such as Roger Fry and Clive Bell began to understand how movement and design were integrated, and the magazine *Drama* published a symposium on the future of ballet.

The cumulative impact of such airing of the issues and more expert press coverage was the evolution of an institutional infrastructure. Leading the bricklaying were two very different characters: Philip Richardson, easily mistaken for a dour bespectacled solicitor in a pinstripe suit, and Cyril Beaumont, a more maverick character who idolised the memory of Oscar Wilde, sported wing collars and kept his hair *en brosse*.*[21] Richardson was the editor of the monthly journal *Dancing Times* and a vigorous champion of the whole sector – ballroom as much as ballet. A staunch committee man, he was the founder in 1920 of what became the Royal Academy of Dance, dedicated to lobbying for the cause and standardising graded examinations and qualifications. Beaumont and his downtrodden wife ran a bookshop in Charing Cross Road that specialised in dance and became a hub for balletomanes. He became a uniquely meticulous chronicler of the Ballets Russes, while churning out a succession of dance-related tomes and running a small literary press in tandem. Beaumont held in particular reverence Diaghilev's pre-war ballet master Enrico Cecchetti, who opened a profoundly influential school in London after the war, and in 1922 Beaumont established a society to codify and preserve Cecchetti's method – one that emphasises strict classical line achieved through careful anatomical development and that remains prevalent in ballet schools today.

By the mid-1920s London was awash with ballet teachers. Pavlova, Karsavina and Massine gave occasional classes when their performing schedules permitted; exiled from St Petersburg, Serafina Astafieva ran the Chelsea School of Russian Dancing in the Pheasantry (now a branch of Pizza Express) on King's Road, Chelsea, and Nikolai Legat worked in Hammersmith. In Notting Hill, Marie Rambert taught Dalcroze alongside ballet; Cecchetti's disciple Margaret Craske had a studio in West Street in Covent Garden, and another true Cecchetti believer, the young

---

* Arnold Haskell, a figure often bracketed with Beaumont and Richardson, was younger than either of them. His influence as Diaghilev's biographer, a critic and champion of ballet began in the 1930s, lies outside the scope of this chapter. See pp. 262–3.

Ninette de Valois, opened the rigorously administered Academy of Choregraphic [*sic*] Art in Roland Gardens, Chelsea. The pupils at all these establishments were almost entirely – 99 per cent in all probability – female.[22] The young Frederick Ashton, mad keen to dance and soon to choreograph, flitted between most of these establishments, and was often the only boy there.

Chelsea's chic terraces were also the epicentre of a new wave of Russian ballet aficionados, focused on *Vogue*'s editor Dorothy Todd and her partner Madge Garland in Royal Hospital Road, the composer Constant Lambert and the dancer Anton Dolin in Glebe Place, and the literary brothers Osbert and Sacheverell Sitwell in Swan Walk (and later Carlyle Square), where Diaghilev and Massine had partied on Armistice Night. Given his extensive connections to the beau monde, Sacheverell in particular could open doors to the new patrons that Diaghilev needed and in 1926, he wrote the scenario for Diaghilev's 'British' pantomime *The Triumph of Neptune*.*[23]

But Diaghilev's London seasons were only periodic, rarely lasting more than a couple of months, and for the remainder of the year there was a hunger for all forms of dance to be satisfied. 'Russian ballet' might have had a special glamour, but it was only one of many attractions in a market where art and show business could co-exist without anyone worrying about 'dumbing down'. Although two of the biggest variety theatres, the Alhambra and Empire, both with pantomime ballet traditions, were declining through the 1920s, and would end up being replaced by cinemas (which often staged live balletic numbers as curtain-raisers to the

* A much-repeated anecdote of the time relates to Diaghilev's misunderstanding of Sacheverell's frequently expressed need, as an officer in the Grenadier Guards, to return late at night to Aldershot, where his barracks were. '*Qui est cette Aldershot?*' Diaghilev asked testily. '*C'est une femme?*'

main film), ballet continued to be allotted a regular fifteen-minute slot on the bills at the Palladium and the Coliseum, with Diaghilev stars such as Karsavina and Lopokova among the headliners, as well as lesser luminaries with exotic names.* Alongside but in no way considered inferior were the spectacular jazzy musicals imported from Broadway with showy tap-dance numbers, such as *Lady, Be Good*, the big hit of 1926 at the Empire, featuring the debonair Fred Astaire in partnership with his sister Adele; and the 'revues', the sophisticated new form of music-hall entertainment offered by the impresarios André Charlot and C. B. Cochran – intimately scaled down for the ballrooms of luxury hotels or restaurants such as the Trocadero, where audiences dined as they watched, but also staged in more conventional theatres such as the London Pavilion and Hippodrome.[24]

Massine choreographed and danced in two of Cochran's revues in 1925 – scenes included *The Rake*, designed by William Nicholson and inspired by Hogarth's engravings, and 'a fantastic spectacle based on the frescoes of Pompeii'.[25] But the big homegrown star here was Anton Dolin, a pupil of both Astafieva and Legat, one of the one per cent of British boys who had studied ballet to a professional standard. After his riotous success hand-standing and double back-flipping with the Ballets Russes in *Le Train bleu*, he became as big a West End draw in the mid-1920s as Noel Coward or Jack Buchanan. Privately homosexual but publicly snapped escorting

---

* A curiosity is a one-act play written by J. M. Barrie, the author of *Peter Pan*, called *The Truth about the Russian Dancers*, which played at the Coliseum for a month in 1920 (and again in 1926 at the Savoy), with designs by Paul Nash. A whimsical fable in which an English nobleman falls in love with a mute Russian ballerina who uses dance as a sign language instead of speaking, it was conceived as a vehicle for Lopokova. In the event, it was Karsavina who took the central role.

pretty girls (or lesbians equally in need of a beard) on his arm, he was also uninhibited about taking the main chance and the bigger pay cheque.

In 1925, he was twenty-one: his autobiography reels off his helter-skelter of engagements:

Archie de Bear engaged me for *The Punch Bowl* review at Her Majesty's Theatre. I made two appearances, dancing first *Hymn to the Sun*, and later, a classic acrobatic new solo to the rather jazzy music of *Alabamy Bound* . . . I had not long to wait before, with Phyllis Bedells as my partner, we began a series of wonderful engagements at the London Coliseum . . . There was *Palladium Pleasures*, a revue . . . I danced – I feel sure – an incredibly bad ballet, *A Flutter in a Dove Cote* with Iris Rowe . . . There was *The Charlot Revue of 1926* at the Prince of Wales' Theatre with Herbert Mundin and Jessie Matthews, which brought stardom and acclaim to my darling Jessie . . . we danced *See Saw Margery Daw* as a pas de deux . . . The Stoll tour and many more long, happy weeks, then to the London Coliseum with Phyllis Bedells and Ninette de Valois as my partners. Cabaret at the Piccadilly Hotel with Phyllis for six weeks at Christmas . . . I danced with Thamar Karsavina at the London Coliseum, *The Nutcracker* adagio, followed by *Le Spectre de la Rose*, twice a day for two wonderful weeks . . . Lew Leslie's *Whitebirds* at His Majesty's was a major disaster financially and not much use artistically. Ninette de Valois was my opposite Apache in the Montmartre scene . . .*[26]

* He did not record his additional appearance on 13 July at a garden party at Hurlingham where, according to the diary of Chips Channon, 'He did a very questionable dance with no clothes save a golden spider rose attached to him.' (Henry 'Chips' Cannon, *The Diaries 1918–1938*, p. 166.)

Fun, yes, but it was all a miscellany of ephemeral sideshows, at the mercy of the whims of producers, often flung together pell-mell and evidently of slipshod quality. Audiences craved novelty and gimmicks and the press colluded. 'Vera Nemchinova, whose legs are insured for the enormous sum of £30,000, will make an effort at the Coliseum matinée on Monday to beat her own world record of spinning unassisted 38 times on one toe,' read one particularly silly but all-too-typical article in the *Daily Mirror*.[27]

Amid an increasing sense of frustration, enthusiasts began wondering why the British couldn't themselves do what the Russians were doing, with the implicit assumption that some sort of hierarchy privileging academic ballet (sometimes fastidiously referred to in this period as 'toe dancing' or 'operatic dancing') over other forms of dance was desirable. Kathrine Sorley Walker has traced the first mutterings of this to a letter published in *Dancing Times* in 1917 from an actress and novelist called Rachel Verney. 'We have a Stage Society in London [a precursor of the Royal Court, mounting non-commercial new plays of artistic merit],' she wrote. 'Why should we not inaugurate a Ballet Society?'[28] Correspondence ensued, most of it broadly supportive, but sceptical of the existence of the native talent or skills – let alone money – to sustain such a thing.

But a seed had been planted and through the mid-1920s various humble initiatives sprung up, stimulated by irritation at what was regarded in sterner quarters as Diaghilev's surrender to Frenchified modishness. The ballet schools mounted modest matinées to showcase their pupils' prowess. At the Lyric Theatre, Hammersmith, Marie Rambert's protégé, a spindly young man called Frederick Ashton, choreographed a witty caprice called *A Tragedy of Fashion*, in which he himself played the role of a perfectionist couturier who kills himself when his creations are met with displeasure. Bookseller and publisher Cyril Beaumont went a step further and planned a more permanent company to be called the Cremorne Ballet: like some bathetic early experiment in aeronautics, it took off promisingly but soon crashed to the ground. There was vague talk about the state providing aid, but that was a long way off.

In 1928 the temperature rose, as Anton Dolin entered the fray with a swaggering readiness to shoot his mouth off. 'He could talk anyone into anything,' recalled Richard Buckle, who as a teenager had been bundled into bed with him at a Marble Arch hotel.[29] Using his stardom as a platform, he bluntly stated *ex-cathedra* views, albeit sincerely aimed at raising everyone's game, that put other people's backs up. 'Taking some pretty tuneful music and putting a few, or too many, pink roses on a ballet dress, and dancing a series of steps, however well and interestingly performed, is not BALLET, and calling it by that name does more harm than good,' he thundered in *Dancing Times*, while taking side swipes at 'the production of Futuristic Ballet without the genius of Nijinska or Massine' and 'the natural expressionistic movement' inspired by Dalcroze at Hellerau. 'All dancing should, and must be, based on the only school of dancing possible – the Russian school,' he concluded. 'And that is the school we must teach in England, and teach our teachers to teach.'[30]

His polemic was useful, though. In terms of what was being taught, the Russian school had already won the battle. He was certainly right to insist that British – or English – ballet had to stiffen up if it was to get anywhere (and a first step, it was suggested elsewhere, might be losing the habit of altering perfectly good English names into more spuriously glamorous 'Continental' forms – Dolin himself having been born Patrick Healey-Kay*). At

* Philip Richardson wrote a short satirical play on this subject, *No English Need Apply*, in which dancers auditioning with exotically foreign names are unmasked as Janet and John. (*Dancing Times*, December 1923, pp. 347–9.)

the end of the decade that vital push would come in particular from two remarkable young women, whose relationship was highly competitive, verging on combative.

Inspired as a child by seeing the unabashedly British Phyllis Bedells take centre stage at the Empire, Ninette de Valois (born Edris Stannus) had everything except money. She certainly did not want for rigorous training with Cecchetti and Legat, the experience of dancing for Diaghilev, inexhaustible energy, fearless determination, a clear eye for her goal and a formidable talent inherited from her military forefathers to lead and command.[31] In 1926, at the age of twenty-seven, she had published in *Dancing Times* a manifesto entitled 'The Future of the Ballet', full of categorical assertions that invited no argument and left no doubt that here was someone who knew exactly where they were going and why.

> Discussing the ballet as a complete theatrical art, there is no question that the teachings of the classic school are the sure and only foundation – limitless in its adaptability it consequently proves its power to meet the varied requirements of the theatre. But the Hellenic School of dancing with Isadora Duncan as its figure head has shown the emotional powers that lie hidden in the theory of broader and freer body movements. The influence of the plastic school on the classic has been greatly felt – and the result has been most satisfactory.[32]

Like Dolin, de Valois earned her bread by dancing around town and, as well as running her school, she provided barefoot choreography for productions of masked verse plays by W. B. Yeats at the Abbey Theatre in Dublin and the Festival Theatre in Cambridge, where her cousin Terence Gray and his colleague Norman Marshall favoured a fashionable style of theatre, imitative of the

Ancient Greeks, involving mime and music. All this kept de Valois very busy, and her manner was consequently brisk.* 'At rehearsals,' Marshall recalled, 'her way of dashing about the stage, scolding, goading and exhorting was so reminiscent of a hockey practice that the company nicknamed her the Games Mistress.'[33]

The other outstanding figure was Marie Rambert. Trained by Dalcroze and having been Nijinsky's assistant on *The Rite of Spring*, she was a cosmopolitan and cultured charmer with a fiercely explosive but warmly affectionate temper. More imaginative and nurturing but less driven than de Valois, 'Mim' Rambert inspired loyalty and love where de Valois earned fear and respect, and round her would cluster the cream of young balletic talent – not only Frederick Ashton, but dancer and designer William Chappell, choreographer Antony Tudor, virtuoso dancer Harold Turner, and two exquisite ballerinas of South African origin, Pearl Argyle and Maude Lloyd, among them.[34]

But first some essential space had to be cleared, and that could be achieved only if the Ballets Russes wasn't dominant. So Diaghilev's death in August 1929 and the company's dissolution was a moment of tragic shock but also of liberation: now was the time to strike. Within months, a committee led by the moving-and-shaking editor of *Dancing Times*, Philip Richardson, abetted by a young balletomane called Arnold Haskell, and including Karsavina,

---

* Interviewed in 1998 on the occasion of her centenary, almost blind and partially deaf but still totally compos mentis, de Valois had lost none of her edge as she put the journalist John Walsh firmly in his place. 'Sit up straight. You look most uncomfortable . . . I don't know what you're talking about. Ask me short questions. And stop waving your hands around.' He ended up charmed and convinced. 'Though [she] can be rude, direct, abrasive and frankly impossible,' he concluded, 'she does have a habit of turning out to be right.' (*Independent*, 5 June 1998.)

Lopokova and her economist husband Maynard Keynes, Dolin, Rambert and de Valois had settled their differences, joined forces and pooled resources to form the Camargo Society,* a subscribers' club that presented new choreography with new music and designs, all of British origin. It lasted only three years and performed very intermittently, but what was important was its creative boldness and integrity. The aim was art, not West End entertainment but, as Haskell put it, 'we met with kindness and indulgence everywhere' and 'this may have made us take matters a little too easily'.[35]

In 1930 de Valois went into business with Lilian Baylis, a sublime eccentric with an evangelical mission to bring high art to 'ordinary' people; she ran an opera and drama company at the Old Vic in Waterloo and was building a new theatre at Sadler's Wells in Islington. For the latter she decided she needed ballet, which de Valois agreed to provide, and in 1931 the Vic–Wells company of six salaried dancers would take permanent root, slowly growing hand to mouth and feeding off plain fare, until it moved upmarket to Covent Garden in 1946 and became the Royal Ballet a decade later. In 1930 Rambert and her playwright husband Ashley Dukes started another 'Ballet Club' and in 1931 they opened their own bijou theatre in a converted church hall at a decent distance from Islington in Notting Hill. Patronised by the beau monde, the Mercury Theatre, which features briefly in *The Red Shoes*, became the chic first home for the modern dance company that still bears Rambert's name. The subsequent histories of the Royal Ballet and the Ballet Rambert are well documented elsewhere.[36]

De Valois and Rambert were truly Diaghilev's children; had he survived another ten years, he might have regarded the maturing

---

* Named after Marie Camargo (1710–1770), the ground-breaking French dancer.

of their modest efforts in a benign paternal light. In Paris, however, the dance scene of the 1920s posed several more aggressive threats to the supremacy of the Ballets Russes and, much to Diaghilev's irritation, the enterprise never quite recovered the lustre that it had enjoyed there before the Great War. Yet none of these rival ventures amounted to anything substantial or enduring – whereas London's little acorns are stout oaks a century later.

Why? The culture of Paris was faster to change than London's and more receptive to the changeable winds and tides of modernism. Jean Cocteau acted as the bellwether, neither radical nor reactionary, always opportunistically where he needed to be and promoting his own interests in a way that made Diaghilev uncomfortable. As Madeleine, wife of the composer Darius Milhaud, later remembered: 'He liked to be in charge of everything, and generally was . . . if he wasn't doing everything, he didn't think he was doing anything.'[37]

But even if Diaghilev couldn't trust Cocteau (who in turn resented the Russian for the way he'd been blindsided over *Parade**), they remained useful to each other. Cocteau had his finger on the pulse of Paris, and was attuned to the new vogue for American popular culture and the music-hall – phenomena alien to Diaghilev with his tsarist background and elevated conception of art. In particular Cocteau was the guiding light for the band of young French composers – christened in the press as Les Six, though they hardly formed a stylistic unity – that congregated in a cabaret bar called Le Boeuf sur le Toit, off the Rue Saint-Honoré. This fashionable institution took its name from a frivolously nonsensical 'pantomime-ballet' in the style of *Parade*, set in Prohibition America, populated by clowns and dwarves and replete with references to slapstick cinema, that

* See pp. 137–40.

Cocteau had himself devised and presented to a score by Milhaud, with designs by Raoul Dufy, at the Théâtre des Champs-Élysées in 1919.

This was Diaghilev's territory, of course – the Théâtre des Champs-Élysées had been the venue for the première of *The Rite of Spring* – and the success of something as derivative as *Le Boeuf* must have been a bitter pill to swallow at a time when the Ballets Russes's post-war return to Paris in December 1919 had been curtailed and dampened by strikes. But to antagonise Cocteau would be to lose access to his circle too, so Diaghilev wisely commissioned scores from three of Les Six – Poulenc, Auric, Milhaud – and in 1924 Cocteau would provide him with the scenario for one of the Ballets Russes's biggest successes of the jazz era, *Le Train bleu*.

Yet only weeks before the première of *Le Train bleu*, Cocteau had also been involved in another more direct challenge to Diaghilev. It emanated from Étienne, Comte de Beaumont, and his wife Édith, a wealthy, cultured, *branché* homosexual couple at the epicentre of Parisian high society and on kissing terms with Diaghilev.[38] In their fabulous mansion in the Rue Masseran, they held extravagant masked balls, for which Étienne designed fanciful costumes and directed *tableaux vivants*. He then went a stage further: infatuated with Massine, he flung a vast amount of money at him to curate thirty dancers in new ballets for a six-week season of avant-garde ballet and drama entitled *Soirées de Paris*, to be staged in La Cigale, a music-hall in Pigalle.

Diaghilev was understandably incandescent with rage. The Ballets Russes was booked to appear at the Théâtre des Champs-Élysées at exactly the same time, May–June 1924, yet many people who owed him loyalty had signed up with de Beaumont – not only the traitor Massine and the unreliable Cocteau but also Picasso,

Satie, Derain and dancers including Lopokova and Idzikowski. Younger talents with hopes of commission were warned: it's him or me. Cocteau slithered disingenuously: 'I wanted to explain to you about a Cigale project which I think should please you,' he wrote to Diaghilev. 'E. de Beaumont wants me to stage [an adaptation of Shakespeare's] *Romeo and Juliet*, to alternate with his music-hall programme . . . So I am doing nothing that is in any way like your productions, and am confining myself to theatre.'[39]

Both parties came to see the other's shows and made their views plain. Diaghilev stood publicly pointing at a poster for *Soirées de Paris* and announced, 'Only my name is missing.'[40] It was a war to the death, but with *Les Biches*, *Les Noces* and *Le Train bleu* as new weapons in his armoury, Diaghilev emerged the outright winner. For de Beaumont, nothing went right. Under pressure to produce an enormous amount of fresh material in a very short time, Massine was more than usually unpleasant in rehearsals and produced work of very variable quality, sinking to the downright trivial.* De Beaumont proved ineffectual on the theatrical ground, the orchestra went on strike and, despite the dazzling range of talent he had hired, the net result was a mess that soon emptied La Cigale and left the de Beaumonts to retreat to their mansion and count the cost. 'I have been through fire and water,' Lopokova shrieked. 'There was not one controlling voice in the situation.'[41]

---

* Three years later, Diaghilev would salvage from the wreckage the one interesting item. Designed by Picasso and with music by Satie, *Mercure* was a cartoon take on Roman mythology consisted of twelve brief and largely static scenes, including one in which the Three Graces were presented by 'muscular male dancers *en travesti* wearing large papier-mâché breasts and pictured in a vertical bathtub' (Vicente Garcia-Marquez, *Massine*, p. 180). This was the only occasion on which the Ballets Russes presented a work that Diaghilev had not commissioned.

More sustained competition to Diaghilev had come from the Ballets Suédois and its rousing manifesto:

*Les Ballets Suédois sont les seuls qui OSENT. Les Ballets Suédois sont les seuls représentatives de la vie contemporaine, les Ballets Suédois sont les seuls qui soient vraiment contre l'académisme. Contre tous les académismes.*

(The Ballets Suédois are the only ones who DARE. The Ballets Suédois are the only representatives of contemporary life. The Ballets Suédois are the only ones who are genuinely against academicism. Against all academicisms.)[42]

This was no empty boast, and over the five years of its existence, Ballets Suédois stole ideas, headlines and audience from Diaghilev, as well as making significant and radical innovations of its own. Underpinning the enterprise were the considerable financial resources of Rolf de Maré, born in Stockholm in 1888 of landed aristocratic stock. Although widely travelled and cosmopolitan, de Maré was an enigmatic soul without Diaghilev's swagger. Based in Paris, he traded throughout his life in Old Masters and contemporary art, eventually bequeathing his outstanding collection to Stockholm's Moderna Museet when he died in 1964.

In 1918 he had fallen in love with a plump Swedish dancer called Jean Börlin, who became his partner (in a relationship not dissimilar to those that Diaghilev had with younger men: Börlin appears not to have been homosexual himself). Börlin's talent as a performer was for vivid characterisation, marked by a puckish energy that reflected his superficially sunny and free-wheeling personality: he also had a rich choreographic imagination, though how much of his inspiration he owed to de Maré remains a mystery.

With the Ballets Russes preoccupied in London during the immediate post-war era, de Maré seized his window of opportunity. He took out a seven-year lease on the Théâtre des Champs-Élysées and commissioned his friend Jacques Hébertot to act as manager and promoter of a company of Scandinavian dancers presenting works created by Börlin. Hébertot was a master of public relations, de Maré pumped in the money and Börlin delivered the goods.

Although it offered obvious points of similarity to the Ballets Russes, Ballets Suédois was no carbon copy. For one thing, none of its dancers was up to much technically. Börlin had studied for a time with Fokine and Dalcroze, but he had no classical grounding and nobody else in the troupe of twenty ever attracted much attention. For another, their success was as much based in ethnic dance as it was in a modernist aesthetic, and almost never featured pointe shoes or the spinning, leaping and bending associated with the Russian school.

Over five seasons, the company kept the Théâtre des Champs-Élysées as its hub, while also touring extensively over Continental Europe. Its two expeditions to London, in 1920 and 1922, made little impression, and in 1923–4 the company travelled to the USA, where it was considered merely bizarre. The company was then disbanded for six months, reviving briefly only to be felled by the cruel winter of 1925 that left French theatres empty. At that point Ballets Suédois was extinguished, not least because de Maré couldn't afford to continue subsidising the operation and his affair with Börlin, now enslaved to the drink and drugs that led to his early death, had drifted to an end.

Ballets Suédois operated on a more extreme mix of styles than the Ballets Russes. Its bread and butter was a series of works drawing on Scandinavian folklore, presented in ethnographically authentic costume, with music drawn from folk tunes and *faux-naïf* settings.

The tone of *La Nuit de Saint Jean*, *Dansgille* and *Les Vièrges folles* ('The Foolish Virgins') was bright, colourful, childlike, threaded with only a minimum of narrative and avoiding any classical technique in the steps. The aim was to charm: the means used were much less sophisticated than Fokine's picture-book homages to Russian culture (*The Firebird*, *Petrushka*), let alone the witty urbanity of Massine's farcical *La Boutique fantasque*. Even if the dancers ended up sick of performing these frolics night after night, audiences simply couldn't get enough of them.

But there was also a much more stringent aspect to Ballets Suédois and in the early 1920s, Börlin and de Maré stole a march on Diaghilev by brazenly incorporating Dada, surrealism, expressionism and the aesthetics of chrome steel and plate glass. *Maison de fous* ('Madhouse', 1920) was a hallucinatory exploration of paranoid schizophrenic delusion; *Les Mariés de la Tour Eiffel* (1921) was a black comedy in which a bourgeois wedding turns into a massacre, following a scenario by the ubiquitous Cocteau and with music by five of Les Six; *Skating Rink* (1922), designed cubistically by Fernand Léger, showed a death-like figure picking a girl out from the zombie-like beings vacuously circulating over the ice. Léger, a man of the Left, became very excited by the possibilities.

Most intriguing of all are *Within the Quota* (1923) and *Relâche* (1924) – both of which should probably be described as mimed playlets, as they appear to have contained almost nothing conventionally danced. Following a plot line devised by Gerald Murphy, *Within the Quota* had music by Cole Porter. Against a backdrop blow-up of a newspaper front page splashed with tabloid headlines, it showed a hapless Chaplinesque immigrant from Sweden (a role taken by Börlin) arriving in New York only to be bewildered and bamboozled by some of the more crass manifestations of the American way of life. *Relâche* (the word used in French to indicate a temporary theatrical closure or cancellation) was billed as a *'ballet instantanéiste'*. The visual conception was Francis Picabia's, interrupted by a fantastical freewheeling twenty-minute film interlude directed by René Clair. The stage was dominated by a wall of 370 metallic discs like car headlights, their intensity of illumination governed by the sound of the revving car engines and parping horns featured in Satie's pounding minimalist score. A chain-smoking fireman and a respectable lady with dark erotic desires – fulfilled by Börlin in bespangled trunks and an octet of gents in evening dress who strip down to their underwear – featured in a piece of wilful pretension that created a brief stir over a handful of performances but proved ultimately sterile.* This was gimmickry without substance: Diaghilev had kept a sharp eye on Ballets Suédois; but its time was soon up, and its legacy would fall more into the genre of performance art that emerged half a century later than it did to dance.

One other Ballets Suédois piece worthy of mention is *La Création du monde* (1923). Designed by Léger, it picked up on one of the most salient trends in 1920s Parisian culture: the fascination with the art of 'primitive' and tribal Africa and the glamour of *négritude*. This had been a fascination for an élite of artists (such as Picasso) before 1914, but post-war all things black became more broadly popular through a major exhibition at the Galerie Devambez in 1919 as well as the influx of blues singers and jazz bands often made up of American soldiers left behind after the Armistice.

In their wake came a nineteen-year-old girl of unique gifts, spotted in a Broadway night club, who signed up for Paris on the

---

* It has occasionally been speculatively reconstructed and restaged in recent years: highlights can be seen on You Tube (https://www.youtube.com/watch?v=yHAYeOU9hkU).

grounds that France might have something better to offer than the subtle slights and overt segregations of Jim Crow's America. Her name was Josephine Baker and in 1925 she became the overnight star of *La Revue nègre* at the Théâtre des Champs-Élysées: Ernest Hemingway famously called her 'the most sensational woman any-one ever saw'.[43] Her utter lack of inhibition was exhilarating: she sang risqué songs and told wicked jokes, but it was the way she flaunted her rubbery body – 'a cross between a boxing kangaroo, a piece of chewing gum and a racing cyclist', as one wag put it[44] – that enthralled.

Bare-breasted, crossing her eyes and emitting a strange whis-tling whinny as she shimmied and slapped her buttocks in a crazy Charleston, her persona took ownership of all the melodramatic clichés of black female sexuality (the '*Vénus noire*' of Baudelaire's poems, '*bizarre deité*', '*démon sans pitié*') by turning them into a romping joke. No woman before her had played such a game in so public a fashion, her panache transcending vulgarity. And not since Nijinsky insinuated androgyny had anyone so boldly stretched the parameters of the erotic. After Josephine Baker, the sexiness of Scheherazade looked old hat.

We do not know if Diaghilev ever witnessed this marvel in per-son, and he left no comment on her. Would he have been charmed or appalled? Would he have felt that he had missed the boat, or recognised that the liberties she took with her body portended the doom of ballet's classical aesthetics even more ominously than had *The Rite of Spring*? One doubts his approval would have been forth-coming: jazz was anathema to him; he disliked Americanisation, and he was indifferent to the female physique. But it is certainly telling that Harry Kessler found nothing and nobody in the company's post-war era so exciting as Baker, 'a genius' for whom he planned a ballet on the theme of the Song of Solomon: 'Miss Baker would be dressed (or not dressed) on the lines of oriental Antiquity while Solomon would be in a dinner jacket, the whole thing an entirely arbitrary fantasy of ancient and modern set to music, half jazz and half oriental, to be composed perhaps by Richard Strauss.'[45]

Nothing came of this, and as she moved to the Folies Bergère and then into the cinema, Baker posed no direct competition to ballet. But her flagrantly flaunted exoticism had raised the temperature in Paris and audiences there found many of the final experiments of the Ballets Russes timid and prim, if not passé, in comparison. In London, they baffled; in Paris, they bored. Was the moment passing?

Having seen off the Ballets Suédois, the de Beaumonts and Josephine Baker, Diaghilev faced one last foe in Paris: his old antagonist Ida Rubinstein.

Two decades after her brief success with the Ballets Russes in *Scheherazade* and *Cléopâtre*, her problem continued to be a combination of too much money and too little talent. Still supremely elegant in her forties but too old to continue discarding Salome's seven veils, this grande dame with impeccably condescending manners, an hourglass figure and darkly beautiful Semitic features used her vast inherited wealth (and that of her lover Walter Guinness) to seek out new vehicles through which to exhibit herself to advantage. In 1928, she established her own company in Paris and commissioned a repertory of seven new works. Never one to do anything by halves, she hired the Opéra, engaged Benois to supervise the designs, Nijinska and Massine to choreograph and (among others) Ravel and Stravinsky to compose scores – the results being *Boléro* and *Le Baiser de la fée*.

Such a roster might have been dazzling, but Rubinstein's insistence on making herself the centrepiece sabotaged the enterprise. For all her exquisite looks, she was as risible in the role of a malign fairy in *Le Baiser de la fée* as she was in *Boléro*, standing on a table in gypsy costume waving her arms about. Why she put herself through it was something of a mystery as she was paralysed by stage fright. Other dancers in the cast such as the young Frederick Ashton sniggered at the 'poor old thing' as she tottered round the stage looking like an ostrich, fluttering and pouting in a desperate effort to mask her incompetence. She had all the dignity and sincerity of Marie Antoinette playing the milkmaid.[46]

Rubinstein's wholesale appropriation of talents that Diaghilev had earlier sponsored caused him intense aggravation – and Stravinsky's participation was the source of a final tiff that was sadly never resolved. At least he could rub his hands in sadistic delight at the mediocrity of what she had produced, reporting back to Serge Lifar after seeing a couple of performances,

> The whole thing was astonishingly provincial, boring and long drawn out . . . it is very useful to look at rubbish, it makes one think . . .
>
> The theatre was full, but as for success – it was like a drawing room in which some respectable person has just farted . . . what is the use of it all? . . . we need someone, a Napoleon or the Bolsheviks, to explode a bomb under these hovels with their audiences, their sluts who think themselves dancers, their millions spent on buying musicians.[47]

So what did he think? And what was the use of it all? A few months later, during his last London season just weeks before he died, Diaghilev wrote an uncharacteristically long and rambling letter to *The Times* in which is embedded the nearest he ever came after his *Mir iskusstva* days to expressing an aesthetic manifesto. An attempt to distinguish his enterprise from the ephemera of

Ida Rubinstein and the Ballets Suédois, it is incoherent and some-times self-contradictory – both radical and conservative, a defence of innovation, an attack on the gimmickry of the avant-garde and an assertion of eternal principles – but, in its muddle,* it comes closer than anything else to summing up the miscellaneous volatile opportunistic eclectic stop-start course of the Ballets Russes:

Sir, – The longer the globe revolves, the less movement we will find on it! Peoples may fight world wars, empires may tumble, a colossal Utopia may be given birth to, but the inborn traditions of humanity remain the same. Social revolutions upset political statuses, but they do not touch that side of the human spirit which leads to beauty. On the contrary, in such moments one has not got the time to busy oneself with aesthetic problems. In a period of this description we find ourselves at the present moment, when individual talent and human genius, always alive, enter like a microbe into the human system, but there it is refused any support.

Our century, without halting, interests itself with new 'Mouvements mécaniques', but whenever new 'Mouvements artistiques' occur people seem to be more frightened of being run over by them than by a motor-car in the street. For 25 years I have endeavoured to find a new 'Mouvement' in the theatre. Society will have to recognise that my experiments, which appear dangerous today, become indispensable tomorrow. The misfortune of art is that everybody thinks he is entitled to his own judgement. When a scientist invents an electrical machine it is only experts

* And possible mistranslation from the original French in which, given Diaghilev's rudimentary command of English, the letter was most likely originally composed.

who assume the right to be competent to criticise, but when I invent my artistic machine, everybody, without ceremony, puts his finger into the most delicate parts of the engine and likes to run it his own way . . .

The new appreciation of my 'Spectacles' of to-day is a series of exclamations: What an 'Étrange', 'Extravagant', 'Repellent' show, and the new definitions of the choreography are 'Athletics' and 'Acrobatics'. The show, before anything, must be 'Étrange'. I can picture to myself the bewilderment of the people who saw the first electric lamp, who heard the first word on the telephone. My first electric bell for the British public was the presentation of the Polovtsian dances of *Prince Igor*. The small audience could not tolerate this eccentric and acrobatic savagery and they fled.* And this only happened in 1911, at Covent Garden. At the very same theatre in 1929 the critics announced that my dancers had transformed themselves into 'athletes' and my choreographic parts were 'pure acrobatics'.

I have no room here to discuss this grave question in detail, but in a few words: the classical dance has never been and is not to-day the Russian ballet. Its birthplace was France; it grew up in Italy, and has only been conserved in Russia. Side by side with the classical dance there always existed the national or character dance which has given the evolution of the Russian ballet. I do not know of a single classical movement which was born of the Russian folk-dance. Why have we got to take our inspiration from the minuet of the French Court and from the Russian village festival? That which appears to you acrobatic is a dilettantic terminology for our national dance step. The mistake really, in fact, goes much deeper, because it is undoubtedly the

* This is untrue. The audience was large, and the reception enthusiastic.

Italian classical school which has introduced into the dance the acrobatic elements . . . in the plastic efforts of Balanchine, on *The Prodigal Son*, there are far less acrobatics than in the final classical *pas de deux* of *Aurora's Wedding*.

Monday next I am presenting to the public two new items. Lifar is, for the first time, in charge of the dances; he is the inventor of the choreography of the *Renard*, and it is there where really one has the first opportunity to talk of acrobatic ballet. It is not all Lifar's principle, but just because he could not see any other form to express the acrobatic music of Stravinsky, as Picasso is the acrobat of outline. Several constructive elements have introduced themselves into the field of acrobatics, and 'Constructivisme' in painting, decor, music and choregraphy is the craze of to-day.

The forms change. In painting and in scenery this craze is finishing. But in music, where we were full of impressionism and sentimentalism, and in choreography, where we paid reverence to the classical dance, 'constructivisme' acquired an extraordinary strength. It was the period of cynical sentimental simplicity . . . and the poor music sank to such banality, even surpassing the ladies' ballads of the end of the nineteenth century. That is why I welcome everything that can help us to forget the fatal errors of the 'Paris international market'. My young countryman Igor Markevitch [Diaghilev's final protégé] will play for the first time his piano concerto. He is sixteen years old. His music is dear to me, because I see in it the very birth of that new generation which can protest against the Paris orgies of the last few years . . . all sentimentalism of melody is absent . . .

Lifar has the same sense of construction and the same dread of compromise. On the outside cover of the score of the *Renard* Stravinsky has written, 'This ballet must be executed by buffoons, acrobats or dancers.' Lifar has taken dancers and real acrobats of the circus, and the task of the choreographist has been to combine the plastic of the circus and dance tricks . . .

The public and the critics will probably be annoyed with my two young friends but they are both debutants and they are not afraid of it.

The more the globe revolves, the less movement we find on it.

I am, &c., Serge Diaghileff[48]

The basic sources for this chapter are Kathrine Sorley Walker, *Ninette de Valois: Idealist Without Illusions*, pp. 5–98; Michael de Cossart, *Ida Rubinstein: A Theatrical Life*, passim; Lynn Garafola, *Diaghilev's Ballets Russes*, pp. 98–143, 211–36, 273–5; Bengt Häger, *Ballets Suédois*, passim; Julie Kavanagh, *Secret Muses: The Life of Frederick Ashton*, pp. 32–137; Vicente Garcia-Marquez, *Massine*, pp. 167–204; Malcolm McCormick and Nancy Reynolds, *No Fixed Points: Dance in the Twentieth Century*, pp. 178–237; Richard Allen Cave and Libby Worth (eds), *Ninette de Valois: Adventurous Traditionalist*, pp. 4–37; *Les Ballets Suédois: Une compagnie d'avant-garde 1920–1925*, passim; Karen Eliot, *Albion's Dance*, pp. 1–28; Jane Stevenson, *Baroque between the Wars*, pp. 281–94.

# 8

# SUCCESSORS

———

From left to right, Christian Bérard, Boris Kochno, René Blum, Vassily de Basil, Serge Grigoriev, George Balanchine

Scepticism bristled in the weeks following Diaghilev's death in 1929. What could ballet's future be without the figurehead who, as the obituary in *The Times* put it, was 'the originator of perhaps the most distinguished entertainment of modern times'?[1] The *Daily Express* was one of many to shake its head: 'I do not think the Ballet will long survive. There is all the machinery, but no driving force. The man who built the machine is dead.'[2] Although the doomsayers would be proved wrong, inasmuch as ballet's popularity would continue to grow for another generation, perhaps they were right to identify a loss of 'driving force': the sense of one personality dominating the scene and setting the agenda was never recovered, and the story of the next thirty years is one in which Diaghilev's disciples and imitators sought both to replicate his achievements and escape his shadow. The bar had been set high. According to the *Daily Mail*, 'This extraordinary man had put his stamp on the age, or perhaps it would be better to say that through him the age – that is the first quarter of the twentieth century – found expression.'[3] Arnold Haskell was even blunter: 'From 1919 to 1929 was the Diaghileff era of modern art.'[4]

Because the organisation ran hand to mouth and relied on last-minute contributions from his patrons, the Ballets Russes had no financial infrastructure, no reserves or capital. To meet its debts, the bulk of materiel – sets, costumes, scores, stored in Paris – was soon sold off as a job lot to a New York impresario who entertained the idea of transferring the company to the USA. Fallout from the Wall Street crash sent this pipe dream up in smoke.

Many in the business assumed that Diaghilev's loyal dauphin Boris Kochno would take up the reins and carry on: bookings and commissions were in hand for 1930 and beyond. But this was not to be; everything simply disintegrated. Despite all his intelligence, imagination and discretion, Kochno did not have the managerial authority to go it alone. Serge Lifar, his rival at Diaghilev's death-bed, tried to muscle in but was rebuffed. Fortunately for all those Ballets Russes associates repelled by his blustering ego, he landed a position at the helm of the Paris Opéra that would keep him grounded – with one unfortunate hiatus, of which more later – until 1958. Massine meanwhile 'drove himself into a frenzy' in his efforts to rally core members of the troupe and find new patronage.[5] But nobody had any money.

In only one place was this no impediment: Monte Carlo. Its economy was a law unto itself, and the opera house in which Diaghilev had based the Ballets Russes since 1924 was sheltered under the umbrella of the Société des bains de mer de Monaco – in other words, the bottomlessly profitable casino – and run by the benign intellectual René Blum, the Jewish brother of French socialist leader (and later prime minister) Léon Blum. Blum had worked harmoniously with Diaghilev and understood the art of ballet: all he lacked was roughness and toughness. These qualities he found in spades in a cadaverous Cossack, formerly an officer in the military police. Born Vassily Grigorievich Voskrezensky but going by the name of Colonel de Basil, he had picked up some experience in the Parisian theatrical and art worlds, but he had no depth of knowledge or sensibility, and relied on others to come up with the ideas. 'A man of action and a keen business man, whose great interest lies in the handling of difficult people' was Arnold Haskell's

nice way of describing him.[6] The company's senior ballerina Alexandra Danilova put it more bluntly: de Basil, she sniffed, 'was not
a gentleman'. A chancer and a fixer would be closer to the truth
– ruthlessly shrewd and totally untrustworthy, though charming
and sympathetic when it suited him, he was driven by commercial
instinct rather than aesthetic vision, and a reluctance to cough up
that became legendary. In his incorrigible pleasure in intrigue, he
was supported by a comic-opera trio named Lidji, Philippov and
Zon who hovered in the background as gatekeepers, stooges and
collaborators. The result, Danilova added, was 'the most chaotic
organisation I have ever known'.[7] This was not simply her personal
pique. 'Probably no one who ever worked for the de Basil Ballet
ended up without a financial grievance,' wrote Kathrine Sorley
Walker. 'Everyone was cheated, one way or another, or at least felt
cheated, which comes to much the same thing.' To be fair, however,
'dispassionately considered, it seems impossible that the company
could have kept going if it had attempted to pay its way honestly'.[8]

Blum was initially awed by de Basil's gangsterish energy and
together they proposed reassembling Diaghilev's personnel and
running a repertory on his lines, for which Kochno would act as
artistic consultant, with Balanchine as principal choreographer and
Diaghilev's staunchest support Sergei Grigoriev as ballet master
and company manager. The first season, running through the first
half of 1932 in Paris and Monte Carlo, was riotously successful, but
de Basil had none of that Wagnerian idealism that had fired the
Nevsky Pickwickians. His aim was flagrantly to showcase star dancers – in particular, a trio of barely teenage girls spotted and bagged
by Balanchine (always a Pygmalion in his attitude to female talent)
in the prestigious dance schools run in Paris by the retired Mariinsky ballerinas Olga Preobrajenska, Lubov Egorova and Mathilde
Kschessinska.

These 'baby ballerinas', as they became known, were Tatiana Riabouchinska, Irina Baronova and Tamara Toumanova – three among many White Russian émigrés of both sexes whose way forward in Europe was ballet. Although all three girls came from upper-middle-class stock, their parents were in no position to pay for the classes. Having lost social status, wealth and possessions in the Revolution, they were reduced to menial jobs or downright indigence, and the teachers generally took their compatriots' children on as charity cases. 'You can pay me back when you become a ballerina,' Preobrajenska told Baronova (and she did).[9] There was no shame in this, and no sense of losing caste or descending to a superior form of prostitution: ballet was regarded by Russians as a supremely dignified profession without language barriers that honoured their cultural identity.

With only a few public appearances already to their credit, the baby ballerinas were barely out of pubescence when they joined de Basil: Baronova and Toumanova were both twelve, Riabouchinska fourteen. The intense interest that they stoked in the popular media during the 1930s brought them a fame that matched that of any Hollywood star. Today the way they would be ogled, prodded, promoted and exploited would very probably be regarded as morally unacceptable if not legally actionable – even if they were maternally chaperoned and never expressed anything but unmitigated delight in what they were doing.

Despite this cracking start, Balanchine and Kochno felt blindsided by de Basil and they both walked away. (Balanchine later described de Basil as 'a crooked octopus, and with bad taste'.[10]) No matter: they did not lick their wounds for long, and Kochno's fashionable and wealthy contacts rallied to helped them out of their hole. Old friends such as Coco Chanel and Cole Porter as well as a new friend, the surrealist Edward James, clubbed together to finance Les Ballets 33: as its name suggests it was an affair *du moment*. But an interesting one: its legacy includes *Anna-Anna* (subsequently retitled *The Seven Deadly Sins*), first fruit of the exile from newly Nazified Germany of Bertolt Brecht and Kurt Weill: a musical entertainment directed by Balanchine and set to Weill's thrillingly acerbic score. Sung by a cabaret chanteuse and a chorale of four male voices, it turns the religious concept of sin on its head as it describes a road journey across fancifully imagined American cities taken by two sisters, both called Anna and mirror images of each other morally. Weill's wife Lotte Lenya sang one Anna and Edward James's louche wife Tilly Losch danced the other. *Dancing Times* described it as 'peculiar but very interesting . . . on essentially German lines' – probably a reference to Kurt Jooss, a choreographer trained in the Hellerau barefoot tradition and terrified by the rise of totalitarianism. His most celebrated work, *The Green Table*, first performed in 1932, dramatised in expressionist style the futility of international diplomacy and the horrors of war. More mimed parable than ballet, it toured Europe as Hitler rose to power and it became a beacon of the peace movement.[11]

Hovering around Les Ballets 33 during its seasons in Paris and London was an egregiously tall, fiercely intelligent and sexually tormented twenty-six-year-old Bostonian called Lincoln Kirstein.[12] Heir to a department-store fortune with which he had established an eloquent literary quarterly, *Hound and Horn*, during his time as a Harvard undergraduate, he had been a paid-up mainlining balletomane since boyhood. To channel his passion, he had been helping Romola Nijinsky write a money-spinning (and self-justifying) biography of her poor mad husband. Her constant deference to the fashionable spirit medium Eileen Garrett made the collaboration exasperating and he was only too happy to devolve this task to a young British balletomane, Arnold Haskell, when he alighted on a bigger adventure – that of taking Balanchine to New York and starting a tradition of distinctively American ballet.

Balanchine initially hesitated. He seemed 'not desperate, exactly, but without any hope', Kirstein wrote in his diary when the project was broached.[13] But with Les Ballets 33 showing no signs of reaching 34 and America a honeypot, he soon came round and professed himself 'willing to risk everything for it'.[14] So in January 1934 the School of American Ballet opened in a studio on Madison Avenue. A few months later, despite grumblings from the tuberculosis that dogged Balanchine, its students performed his first transatlantic creation, *Serenade*. Set to a suite for strings by Tchaikovsky, it is a work of romantic farewell to Europe rather than an exuberant welcome to America, but as Balanchine's love for the New World burgeoned – he was particularly fascinated by the idea of integrating black- and white-skinned dancers and exploiting a physique that tended nationwide to the tall, athletic and robust – the ethereal melancholy of the wan sylphide would yield to the breezy energy of the drum majorette and embrace the razzmatazz of Broadway and Hollywood. It would be a slow, uncertain start, but the field was wide open and another major chapter in the history of ballet had begun.[15]

Meanwhile the Ballets Russes de Monte Carlo flourished under de Basil, holding lengthy seasons in London – five months in 1933 at the Alhambra (the theatre at which Diaghilev had presented *The Sleeping Princess* a decade previously) and two months in 1934 at the more prestigious Covent Garden. Comparisons were favourably made with Diaghilev's glory days; some people even appeared to have forgotten them. 'Colonel de Basil's company exploded on London', wrote Lesley Blanch in her memoir, 'and overnight, the mystique of ballet and balletomania came into being'[16] – as if Nijinsky and Karsavina had never existed. 'De Basil's Ballets Russes have surmounted the seemingly impossible situation created by Diaghilev's death,' proclaimed Adrian Stokes. 'They have proved themselves the rightful successors.'* Such was his enthusiasm that he made over a great part of a legacy from his wealthy stockbroker father to the company.[17]

Massine had stepped in to fill the vacancy left by Balanchine and proved the bigger fish, bringing with him a chestful of Diaghilev's legacy, as well as the sets and costumes he had acquired as a job lot from the defaulting New York impresario.[18] Restagings of the perennially popular pre-war Fokine repertory such as *Les Sylphides*, the Polovtsian Dances from *Prince Igor*, and *Petrushka*, as well as Massine's *La Boutique fantasque* and *Le Tricorne*, would remain the company's bread and butter. Massine also revamped *Le beau Danube*, a Viennese confection that he had choreographed to Johann Strauss's waltzes for de Beaumont's ill-fated *Soirées de Paris* in 1924. With Massine himself playing a dashing hussar caught between his lady love (Riabouchinska) and a flirtatious street girl (Danilova), the irresistible lilt of the music, the chocolate-box setting and a dazzling finale, this also proved a bankable and durable hit.

Massine had other things on his mind than crowd-pleasers, however. His private life was a mess: now in his mid-thirties, he was negotiating an unsatisfactory *ménage à trois* with his second wife

---

* But many with long rosy memories had reservations. 'When my children took me to see the reincarnation [of Diaghilev's Ballets Russes] – Toumanova, Baronova, and, my favourite of the three, the flame-like Riabouchinska – they were deeply shocked when I maintained that even these were not in the same class as Pavlova. I doubt, myself, if anything less feudal than czarism could produce quite that disciplined perfection . . . certainly not the absolute flawlessness of the corps de ballet, every pose and movement in every corner of the stage, at each several moment, utterly right. And will there be another male dancer quite like Nijinsky in a thousand years?' (Ralph Furse, *Aucuparius*, p. 43.)

Eugenia Delarova and the German-Norwegian ballerina Vera
Zorina, who slit her wrists at one desperate moment in the affair.
But with the cold heart of genius he was also fomenting a succession of serious large-scale works that mark the peak of his creative
achievement.

Described by his biographer Vicente Garcia-Marquez as 'a
turning point in the history of twentieth-century dance',[19] their
principal innovation was the use of a symphony of the romantic
period as their scores. Outside Russia (where the practice had briefly been tried out in the early 1920s), this was unheard of at the
time and a break with the previously unquestioned custom of using
either dance suites or music composed bespoke for a scenario. The
ethics of Massine's appropriation split opinion: purists complained
that something complete in itself was being redundantly illustrated,
without the composer's co-operation; but others, notably the great
critic and Wagner scholar Ernest Newman, claimed Massine's visu-
alisations to be revelatory of 'the inner life of the work', providing
imagery that 'enhanced' one's listening.[20]

The subject matter of the symphony ballets varied, but choreographically they owed much to the flattened perspectives, bas-reliefs
and hieratic poses characteristic of the classical, Byzantine and
pre-Renaissance Italian art to which Massine had been introduced by Diaghilev two decades previously. First, in 1933, came
*Les Présages*, set to Tchaikovsky's Fifth Symphony. Reflecting the
composer's obsessive fatalism, it dramatised man's struggle against
destiny through a central character identified as Action (danced by a
woman) battling against hostile forces. With its sculptural tableaux
inspired by the friezes on Ancient Greek temples and the 'comets,
cosmic thunderbolts, spouting hearts and Dalíesque rainbows'[21]
swirling over André Masson's expressionistic designs, 'the preten-
tiousness of its theme . . . its mystic glooms . . . confused symbolism

and indeterminate philosophy'[22] impressed and perplexed in equal measure. What precisely it was intended to mean not even the dancers could have told you, since Massine was notoriously reluctant to explain anything in the rehearsal room.

Six months later came *Choreartium*, to Brahms's Fourth Symphony. This time any allegorical baggage was discarded, leaving only an attempt to interpret the ebb and flow of the music choreographically in an unspecific classical setting. In Arnold Haskell's words:

> Brahms' Fourth Symphony contains no obvious theme. It is definitely abstract, and not programme music. To translate it into choreography it needs a sculptor of the heroic, a Michael Angelo in human material. The result is forty minutes of individual and group movement, always beautiful, logical and yet surprising, with every member of the huge cast an individual and at the same time part of a fresco. There is repose in plenty. The eye has to time to wander from group to group and to dwell on their contours. There is a remarkable series of entries and exits, and a variety of moods that makes the absence of subject no loss . . . Such a feat on this scale has never before been attempted in choreography. It is the birth and triumph of pure dancing.[23]

The climax of this phase of Massine's oeuvre came with *Symphonie fantastique*, first performed in 1936. Following the programme laid out in the score by Hector Berlioz, it consisted of five scenes depicting a variety of mythical or imagined landscapes – a ghostly chamber, a dazzling ballroom, a pastoral idyll, a prison courtyard, a witchy cavern – through which a Byronic artist moodily passes, hallucinating the elusive image of his unattainable beloved, incarnated by the ineffable Tamara Toumanova. As in *Choreartium*, the choreography was boldly sculptural, and even those critics such as Edwin Denby who disliked the basis of the enterprise were ready to admit its 'astonishing inventiveness' and 'sense of dramatic variety and climax'.[24] As pure theatre, it was breathtaking.

Massine played the part of the composer: of dancing, he did little, but his sheer stage presence was electrifying. Although he had become celebrated for his ability to vanish into other characters and present graphic caricatures, here he admitted a degree of self-exposure, dramatising the isolation and frustration of the creative artist and the restlessness of his torrid love life.

———

De Basil's company had arrived in New York in 1933 under the aegis of a canny impresario called Sol Hurok. The Jazz Age might have drawn everyone out on to the ballroom floors and from the late 1920s an avant-garde aesthetic based on bare feet and natural gravity was budding in the work of Doris Humphrey, Mary Wigman and Martha Graham (with whom in 1930 Massine briefly collaborated on a revival of *The Rite of Spring*). Several of Pavlova's colleagues had lingered on after her final tour in 1925, drifting towards the bright lights of Broadway and the big bucks of Hollywood or establishing little academies in the boondocks. But the classical style was marginalised as a hokey European import for a genteel élite, at best an ornament to opera: Diaghilev hadn't returned to the United States since the First World War, and nothing of consequence had subsequently materialised. So ballet had never been fully adopted in the USA – which is precisely why Hurok, like Kirstein and Balanchine, was so excited about investing in it.

Hurok paved the way with a massive publicity campaign highlighting the allure of the baby ballerinas and launching the season with that trusty tactic – an opening-night gala papered with an audience of bejewelled dignitaries whose red-carpet arrival guaranteed front-page coverage. Even so, with theatres slumped in the pit of the Depression, box-office takings got off to a slow start, only picking up after a few old favourites were shoehorned into the programme.

There was also a gimmick, in the form of a 'new ballet with an American theme', flung together in haste by Massine on the unpromising subject of the construction of the transcontinental railroad. *Union Pacific* celebrated the melting pot through affectionate caricatures of Irish, Chinese, Mexicans and Mormons, marking the joining of the west- and eastbound tracks with a wham-bam finale, but despite its hoe-down tunes (arranged by a Russian composer, Nicolas Nabokov), ethnic diversity and local colour, it just didn't seem authentic. Whether Russians had any business deciding what was truly American was a question that became increasingly contentious among the intelligentsia. When Lincoln Kirstein wrote his thrillingly arrogant and opinionated polemic *Blast at Ballet* in 1938, he complained, 'It has been ordained that all ballet on this continent should be Russian, or else it isn't really ballet at all . . . Americans have been led to believe that Russianballet is one single word.'[25] Why could it not be American? Yet it could also be said that, thanks to de Basil's company, the USA finally saw the point. The mass public suddenly couldn't get enough of ballet with the adjective 'Russian' indelibly attached and by the mid-1930s receipts for the tours had reached the magic million-dollar mark. Vicente Garcia-Marquez justifiably claims that at this moment ballet became 'the most popular form of entertainment available on a grand scale throughout the country after cinema and radio'.[26]

The itineraries Hurok organised were relentless and the troupe's resilience in the face of whistle-stop schedules of eight shows a week, crisscrossing the continent a distance of 20,000 miles via a chartered eleven-car train or a cortège of buses, remains astounding. No unions protected anyone's rights; rehearsal might be last minute on stage, improvised in hotel lobbies or resumed after a performance; daily class would be held whenever and wherever – on occasion in roadside fields, with cattle railings used as a barre. As a hanger-on, Haskell remembered these tours as being of 'deadly monotony: lack of sleep, tasteless food, inane interviews and creative frustration'.[27] Although there were several British and North American dancers in the ranks, Russian was the company's lingua franca, and Russian customs, festivals and observances were religiously kept. Conditions were spartan and everyone had to muck in, but poker and pets whiled away the tedious hours between destinations. The lack of privacy must have hampered any love affairs. The bottom line, as Baronova later recalled, was that 'we were young, and we adored it all. And sometimes we even got paid.'[28]

The boom imploded as well as exploded. In 1935 the always uneasy partnership of Colonel de Basil and René Blum collapsed. Blum's reported quip that 'De Basil has just bought my car from me with my own money'[29] suggests the underlying problem – Blum's total lack of trust in someone who was ready to sink to anything if it worked to his advantage – but the final straw seems to have been de Basil's determination to reorient operations away from Blum's base in Monte Carlo and towards the more lucrative London and New York. Blum would continue to run his own company with Fokine at the helm, and between 1935 and 1937 he and de Basil went head to head in summer seasons in London – de Basil at Covent Garden, Blum at the Alhambra. But de Basil always had the edge: more stars, more popular repertory, more money.

Most bitterly contested were the skirmishes over the services of ballet's two biggest box-office draws.

No other choreographer had the same traction with the public or the same success rate as Massine. His genius, industry and commitment were undisputed, but they came with a very high price tag: craving both the money and power that gave him artistic independence, he sold himself to the highest bidder, without sentimental loyalty. And where he went, others would follow.

The baby ballerinas presented a different challenge: not yet consenting adults, they travelled with their mothers, who supervised literally every move they made and became legendary for petty acts of sabotage aimed at advancing their particular daughter's cause. According to Danilova, they were 'really very tiresome . . . forever glorifying them, smothering them, and pitting them against one another'. Mama Toumanova, who doubled as a faith-healer, fortune-teller and poker queen, was particularly trying. 'She never stopped saying her daughter was a genius,' recalled Baronova, 'and Tamara behaved accordingly.'[30] Such was the way Mama trumpeted that nobody could pirouette or bourrée like her Tamara that some wag in the company sneered, 'And nobody could fart like Tamara either.'*[31]

The baby ballerinas weren't the first of their kind. Infant dancers had long been commonplace in variety halls, and Alicia Markova had been barely fourteen when Diaghilev had signed her up in 1925. Yet she had been fragile in health and physique and presented herself on stage as an exquisitely serene child. The baby ballerinas, in contrast, did not act their age: robust troupers, they had no inhibitions and their readiness to perform full out, night after night in any circumstances, lent them an adult sexuality that verged

---

* 'Ballet fathers are seldom seen; it is ballet mothers who dominate, so that I have often wondered if the ballerina is not perhaps the flower of some immaculate conception.' (Lesley Blanch, *Journey into the Mind's Eye*, p. 212.)

on the transgressive. Darlings of the tabloid press, they were also role models for girls at a time when teenage culture had not yet been invented, and the accepted image of youthful femalehood vacillated between winsome Mary Pickford and cheerful Deanna Durbin. Thrillingly, there was something unsafe about their glamour and talent. They learned fast; their bodies were in the making, wonderfully pliable and willing. 'We were as strong as steel,' Baronova recalled.[32] To call them precocious would give a misleading impression of prim daintiness: they weren't airbrushed nymphs in Alice hairbands and short white socks, but women of daring energy and confidence shamelessly in control of their bodies, expressing on stage a wide variety of emotions *sans pudeur*.

Their talents were authentically prodigious. Frustratingly, fragments of film that survive on YouTube can leave them looking merely quaint – and by today's standards, slapdash – but their wholehearted exuberance was electrifying. The three of them appeared together on stage very occasionally (in *Les Sylphides*, for example), but their personalities were very different and, rather like the Fab Four thirty years later, the fans all had their favourites.* A year and a half older than the other two, the doe-like Riabouchinska was blessed with a spontaneous lyricism and mercurial lightness that Ralph Furse described as 'flame-like'.[33] Less ethereal in manner and more impulsive in character, the sweet-natured extrovert Baronova was the most readily adorable of the trio as well as the most classically polished. Toumanova's raven-haired allure made *Cotillon*, another Balanchine novelty, particularly successful: based on the simple premise of an innocent girl swept up in a fashionable ball, it was perfumed like Fokine's *Carnaval* and Nijinska's *Les*

---

* Oddly, only one photograph of the trio posing together appears to have survived. It is reproduced in plate 20.

*Biches* with erotic ambiguity and what one critic called 'the loveli-
ness of corruption'.[34] As she matured, Toumanova's dark enigmatic
beauty earned her the sobriquet of 'the Black Pearl' and she exuded
romantic mystique in the grand manner.

Not surprisingly, the babies were much courted. When the company visited Berlin in 1936, Goebbels, something of a balletomane,
had quietly assured de Basil that no questions would be asked about
anyone's racial make-up.[35] The Reich leaders turned out in force
and Hitler went backstage to kiss Riabouchinska's hand after the
performance. He was later reported to have hung a full-length portrait of her in his apartment. Hitler could not have known that this
blonde Aryan beauty had just married a Jew in the company, David
Lichine (something of a Lothario, previously married to another
de Basil dancer of barely legal age, Lubov Rostova, who in 1935
was reported in the *Evening Standard* to have 'fallen from the window in her hotel' in dubious circumstances and sustained horrible
injuries on some railings).[36]

Poor Danilova, twice the babies' age, supremely accomplished
and very much the grande dame! Frequently she found cherished
roles taken from her and her advice ingenuously solicited. Even in
her autobiography, written forty years later, the irritation rankles:
the girls were 'each in her own way, quite sweet', but 'they did not
know how to behave'.[37] What made things worse was that Danilova
was having an affair with Gerry Sevastianov, a dashingly handsome
and urbane White Russian who had graduated from being de Basil's
chauffeur to his aide-de-camp. As his ardour for Danilova cooled,
he had turned his attention to the fifteen-year-old Baronova, who
became naively infatuated. Furtive trysts ensued, but Danilova was
not fooled and there was an awful scene backstage. Baronova won
out a year later: while touring in America, she evaded her mother's
chaperonage and eloped with Sevastianov, twice her age, crossing a

state line from Ohio to Kentucky, where the legal age for marriage was seventeen. Baronova, still sixteen, lied to the registrar. Only two years later did they celebrate their union in a Russian Orthodox church.*38

Dominated by her fanatically possessive mother and wedded to her profession and the fame that accompanied it, Toumanova seems to have remained single until in 1944 she married Casey Robinson, screenplay writer for some of Bette Davis's romantic melodramas. Mama Toumanova came along too; Robinson must have been a patient man.

Nobody fed the reputation of the baby ballerinas more assiduously than Arnold Haskell: it is even thought that he coined the term.39 A banker's son, born in 1903, he was completely obsessed by the age of ten, tracking every move of star dancers the same way that other boys of his tender age idolised polar explorers or Olympic sportsmen. As a law student at Cambridge, he was enchanted by the magic of *The Sleeping Princess* and befriended the young Dolin and the even younger Markova. In 1925 he visited Monte Carlo, where he briefly met Diaghilev. Slender, dapper and refined, he was blessed with a ready wit and an engagingly fluent prose style. In 1935 the *Daily Telegraph* appointed him the British press's first ever dedicated ballet correspondent – itself a sign of the art's new status, the field being previously assigned to classical music experts – but he remained in post for only three years, perhaps because he felt unable to be fearlessly frank.†

Less critic or historian than cheerleader, he was licensed by de

* The marriage ended in 1944, but after the death of her second husband, a British ex-army officer, Baronova returned to Sevastianov.
† After the Second World War, he became director of what is now known as the Royal Ballet School, while continuing as a prolific lecturer, broadcaster and pundit.

Basil to travel with the company on their American tours, mixing freely with the dancers and reporting titbits to his column in *Dancing Times*. He popped up everywhere else too. If Cyril Beaumont in his bookshop was ballet's meticulous chronicler, Haskell was its public champion and spokesman – privy to whispers from the wings, a welcome guest at after-show parties and confidential lunches, revered as a fount of wisdom by his readers and trusted as a safe pair of hands by the professionals. Although no whiff of scandal lurked around this complicity (Haskell was happily married to a Russian heiress without balletic connections), he would later admit that 'in some respects I went overboard in my enthusiasm'.[40]

Haskell wrote over twenty books about ballet. The first was *Balletomania: The Story of an Obsession* (1934), a loosely autobiographical account, described on its jacket blurb as 'a book of gossip and history, of comedy and tragedy, of triumph and disaster, about the most lovable of all the arts', which *Dancing Times* felt was marred by 'unswerving idolatry of everything Russian';[41] the second was his pioneering but inevitably inhibited and eventually redundant biography *Diaghileff* (1936).

Haskell led a fashion for books on his speciality – the British Library catalogue for the years 1934–9 records literally hundreds of ballet-related titles, embracing manuals and monographs, pamphlets, primers and picture books, as well as such general surveys as *Talking of Ballet*, *The Birth of Ballets Russes*, *Ballet-hoo*, *Prelude to Ballet*, *A Pageant of the Dance and Ballet*, *Invitation to the Ballet*, *Dancing around the World*, *The Symphonic Ballet*, *Ballet Go-round*, *Ballet Panorama*, *Ballet in Action*, *Balletomane's Scrapbook*, *A Prejudice for Ballet*, *Footnotes to the Ballet* and *Tribute to the Ballet* (the latter a volume of atrocious verse on balletic themes by the poet laureate John Masefield).

An editorial in *Dancing Times* harrumphed: was the craze getting out of hand?

The past season will also be known on account of the perfect glut of books on the ballet – good, bad and indifferent – that it has brought forth and for the enthusiasm shown at many performances, particularly at Covent Garden. I am not at all sure if this enthusiasm has not been a little overdone and if it is not a little unhealthy. The out and out ballet fan who can never see a fault in the object of his adoration is apt to become a little wearisome and the vociferous applause at the fall of the curtain does not always ring true. If our audiences were a little more critical and little less prone to idolise certain dancers it would be the better for ballet.[42]

Herbert Farjeon wrote a satirical song on the subject for his 1938 revue *Nine Sharp*:

How we screamed and shrieked and hooted, how we whooped
    and how we howled!
We were ravished and uprooted – we were frequently
    disembowelled!
You will never know the throb, the glow, the bliss, that we knew
    then
When Bolonsky danced Belushka in September 1910.[43]

The implication of that last line serves as a reminder that ballet-omania was not a new phenomenon so much as one that came in waves: those gazing through *Spectre de la rose*-tinted spectacles imprinted with images of Karsavina and Nijinsky felt entitled to look down their noses at young things whose memories reached back no further than the baby ballerinas (a snobbery that persists today among survivors of the 1960s who saw Margot Fonteyn or Suzanne Farrell).

But the market couldn't get enough of it all. In 1938, Haskell's Pelican paperback baldly entitled *Ballet* sold over 100,000 copies at sixpence.[44] An even bigger seller was Caryl Brahms's heavy-handed but light-hearted whodunnit *A Bullet in the Ballet* (1937, written with the help of S. J. Simon), centred on the fatal shooting of a Russian male dancer during a performance of *Petrushka*.* Full of in-jokes that could have been appreciated only by the cognoscenti, it includes a thinly disguised portrait of Massine as Nicolas Nevajno, a choreographer infatuated with aluminium and black shirts.

Another enormously influential book was Noel Streatfeild's *Ballet Shoes* (1936), a novel that ministered to the fervent, often nun-like vocation towards ballet that commonly infected girls aged about ten. Streatfeild's character the wilful Posy Fossil is one such: she passes through the dance academy run by the expatriate Russian ballerina Madame Fidolia (described as 'very odd looking', with 'black hair parted in the middle and drawn down tight into a small bun') and ends up going off to Czechoslovakia to study with the great Manoff, identified as a peerless Petrushka in the Marmaro Ballet.

Goaded and guarded by their mamas, thousands of stage-struck hopefuls such as Posy Fossil aspired to pirouette in pointe shoes and transcend the otherwise constricted and sedentary range of possibilities open to respectable women. One can only guess at

---

* Brahms wrote two feeble sequels: *Casino for Sale* (1938) and *Six Curtains for Stroganova* (1945), both featuring some of the same characters in balletic settings. In 1946 a staged version of *A Bullet in the Ballet* starring Massine and Baronova toured the British provinces with some success, but never made it to the West End. Other similarly themed balletic thrillers include *Death in the Fifth Position* (1952) by Edgar Box (a nom de plume of Gore Vidal) and *Death Comes to the Ballets Russes* (2015) by David Dickinson.

their sociological roots, but it appears that most of those who made it into the business were either of colonial stock or sprang from the lower middle class. Graceful deportment nurtured by the dancing class was an accomplishment on a par with the cut-glass diction favoured by elocution teachers – an agency of upward social mobility – and through to the 1960s, the romance of the feisty young ballet student fighting snootiness and prejudice to reach her goal remained a common fictional trope, evident in vacuous novelettes by Lorna Hill, Marie-Jeanne and Jean Estoril as well as comic-strip heroines such as *Bunty*'s plucky Moira Kent. (A survival of this is the bland 2016 French animation *Ballerina*.) Before supermodels or rock stars entered the mix, only Hollywood pin-ups could rival the ballerina as a girlhood fantasy.

Of who else made up the audience we know frustratingly little. Prices in the mid-1930s at Covent Garden ranged from a place on the gallery bench at two shillings to a stall at fifteen shillings; at the Vic–Wells, half that, down to sixpence on a back-row bench. As two shillings was about what you could expect to pay for a dozen large eggs or admission to a dance hall – and as the extensive coverage of ballet in the popular press suggests – it is reasonable to assume that tickets were affordable by ordinary working people who took up a significant percentage of the cheaper seats.*

There was a sense in Britain through the latter half of the 1930s that ballet had entered the mainstream and grown to solid adulthood. 'Everybody is agreed that enthusiasm for ballet is one of the outstanding artistic characteristics of our time,' wrote Francis Toye

* Taking inflation at an average of 5 per cent per annum into account, this would approximate today to £7 and £60; actual prices at the Royal Opera House currently range from roughly £5 to £120 and at Sadler's Wells from £12 to £60. But in the 1930s, there was no state subsidy and the economy was in a slump.

in the *Illustrated London News*. 'There is a large and constant public and, at long last, there seems to be slowly emerging a not unintelligent attitude towards the art in general as distinct from mere adulation of its interpreters.'[45]

But there was idle hysterical chatter too. 'In London during the last half of the Thirties, ballet was the new fashion, its young stars graced the pages of the glossy papers, it was a rave for the young generation,' wrote Leslie Baily,[46] and some found it suspiciously high-pitched. Describing an evening at Covent Garden in 1936, the composer Vernon Duke noted a phenomenon that was toxically turning into the damaging cliché that male dancers in tights were 'pansified' effeminates and 'queers' and that men who took pleasure in watching ballet were no better:

The resplendent parade of homosexuals, shy and blatant, simpering and booming, dressed with the unmasculine exaggeration of every caprice of fashion so typical of their ilk, was something to see; the boys were on the town and Covent Garden was their citadel. Ten years later Cecil Gray [a cocaine addict and alcoholic] summed it up fearlessly in *Contingencies*: 'Ballet, in fact, is the homosexual art form par excellence . . . and at performances of the Russian Ballet the character of the audience was frequently such as to render one's presence in the midst of it – if one happened to be comparatively normal – so acutely distasteful that one preferred to stay away altogether.' . . . The spectacle before me was indeed macabre. But the wildly chattering 'gay' boys (according to Gray, 'those who share homosexual propensities refer to themselves and each other as being "queer"'. Horrors! Gay is the word) seemed affable enough and quite a few of them waved at me with Hellenic grace.[47]

Aspersions were cast at women as well. In the *Evening Standard*, the radio personality Stephen Williams complained, 'I should enjoy ballet very much if the intervals were not marred (for me) by willowy young men who call each other "darling" and lissom young women who lean against each other in rapture.'[48]

Like all myths, this one contains an element of truth – a camp element in the audience had long been registered. But Caryl Brahms was off the mark in *A Bullet in the Ballet* when she made reference (remarkably candid for its time) to the prevalence of 'unnatural sex' within Stroganoff's ballet company. Here the murdered man, said to have had affairs with both men and women, is described as 'a sex maniac and – er – a homosexual'.[49] There is absolutely no solid evidence that this accurately represents a significant portion of de Basil's male ranks, or Diaghilev's either. Haskell's contemporary assertion that 'of the outstanding male dancers that I know, and I know them all, not one is effeminate in manner, and very few indeed are not thoroughly normal' may sound primly ridiculous to us now, but it is probably true.[50]

Yet the 1930s saw the growth of more sternly critical voices making more than rapturous sighs and giggles. As well as Haskell and Beaumont, one might also point to the highly wrought reflections of the art critic Adrian Stokes in his books *To-night the Ballet* (1934) and *Russian Ballets* (1935), and to the (unpublished) diaries of the Oxford-educated barrister's son Lionel Bradley, a librarian who left meticulously observant reviews of every performance he attended – a blogger *avant la lettre*. From the other end of the social spectrum came Edward Haddakin, a railwayman's son from York who started life as a merchant seaman and began writing ballet reviews in 1935 under the name of A. V. Coton while still a policeman in Bethnal Green; after the war, he became ballet critic of the *Daily Telegraph*. In the USA, the discourse was also developing: to balance the *New*

*York Times*'s John Martin, ardent champion of the barefoot aesthetic of Martha Graham, came Edwin Denby, one of the most subtly poetic of all commentators on ballet, who wrote his first columns in 1936, his sensibility both classical and romantic.

The cinema started cashing in too.[51] In 1916 Pavlova had made a silent movie, *The Dumb Girl of Portici*, but the advent of the talkies opened up new possibilities, at first focused on the drama of Nijinsky's life. In 1931, a film called *The Mad Genius* presented John Barrymore as a thinly disguised Diaghilev figure attempting to exert a Svengali influence over a protégé. Three years later, Alexander Korda, whose productions of *The Private Life of Henry VIII* and *The Scarlet Pimpernel* had made British studios a rival to Hollywood, bought the rights to Romola's biography of Nijinsky with the idea of turning it into a showcase for his star (and girlfriend) Merle Oberon, based on a plot line similar to that of *The Mad Genius*. A young Hungarian writer, Emeric Pressburger, was hired to develop a screenplay using Hans Christian Andersen's dark parable *The Red Shoes* as a frame. Meanwhile Korda's rival Michael Balcon was planning for his newly acquired Ealing Studios 'a real crime story against a background of Russian ballet . . . in colour' (*A Bullet in the Ballet* perhaps?).[52] War prevented both projects from progressing. But in 1946, at the height of his richly creative partnership with Korda's former assistant Michael Powell, Pressburger dug the aborted script out of his back drawer and he and Powell began to think about it again . . .

At the same time, ballet – as opposed to show, jazz or tap dancing embodied in the art of Fred Astaire – was exerting a fascination on Hollywood, both as subject matter and as the basis for a visually exciting musical interlude. This is most lastingly evident in the 'Dance of the Hours' sequence of Walt Disney's 1940 cartoon *Fantasia*, where the dancing of the ostrich Madame Upanova is parodically but precisely based on observations of Irina Baronova in action.[53] But the first successful full-length talkie set in the world of ballet came from France in 1937: *La Mort du cygne* (Anglicised as *Ballerina*) concerns a timid girl infatuated with a star ballerina; it was ineptly remade in 1947 by MGM as *The Unfinished Dance*, with Margaret O'Brien as the girl. From the late 1930s to the early 1950s, films such as *Waterloo Bridge* (with Vivien Leigh); *The Men in her Life*; *Dance, Girl, Dance*; *Specter of the Rose*; *Never Let Me Go*; *On Your Toes*; *Days of Glory* (with Toumanova); *The Red Danube* and *Limelight* (with Charlie Chaplin and Claire Bloom) presented ballet dancers as dramatic characters, while sequences featuring classical ballet dancers emerged in *Night and Day*, *Tonight and Every Night*, *The Band Wagon* and *Escape Me Never* among others. A generation later came *The Turning Point*, followed by *White Nights*, *Billy Elliot* and *Black Swan*. Common to them all is the theme of aspiration – the struggle of the neophyte dreaming of stardom, pitted against some sort of obstacle, antagonist or prejudice.

———

Through the latter half of 1937 London was *en fête* for George VI's coronation. Colonel de Basil's company continued to dominate Covent Garden, where it provoked, according to *The New Yorker*'s correspondent Janet Flanner, 'a pandemonium of applause . . . even when Diaghilev was alive, we never saw a first night at which both spectators and dancers were more brilliantly ebullient'.*[54] The season broke all box-office records and appeared on the new medium

---

* 'At Covent Garden,' Flanner continued, 'you may smoke during the ballets, and between acts eat strawberries and cream at the bar. As the long summer season drags on, top hats disappear, ballet love becomes intense, and balletomanes sit sweating in flannels.'

of television, with commentary by the inevitable Arnold Haskell. Novelties included *Francesca da Rimini*, a dance drama in Fokine's heavily mimed style that marked Riabouchinska's husband David Lichine out as a promising choreographer; and Fokine's *Le Coq d'or* – a hit in 1914 for Diaghilev when it was presented as a full-length danced version of Rimsky-Korsakov's opera and an even bigger hit a quarter of a century later, as reworked with an orchestral suite from Rimsky-Korsakov's score, designed by Natalia Goncharova in the sumptuously coloured naive manner of a children's picture book.

But the Russians weren't having it all their own way in London, and the prime threat wasn't from their compatriots. Coming up fast on the outside lane was a home-made vehicle that was steadily gathering traction: the Vic–Wells Ballet, housed in the ugly new Sadler's Wells Theatre that had opened in suburban Islington in 1931. Here, sustained by next to no money, presided the inexorable Ninette de Valois. Her main asset was Alicia Markova – still imperturbably serene in her virginal mid-twenties – until she left in 1935 to establish her own touring company with Anton Dolin. Undaunted by that loss, de Valois brought on the Vic–Wells's own baby ballerina, a fifteen-year-old ingénue called Peggy Hookham, who adopted the more exotic stage name of Margot Fontes (her mother's maiden name), soon adjusted to Fonteyn. Like Baronova and Toumanova, she had Russian teachers and an over-bearing mother: unlike them, she had weak feet and only passable technique. Wide-eyed charm, natural musicality and graceful proportions were her chief gifts, and there was something touching and engaging about her lack of steel or dazzle. How far could she go?

One promising ballerina wouldn't have been enough to elevate the Vic–Wells to the top league, but it was de Valois's good fortune (based on cool judgement) that she had also bagged a plausible partner for Fonteyn in the flamboyant Australian Robert

Helpmann; a nascent genius of a choreographer in Frederick Ashton; a highly cultured music director in Constant Lambert; and the co-operation of ballet master Nikolai Sergeyev, a St Petersburg émigré in possession of uniquely valuable records of nineteenth-century choreography that allowed the classic Tchaikovsky ballets of Petipa and Ivanov to be reconstructed. Upcoming dancers such as Harold Turner, June Brae and Pamela May were out and proud British and felt no need to turn their names pseudo-Slavic. The shortage of money was a healthy stimulus to experiment and risk. In sum, the English were stealthily finding their own way of doing ballet, informed by the Russian school but not imitative of it, and even if the Vic–Wells couldn't yet hold a candle to de Basil's company in terms of *éclat*, its courageous resourcefulness and gently poetic imagination was earning it a loyal patriotic following.

Meanwhile the Russians were coming adrift, as the skirmishes, poaching and in-fighting intensified. In 1937, Blum had thrown in the towel* by selling out to a New York plutocrat, Julius 'Junkie' Fleischmann, who appointed as director another Russian expatriate – one Serge Denham, born Sergei Ivanovich Dokouchiaev, formerly a vice-president of Bankers Trust.

Denham's company became the Ballet Russe de Monte Carlo – as opposed (spot the difference) to the Ballets Russes de Monte Carlo. To avoid confusion, this chapter will henceforward refer to them via the convenient shorthand of Denham's Ballet Russe de Monte Carlo and de Basil's Ballets Russes, even though both companies passed through repeated minor changes of nomenclature – sixteen times over twenty years in de Basil's case. This is not to mention several other ephemeral and opportunistic outfits that came and

---

* Five years later, having returned to France, he was deported to Auschwitz, where he died.

went through the pre-war era, using some variant of those magic words as balletomania reached a new peak of intensity, fuelled by a series of feuds and lawsuits, treasons and stratagems, factions and defections, that recall nothing so much as the bloody campaigns of the Wars of the Roses.

Early in 1938, it briefly seemed as though peace had broken out, with the announcement that de Basil's Ballets Russes and Denham's Ballet Russe de Monte Carlo had merged into one entity, assembling all the greatest dancers of the era. In the *New York Times*, John Martin hailed the end of 'a campaign of extermination which . . . might have been conceived by Gilbert and Sullivan'.[55] London also heaved a sigh of relief: 'It almost seems too good to be true,' reported *Dancing Times*.[56] Indeed it was – only a month later, the fighting resumed.

The details of the schism are tedious and inconsequential, but the flashpoint was that Sol Hurok, on whose organisational skills and network of contacts de Basil depended for his American tours, was sick of the Colonel's shenanigans. So was Massine, who had never been granted the artistic control he considered rightfully his, and both men had now signed up with Denham. De Basil, however, continued to retain the better ensemble of dancers on contract and rights over most of the cherries in the repertory, including Massine's *La Boutique fantasque*. Massine had sued de Basil in an attempt to have the rights over his own ballets reverted, but had only partially succeeded. The courts judged that de Basil could retain what he had commissioned and paid for.

The merger between de Basil's and Denham's operations had been negotiated in New York, but de Basil – who was in Europe at the time and whose English was far from fluent – had foolishly signed the contract by the proxy of Baronova's husband Gerry Sevastianov. Effectively, the small print was pushing him out, passing his power to Hurok (who saw Sevastianov as a useful ally) and forfeiting his rights to present Massine's hits. When the terms became clear to him, de Basil reneged and began litigation to quash the agreement. While it was *sub judice*, however, he was forced to withdraw nominally in order that the company could continue to perform. Drably renamed (for tax-exemption reasons) Educational Ballets Ltd, de Basil's Ballets Russes appointed a new board of directors and put its operations under Sevastianov's more emollient management.

Then there was a scramble over contracts as the stars opted to shine in separate galaxies: Baronova and Riabouchinska remained with Educational Ballets Ltd, which moved into Covent Garden in June; Toumanova went to and fro; Danilova and Markova plumped for Massine and Denham's Ballet Russe de Monte Carlo as it simultaneously took possession of Drury Lane, a stone's throw away. Despite endless unedifying legal squabbles, both companies triumphed with the critics and public, feeding off each other's success, and press coverage of the black comedy of it all spread globally. Audiences alternated between the theatres, often switching between auditoriums in the intermissions and scrawling partisan graffiti on posters. The dancers thought it all tremendously amusing and it was said that both managements remained the best of friends, dining together in the Savoy Grill after shows and mutually toasting their respectively high box-office takings.

But the duplication made no sense. Haskell voiced his exasperation in an open letter addressed 'To All Concerned in the Management of Russian Ballets', significantly referencing the Vic–Wells:

You have all been quarrelling, not in the usual backstage fashion but with a bitterness that is damaging to your work and that enriches the legal profession at your expense . . . You must know that the time is past when the British public will accept anything with a Russian label. We are used to the best. We have an admirable company of our own that performs *at popular prices for nine months* in the year.[57]

His jeremiad went unheeded. But Haskell was right: the brand overall would be weakened by the split. After three decades of astonishing productivity, Russian ballet had never been more broadly popular, yet from this moment onwards, the phenomenon began to burn out, its creative impetus failing and its surprise value spent. Two companies with identical aims and characters couldn't occupy the same territory for long, drawing on the same limited stock of stars; Fokine, Massine and Nijinska had done their best work, and Balanchine was floundering on Broadway and in Holly-wood;* David Lichine, the best hope for a Russian choreographer to succeed them, would never rise to their level; and the diaspora of talent that had come west in the wake of the Revolution came to an end.

When legal settlements were made in 1939, Colonel de Basil regained control and Educational Ballets Ltd reincarnated itself as Original Ballet Russe. An autumn season in Berlin was scheduled, but when the outbreak of war made this impossible, the company embarked on a perilous six-week ocean voyage to the haven of Australia, where it spent nearly nine months. This was its third visit to the Antipodes; distanced from the crisis in Europe, the dancers

* There was no love lost between them. In the words of Frederic Franklin, who worked with them all: 'Nijinska hated Balanchine and Balanchine hated her, and Balanchine hated Massine, and Massine hated them both, and Fokine you couldn't get near.' (Quoted in Jack Anderson, *The One and Only: Ballet Russe de Monte Carlo*, p. 78.)

relaxed into a steadier schedule of performing lengthy seasons in a few widely spaced cities.

Sailing back across the Pacific to Los Angeles, they started more American touring and ended up in Cuba, where in March 1941 seventeen juniors went on strike after drastic pay cuts were implemented by the tour organisers. Paralysed between the pro- and anti-factions of the dispute, the company was stranded in Havana, obliging some of its members to eke out an existence doing turns in dance halls and cabarets. Another factor behind the strikers' disaffection was the lure of the better-organised and -financed Ballet Theatre, an enterprise launched in 1939 and based in New York. Comparable in its artistic aims to de Valois's Vic–Wells in London, it was buttressed by the immense wealth of its prime founder Lucia Chase and it was in the mood to hire. Led by its star couple Alicia Markova and Anton Dolin, it had just poached the services of Baronova and the managerial expertise of her husband Gerry Sevastianov from de Basil and the money was there to bag many more. With young choreographers Jerome Robbins and Antony Tudor on board, the force was with it.

Eventually de Basil's depleted troupe limped back from Cuba to the USA. From this point onwards, running low on talent and ideas, the quality of the company went into irreversible decline as the competition mounted. For the remainder of the war, it toured Central and South America, where there was invariably a ready welcome, especially when kitschy new Latin 'folkloric' work was presented. But the stress of churning it out, travelling in often primitive conditions, was profoundly exhausting, and several leading dancers decamped. A ragbag replaced them along the way and the company's style was left miscellaneous, characterless.

In the summer of 1947 – ironically, just as *The Red Shoes* was being filmed – de Basil's Ballets Russes returned to Covent Garden.

Although the reception was affectionate, the moment had passed and what they offered was old hat. Haskell later described the season as 'a pathetic anti-climax'.[58] Cyril Beaumont's record is peppered with adjectives such as 'prosaic', 'dated', 'overblown', 'stilted' and 'ragged'.[59]

Since 1938, British ballet had stolen a march and become a source of patriotic pride, attracting audiences from all social classes and reaching beyond the metropolitan base on which Diaghilev and de Basil had focused. Three remarkable women led the field: Mona Inglesby, who borrowed money from her industrialist father to set up International Ballet, presenting a largely classical repertory with Inglesby herself as prima ballerina; Marie Rambert, whose small company focused on new work; and Ninette de Valois, whose Vic–Wells Ballet had been renamed the Sadler's Wells Ballet in 1941.

None of them was a pushover, but de Valois's supreme political acumen gave her the edge. In contrast to the chaotic democracy of the Russian companies, where 'discipline is far from strict' and individuals 'agitate' and 'succeed',[60] she ran the company, according to Haskell, more or less as 'a totalitarian state' and got what she wanted from her minions. Despite inevitable shortages of everything from pointe shoes to male dancers over the age of eighteen (subject to the call-up), the Sadler's Wells Ballet did sterling wartime service. Touring the country after escaping from the neutral Netherlands during the Nazi invasion (one of the most thrilling yarns of the period), it braved air raids and rationing to raise morale by reminding audiences of beauty and producing work such as Ashton's *Dante Sonata* and Helpmann's *Miracle in the Gorbals* that spoke to the nation's heart during its hour of crisis.

In 1946 de Valois reaped her reward when Sadler's Wells Ballet was invited to make its permanent base at Covent Garden. Here a home-grown choreographer Frederick Ashton and ballerina Margot Fonteyn reached new peaks and a lavish production of *The Sleeping Beauty* demonstrated that the British – or was it the English? – could now inflect that distinctively Russian homage to French absolutist grandeur with a charm and lyricism of their own. The lustre of the Ballets Russes was permanently eclipsed. In Paris, the story would be the same: the world wanted something else. Colonel de Basil died in 1951 and the following year his shrivelled company was liquidated.

How does its achievement add up? Aside from Massine's symphonic ballets of the mid-1930s – works that dated quickly, but left possibilities for posterity – nothing subsequently staged by the company was of significant originality. Although some notable composers and artists were commissioned on the advice of others, de Basil lacked Diaghilev's flair or daring and the only other novelty to enjoy widespread popular success was Lichine's Biedermeier pastel *Graduation Ball*, first performed in Australia in 1940 and still doing the rounds thirty years later. Yet what was lacking in cutting-edge innovation was made up in sheer pizzazz – at its best in the mid-1930s, de Basil's Ballets Russes danced like fury and coruscated with personality. Nobody merely went by the book, there was never anything faceless or regimented about its attitude and its baby ballerinas enjoyed a level of popular recognition matched in the twentieth-century balletic annals only by Pavlova, Nijinsky, *The Red Shoes* and the Fonteyn and Nureyev partnership.

The story of Denham's Ballet Russe de Monte Carlo is longer in duration than de Basil's but shorter in artistic significance. Its activities and reputation were almost entirely confined to North America. It started with great *éclat* in 1938, however, as Massine went full throttle and cooked up another of his frou-frou farces in *Gaîté Parisienne*, complete with show-stopping cancan. It instantly became hugely popular, and in 1941 Warner Brothers filmed a truncated version in Hollywood, distributing it as a showcase for the new process of Technicolor.

Alongside this confection, Massine – nothing if not versatile – also unfurled *Seventh Symphony*, choreographing archetypal forces of elemental creation and destruction to Beethoven's 'apotheosis of the dance'; and *Nobilissima visione*, a balletic oratorio on the early life of St Francis to solemn music commissioned from Paul Hindemith. Sublime if you loved it, sanctimonious if you hated it. Edwin Denby was left stone cold by his response to Beethoven: 'It occupied the mind as long as it lasted, and left no reality, no secret emotion behind . . . every gesture is visually clear, but every gesture is at the same pitch, hit equally hard,' and he called what Massine brought to Hindemith mere 'slinky posturing'.[61]

In 1939 there followed *Rouge et Noir*, a portentous political allegory of the imminent war, with Shostakovich's First Symphony as the score and Matisse's designs in coded primary colours. Rather more sensational was *Bacchanale*, an orgiastic romp with blatantly phallic and vaginal scenery and costumes by Salvador Dalí. Psychoanalytically surreal if you loved it; obscenely vulgar if you hated it.

It was an astounding run, but it came to a speedy end. Four lighter-weight new ballets of 1940 and 1941 successively flopped, as the American public began to tire of both Massine's jokiness and his pretensions, in particular his habit of moulding dancers into pyramidal tableaux 'clicking into position as though placed there by a gigantic hand working a jigsaw puzzle', as one critic put it.[62] Undaunted, he began agitating for more control, more rehearsal time and more money. This was impolitic. Having been Denham's prime asset, he was now his major liability, and with the waning of the vogue for the symphonic ballet (always riskily expensive to produce), Denham was only too happy to see the back of him. In one of those peremptory volte-faces endemic to this era, Massine moved to Lucia Chase's rival Ballet Theatre. He wouldn't be happy there for long either, and at the end of the war he returned to Europe to enter the last phase of his astonishing career.

Denham was a more cultured and courtly man than de Basil, and his suavely deferential manners made him adroit at wooing, wining and dining wealthy donors. But the impresario Sol Hurok, who jumped ship from Denham and landed at Ballet Theatre at the same time as Massine, disdained his taste and delusions of grandeur: 'No sooner did he find himself in the atmosphere of ballet than he, too, became infected with Diaghileffitis, a disease that, apparently, attacks them all, sooner or later,' he sighed contemptuously.[63] The symptoms did not include a flow of original ideas. His one stroke of inspiration – or luck, or judgement – lay in commissioning Cecil B. de Mille's niece Agnes.* In 1942 she delivered him the golden egg of *Rodeo*, a rough-and-tumble ballet about bucking broncos and steer-roping that radiated all the 'sense of what it felt like to be an American'[64] that similar essays by Massine had previously strived but failed to render. Russian dancers turned up their noses at its backslapping, toe-tapping hootenanny, but it caught the mood of the times – and de Mille went on to choreograph *Oklahoma!* in the same vein.

With the help of *Rodeo* and a long stint on Broadway in the musical *Song of Norway*, choreographed by Balanchine, Denham's company weathered the war. It then continued as a hardy road show, bringing innocent pleasure and a whiff of glamour to millions as it traversed North America from Albuquerque to

---

* In 1940, she had choreographed *Black Ritual* for Ballet Theatre's pioneering but sadly short-lived unit consisting entirely of young African American women. It was considered unsuccessful.

Kalamazoo, feeding the dream to a generation of baby-boom youngsters. (One such was a ten-year-old girl called Roberta Ficker who in 1955 did 'a little something' as Clara in *The Nutcracker* when Denham's Ballet Russe de Monte Carlo came to Cincinnati; as Suzanne Farrell, she went on to become perhaps the greatest of Balanchine's muses.)[65]

Tenacious and tireless, it was a gallant enterprise. Through the 1950s, however, its identity crumbled as the Russian component dwindled and the company's make-up became increasingly miscellaneous in terms of both nationality and training – not so much Ballet Russe de Monte Carlo (it never returned to Europe post-war) as Ballet Russe de Americana. To meet popular demand, it was reduced to presenting endless rounds of the same bread and butter, relying on a shrinking repertory of sugar-plum favourites and the top billing of 'marquee' partnerships such as those of Alexandra Danilova and Frederic Franklin, and Alicia Alonso and Igor Youskevitch. A whiff of circus sawdust lowered the tone. Denham's infatuation with – and promotion of – the Polish ballerina Nina Novak did neither him nor the company any favours. Diaghilev had had the sense to be susceptible only to the supremely talented.

Yet Denham wasn't a bad boss. Unlike de Basil, who would go to extraordinary lengths to avoid paying anyone anything, Denham remunerated his dancers meticulously and kept rigorous accounts. Until its natural death in 1962, his organisation remained admirably productive, efficient and financially viable (the only drawback to his prudence being his readiness to bring down the curtain prematurely to avoid overtime payments). But had it never existed, the history of ballet wouldn't look substantially different.

———

Many other companies followed in the Ballets Russes tradition, based on the increasingly rickety principle of one quixotic male infected with 'Diaghileffitis' in pretty much unfettered charge and reliant for financial oxygen on the box office and occasional cheques from susceptible wealthy ladies. In *Blast at Ballet*, Lincoln Kirstein had warned: 'There can be no second Diaghilev . . . beware the little men who seek periodically to revive either his own work or those aims proper to his time.'[66] But there would be many such little men.

One of the more notable was George de Cuevas, an arriviste of obscure Chilean origins – rumour had it that he had been a shoe-shiner in Santiago – with a bogus claim to the title of marquis.[67] What distinguished him from his peers was his key to a treasure trove containing the inexhaustible fortune of his wife Margaret Strong, a principal heir to her grandfather John D. Rockefeller. She had met the penniless de Cuevas in the Faubourg Saint-Honoré salon of the couturier Prince Felix Yusopov (in his previous life, Rasputin's assassin), where de Cuevas had landed up as a receptionist. A shy and studious creature without social confidence, Strong was captivated by de Cuevas, who played the exquisite Parisian dandy and paid her elaborate court. After they married in 1928 and had three children, de Cuevas began to dig into his new-found wealth. While curating an art exhibition at the 1939 New York World's Fair he contracted an incurable case of Diaghileffitis, and five years later landed on the idea of launching a ballet company that would minister to both his *folie de grandeur* and his penchant for handsome young men.

Although big names and big money were lavished on Ballet International, its first season in New York flopped, not least because de Cuevas was merely a dilettante with no idea what he was doing. Undaunted and unchastened, he looked to Europe where rich pickings were to be had. In 1945, having been forbidden to dance in

France pending investigation into his collaboration with the Nazis, Serge Lifar had corralled stray Russian dancers and set up a company in Monte Carlo. When he was partially cleared a year later,* he returned to Paris to lead the Opéra and de Cuevas bought him out. The result was the Grand Ballet du Marquis de Cuevas, a magical place where money seemed to be no object: Nijinska was engaged as ballet mistress; big names such as Alicia Markova and André Eglevsky were imported as guests; and Rosella Hightower, one of a slew of post-war ballerinas from native American stock, became the resident star attraction.

Even less expert than Denham, de Cuevas was a romantic with *ancien régime* snobbery and scant intellect – he therefore privileged the nineteenth-century classics and what new work he commissioned was largely decorative and superficial. But the company served its honourable purpose, and like Denham's Ballet Russe it brought the comfort of glamour to war-wounded cities still in dire need of it. Happily for those he employed, de Cuevas was also mildly benign in temper, interfering little in rehearsal and distributing generous salaries. Airily delegating the execution of his wishes and conducting any business through a bedroom levee, he preferred to expend his limited energies on cultivating his toilette and profile in café society. His weakness was a vulgar craving for *réclame*, and twice in his life he hit the front pages with a swagger.

In 1953, against the background of a general strike in France and the Korean War, he wasted a reputed $100,000 on an extravagant

---

* Not without controversy. Lifar regarded the Nazis as potential liberators of Russia from the Bolsheviks he loathed, and he had undoubtedly treated the Wehrmacht forces occupying Paris with friendly respect. But at his trial, he claimed – as many did – to have secretly helped many Jews to escape or evade arrest. (See Mark Franko, 'Serge Lifar et la collaboration'.)

folly of a costume ball held at a country club near Biarritz. To entertain the 2,000 guests – a smattering of film stars and titled nonentities, along with the dross of café society – Nijinska staged the second act of *Swan Lake* and Dalí provided decor. Bewigged and white-stockinged flunkeys carried flaming torches, 3,000 champagne corks popped, and de Cuevas, costumed by Balmain in gilded silk as 'le Roi de nature', presided over the revels. 'A pagan, barbarous orgy,' thundered the Vatican's mouthpiece *L'Osservatore Romano*,[68] but the real problem, according to witnesses, was that it just wasn't that much fun – basically a publicity stunt that backfired without any of the ravishing elegance of Diaghilev's glorious fête at Versailles thirty years previously.

In 1957, an equally silly event was staged. Serge Lifar, always spoiling for a fight, was enraged when de Cuevas's company had the temerity to make an unauthorised alteration to his ballet *Noir et blanc*. Lifar publicly berated de Cuevas, who slapped Lifar in the face with a handkerchief and refused to apologise. Lifar then challenged him to a duel,* and the two idiots agreed to fence with épées at a location near Paris, kept 'secret' to avoid prosecution but attended nevertheless by a horde of paparazzi. Lifar, fifty-three, made great theatrical play of his swordsmanship; de Cuevas, seventy-two, made only a few desultory lunges yet somehow managed to nick blood from Lifar's arm. Honour being satisfied, both men burst into tears and embraced as the cameras snapped obligingly. (A footnote to this footnote: one of de Cuevas's seconds was the young Jean-Marie Le Pen, then a Poujadiste deputy recently released from the Foreign Legion.)

* This was not the first time: Lifar had also hysterically challenged Massine to a duel in 1938 over a cut the latter had made in *Swan Lake*. 'Go take a powder,' the phlegmatic Massine snorted in response. (Jack Anderson, *The One and Only*, p. 30.)

Margaret de Cuevas took no interest in the ballet. It 'got on her nerves', according to de Cuevas's secretary, and she became increasingly reclusive and eccentric. Her intermittent efforts to discipline her husband's folly failed, and although she continued to write the necessary cheques, the company folded a year after his death in 1961. Its last fling was a revisiting of that mythic episode in Diaghilev's enterprise *The Sleeping Beauty*, mounted in a staggeringly elaborate production that cost twice as much as the ball – de Cuevas, now ailing, had to sell his apartment on the Quai Voltaire to finance it. A stylistic farrago – Nijinska stormed out of rehearsals in a rage – it marked another stage in the decadence of the Russian ballet but drew the crowds: Rudolf Nureyev briefly appeared in it shortly after his defection from Soviet Russia.

Europe and North America were oversupplied with pallid carbon copies of companies such as de Cuevas's, following the template of Diaghilev's enterprise without either the funds or the vision to sustain themselves. This meant constant circulation of versions of the nineteenth-century repertory plus Fokine's pre-First World War creations, with the addendum of a few short new works (seldom of any lasting merit) based on classical style. The showcasing of big names of the -inska and -ovsky variety persisted, but decreasingly so, as the wave of White Russians reached retirement age and went unreplaced. In Britain, International Ballet survived until 1953, competing with Sadler's Wells Ballet and from 1947 to 1949 with the ephemeral Metropolitan Ballet. More durable was Festival Ballet, now morphed into English National Ballet, established in 1950 to capitalise on the cultural bonanza of the 1951 Festival of Britain. Here the partnership of Alicia Markova and Anton Dolin (seamlessly at one with each other on stage, irritably fractious off it) played itself out into the 1960s, with the tubby and amiable figure of Julian Braunsweg taking the role of Diaghilev.[69]

What inexorably killed such companies off in Europe was not only the ever increasing expense of touring but also the competitive advantage given to an élite of companies selected for state subsidy – an element of post-war social policy that encouraged solid governance and allowed the favoured few decent premises, administrative stability, and the chance to plan strategically rather than opportunistically. Those denied this cushion were forced to cut corners and play it safe for the short term: standards and morale slipped in consequence. By the mid-1960s, Diaghilev's model of reliance on audiences and wealthy sponsors, combined with a wing and a prayer, had become untenable.

Meanwhile exponents and witnesses of the Ballets Russes's glory years died, memories faded, tastes changed, time marched on – and since ballet is an art so delicately transmitted by hand and eye rather than book or record, many finer threads were inevitably broken. When, in 1957, David Lichine, a prominent member of the 'de Basil' wave of Russian ballet, was slated to stage *The Nutcracker* for London Festival Ballet, he asked the last surviving member of the Nevsky Pickwickians, eighty-seven-year-old Alexandre Benois, to design the show. The two men, separated by a generation divided by the First World War, held preliminary discussions as if across a chasm. 'I cannot collaborate with you, young man,' Benois concluded. 'What you envisage is not *Casse-noisette* as I know it. You have no feeling for time or period and your conception hasn't anything to do with the magic story of my childhood.'[70] Benois finally relented, and their production remained a Christmas perennial at the Royal Festival Hall into the mid-1960s, neutered of any artistic significance and of interest only to nice little girls and their sentimental mamas.

Yet perhaps the *coup de grâce* for the Ballets Russes came, ironically, from the country in which it had all started. In July 1956 the Bolshoi arrived in London from Moscow for the first time, returning regularly in summers thereafter; visits to New York and American tours followed from 1959. There was a political context to these sorties: the Cold War was warming up, and trade in culture, like the space race, had an edgy undercurrent of competition and aggression. Beneath the superficial smiles and cordial handshakes of cultural exchange and international friendship, both sides were secretly out to score points and prove that they could do it better.

Initially Russia won hands down with the hard blast of Soviet ballet, cast in the mode of crude Stalinist realism and disdainful of Diaghilev's refined modernist aesthetics, but so raw, bold and energised that it transcended its own vulgarity. This was ballet *brut*, epic in emotion, all guns blazing and no hostages taken. The Ballets Russes tradition, now half a century old and fast running out of steam, was left looking feeble and jejune in comparison. Throughout the 1960s, return visits to Europe and America by both the Bolshoi and the Mariinsky (renamed the Kirov by the Soviets) led to the idea that in terms of power and quality of dancing (if not choreography), the advantage lay behind the Iron Curtain.

Devoid of any Nijinskian note of effeminacy, the men in the company jumped and turned and lifted like Olympic champions, but it was the Bolshoi's prima ballerina Galina Ulanova whose impact proved overwhelming. Although she was in her late forties, she gave a magical illusion of youth, dancing with such open heart and proletarian soul that her opposite Western numbers such as Fonteyn were made to look preciously middle class. Not for Ulanova the princely favours and Savoy suppers enjoyed by her predecessors either. The utter simplicity and naked honesty she radiated, according to Jennifer Homans, seemed 'to stand both for and against: for the socialist state and its accomplishments but against its empty, canned slogans, its deceptions and lies'.[71] Later the sensational front-page defectors from the Mariinsky Rudolf Nureyev (in 1961), Natalia Makarova (in 1970) and Mikhail Baryshnikov (in 1974) – all in search of the artistic freedom and challenge denied under sclerotic communist tyranny – would only compound the view that the Russians did ballet better than anyone. But the Diaghilev moment was over.

The basic sources for this chapter are Arnold Haskell, *Balletomania Then and Now*, passim; Kathrine Sorley Walker, *De Basil's Ballets Russes*, passim; Vicente Garcia-Marquez, *The Ballets Russes: Colonel de Basil's Ballet Russes de Monte Carlo*, passim, and *Massine*, pp. 207–362; Jack Anderson, *The One and Only: Ballet Russe de Monte Carlo*, passim; 'The Ballets Russes 1932–1962: A Symposium', *Dance Chronicle*, xv/2 (1992), pp. 191–220; Malcolm McCormick and Nancy Reynolds, *No Fixed Points: Dance in the Twentieth Century*, pp. 265–393; Robert Gottlieb, *George Balanchine: The Ballet Maker*, pp. 75–113; Irina Baronova, *Irina: Ballet, Life, Love*, passim; Martin B. Duberman, *The Worlds of Lincoln Kirstein*, pp. 193–326; Victoria Tennant, *Irina Baronova and the Ballets Russes de Monte Carlo*, passim; Jane Stevenson, *Baroque between the Wars*, pp. 281–94; Michael Meylac, *Behind the Scenes at the Ballets Russes*, pp. 41–283; *Ballets Russes*, film (DVD), directed by Danya Goldfine and Dan Geller.

# 9

## SURVIVORS

———

Richard Buckle

Because a dancer's training cultivates firm posture, respiratory stamina, strong muscles and healthy appetites, ballet promotes long lives, and luminaries of Diaghilev's era born before the invention of the combustion engine survived to witness men on the moon, the Bee Gees at no. 1, and Margaret Thatcher leading the Conservative Party.

Tamara Karsavina, for instance, queen of the Ballets Russes's first seasons, lived on until 1978 and the ripe age of ninety-three.[1] During the 1920s, she had continued to perform sporadically with Diaghilev and freelance all over Europe and the USA, but something of her magic had faded with the First World War and in 1932 she wisely retired from the stage to devote herself to her family. After her somewhat feckless if warmly affectionate husband Henry Bruce died suddenly in 1951, she was left marooned in a hopelessly impractical and increasingly dilapidated Queen Anne terraced house on Frognal in Hampstead. She loved it tenderly and made the best of its shortcomings: the reception rooms were charmingly furnished and, in a squalid little kitchen, exquisite meals were cooked. But the roof leaked, pipes froze, dust thickened, ceilings collapsed, mice scuttled and the garden grew like the foliage enshrouding the Sleeping Beauty. Money had flowed in and out, mostly out. Devoted to her son and grandchildren and loyal to a close circle of friends, Karsavina ended up living frugally, but generously towards others, at the very limit of her means. She was too proud to ask anyone for help.

One of the great beauties of the Edwardian era, in old age she maintained her dignity even as she crumbled into something faintly grotesque. Barely five foot tall and chronically arthritic, she sat ramrod straight, only her neck and arms still undulating with the liquid grace of her schooling. As her once lustrous black hair thinned and greyed, she adopted a mauve wig, and her fabulous dark eyes became heavily lidded and lizardy. Her pious devotion to Russian Orthodoxy, its feasts and rituals, never diminished, but she loved her adopted nationality deeply and acquired a remarkable fluency in its language, writing essays and memoirs in a meticulous bel-letrist prose informed by her immersion in Dickens and Lamb. Free though she was from vainglory or pomposity, her presence had an effortless regality – Byzantine emperors were rumoured to be among her ancestors – that commanded awed respect. To all but a chosen few she was 'Madame Karsavina'. 'I felt like a very inferior mandarin received in audience on the steps of the Temple of Heaven,' wrote the critic Richard Buckle of his first encounter with her.[2]

It is commonly said that ballet dancers have very short careers, but this is misleading: although they may perform on stage for only twenty years, many of them go on to teach and coach, and the older they grow, the more valuable they become as vessels of arcane knowledge that cannot be communicated by notation or even film. Karsavina had a store of such wisdom to offer, dispensed post-war through her active vice-presidency of the Royal Academy of Dancing and the mentoring of British ballerinas in the mysteries of the Russian roles that she had once performed. To Margot Fonteyn she explained that the Firebird must be danced without 'human emotion . . . you are a wild bird, Margot, you must use your arms, you must *beat* your arms . . . you've never felt a human hand on your body before, you've never been caught, and it's terrible'.[3] For Moira Shearer and Antoinette Sibley she unlocked the nuances of mimed passages in *Giselle* and *Swan Lake*. 'I knew the gestures', Sibley told Barbara Newman, 'but to see her do it was like listening to Beethoven after just learning the scales . . . the moment she started to move, you understood everything.'[4]

Karsavina's remained a rich and fulfilled life: that of her stage partner Nijinsky became an empty tragedy as his descent into madness proved irreversible. Confined in 1919 to a Swiss sanatorium after his last dance in the ballroom of the St Moritz hotel, he alternated between long periods of catatonic docility and episodes of violent self-harm and compulsive masturbation during which he refused to eat. Doctors diagnosed 'non-functioning of the glands' and gave his disease futile names; visits to Lourdes and fashionable quacks such as Dr Coué proved fruitless.[5] Having delegated his care to her sister and transferred him to a dismal Paris apartment (which Diaghilev and Lifar visited), Romola decamped to America to pursue hare-brained money-making schemes and lesbian love affairs. When she returned to Europe in 1929, she found Nijinsky's mental state so alarming that she sent him back to the sanatorium. Both Freud and Jung refused to address his case – his mania was too acute for their psychologies.

Partly to pay huge medical bills and partly to fund her own extravagant lifestyle, Romola then wrote a shamelessly skewed biography of her husband (ghosted by young balletomanes Lincoln Kirstein and Arnold Haskell, not to mention contributions from the spirit world via the medium Eileen Garrett) and edited a highly redacted version of the mad diary he had written in 1919 – her intention being to blacken Diaghilev, vindicate her own behaviour and present the world with a palatable idea of Nijinsky as a troubled romantic genius. The books became bestsellers and their version of events was broadly accepted, so at one level the strategy worked.

During the late 1930s, insulin shock therapy was in vogue as a treatment for bipolar conditions. In the short term it appeared to stabilise Nijinsky's state of mind, leading Romola to drop implausible hints that Nijinsky would one day emerge to dance again. In 1940, the pair moved back to Romola's native Budapest, and then to Vienna. After the war, Romola continued to intimate that Nijinsky was 'in considerable recovery' and planning 'an advanced institute for the study of the dance' that UNESCO had 'expressed an interest' in supporting. Of course, this was moonshine. In 1947 the couple was granted residency in England. Here Nijinsky seemed to observers merely apathetically vacant – Arnold Haskell described him as looking like 'a suburban commercial traveller'. An English balletomane, Margaret Power, became his devoted carer and won a degree of his trust: she played unruly games of ping-pong with him and indulged his pleasure in 'piling things up and knocking them over'.[6] In 1950, at the age of sixty, he died from kidney failure in a rented house near Windsor. Serge Lifar and Anton Dolin, neither of whom had seen him dance, were among his pallbearers at his funeral. He was first buried in Finchley, until his remains were removed to the Cimitière de Montmartre in Paris in 1953. Poor Margaret Power had to identify the mouldered corpse before it could be licensed for transfer.

Reviled and resented as a parasite and fantasist by almost everyone who had known Nijinsky professionally (including his sister), Romola died in 1978, two weeks after Karsavina.* As the widow keeper of the flame, her machinations in pursuit of money (often via litigation) had been ceaseless and her dishonesty was often reprehensible. But there were forces other than hers feeding the myth

---

* Nijinsky's daughter Kyra eventually married the conductor Igor Markevitch, Diaghilev's last lover; she died in 1998. The younger Tamara Nijinsky, who may or may not have been fathered by Nijinsky and who was altogether written out of the story by her undoubted mother Romola, died in Arizona in 2017.

of Nijinsky too. No record of him in motion remains (of Karsavina there are a few flickering fragments). Words and studio photographs are posterity's only evidence – an absence that has allowed the fantasy to become all the more intense, often in relation to his ostensible ability to hover supernaturally in the air. 'Although denied a glimpse of Nijinsky in the flesh', Lincoln Kirstein needed only

a reproduction of an etching (by Troy Kinney, I think), which
for the moment almost filled this gap. Nijinsky stood in absolute
physical and spiritual balance, profiled in silhouette, clad in the
black velvet tunic and full white silk sleeves of the male soloist in
Fokine's *Les Sylphides*. There was a deeply mysterious, breathless
stasis in his stoic silence, something at once commanding, elegant
and very wild. He was the incarnation of Chopin's sonorities as
I heard them from my sister's piano practice, and this etching
became an icon to which I constantly referred as the sum of
masculine possibility.[7]

The clichés of *le dieu de la danse* and 'Clown of God', stoked by the megalomaniac claims to divinity scribbled in his mad diary, became etched to his memorial.* The press would lazily label any young male dancer of note the 'new' or 'second' Nijinsky as soon as he executed a passable *grand jeté*. Another dimension of his fame was perpetuated by a magnificent stallion that stunned the racing world in 1969–70: he was named Nijinsky by his owner who had heard the (unsubstantiated) tale that on his deathbed the dancer had muttered his wish to be reincarnated as a horse.

Gay writers – playwrights Terence Rattigan, Terrence McNally

---

* The stories even extended to the size of Nijinsky's penis – the columnist Tom Driberg reports a canard that he could auto-fellate. (*Ruling Passions*, p. 66.)

and Robert David MacDonald, critic Kevin Kopelson, poets Frank Bidart and Wayne Koestenbaum among them – have identified with the erotic tragedy of the sophisticated older man infatuated with a restive and farouche youth who briefly obliges but then betrays him. Released in 1980 as homosexuality began to flow into the cultural mainstream, Herbert Ross's mediocre film *Nijinsky*, with Alan Bates halfway plausible as Diaghilev and some fine ballet sequences, draws on events between 1911 and 1916. In terms of historical authenticity, it ranks on a level with *The Crown* or *Downton Abbey*, but its most wilfully fanciful aspect is its portrait of Nijinsky (George de la Peña) as an impulsively affectionate and chatty extrovert, rather than someone of eerie detachment, 'who ate and drank with curious stolidity, moved unnoticeably from room to room, smiled without meaning and spoke rarely'[8] – a blank, an absence, an enigma even to himself.

Embodying a glory irretrievably lost across cultural chasms blasted by two world wars, Karsavina and Nijinsky became deities enshrined in a mythology of the Ballets Russes. They were the past and not to have seen them was to have missed sight of the greatest glory; but what could keep the tradition developing and where did ballet's future lie? Until 1945, the companies administered by Colonel de Basil and Serge Denham seemed to keep the flame burning with the possibilities opened up through Massine's symphonic ballets, underpinned by a broad popularity based on gorgeous spectacle and the dazzle of the baby ballerinas. Yet this formula turned hard and stale, trapped on a relentless carousel of touring governed by ruthless commercial imperatives.

It was from Paris that fresh impetus initially came – its urgency charged by energies and experiences pent up during the city's four years under Nazi occupation. Diaghilev's secretary Boris Kochno was the key figure in this movement. His early literary ambitions had dwindled, but he had taste and erudition as well as an interesting address book. Through the 1930s he had ducked and dived around the ballet world, scratching a living from ideas, articles and consultancies, and exploiting his facility for devising simple narratives for ballets that choreographers could then develop – two of his more durable achievements being the ground plans for Balanchine's *The Prodigal Son* and *Cotillon*. His relationship with Serge Lifar, director of ballet at the Opéra, was uncomfortable, and after their tussle at Diaghilev's deathbed, there were further quarrels over the inheritance of his chattels. But the deeper division between them hinged on this question: whose account of the story would prevail? Kochno had the understanding, but Lifar shouted more loudly.

Lifar's great love affair was with himself; Kochno flitted between many others, but everything changed when in 1929, shortly after Diaghilev's death, he became intensely involved with the stage designer and painter Christian 'Bébé' Bérard in Paris. A big fat dirty chain-smoking, heavy-drinking and opium-addicted character, adorable and impossible, Bérard embodied the exuberant spirit of Left Bank bohemia. He and the laconic Kochno were oddly paired, but for twenty years, surviving even the Nazi occupation, they lived together as one of Paris's most unabashed homosexual couples, in a magnificent apartment near the Place de l'Odéon that became a magnet for everyone fashionably artistic, including Diaghilev's old-timers such as Chanel and Cocteau. Bérard may have been an almighty mess of a person, but he was blessed with continuous and apparently effortless creativity, his style characterised by a wonderful light touch that could draw visual magic out of the simplest materials and effects – a gift immortalised in the gorgeously mirrored and windswept dreamscape he created for the Beast's chateau in Cocteau's 1946 film *La Belle et la bête*.

The lessons Kochno had learned at Diaghilev's side bore fruit only in the vicious winter of 1944–5 when Paris was free but freezing.

With Bérard to inspire him, he returned to the theatre that had seen the première of Nijinsky's *The Rite of Spring* to become the artistic director of the newly formed Ballets des Champs-Élysées.[9] Nobody had much money and there was little food, but these were privations that proved an incentive. Two cold and hungry young men of outstanding talent emerged on stage, with nothing to lose: they were the blue touchpaper that would ignite Kochno's enterprise and give ballet the post-war push it needed.

Half Italian and the high-spirited son of a restaurateur in Les Halles, Roland Petit had entered the lowest ranks of Lifar's Opéra in 1940 at the age of sixteen. By the time he was twenty he had had enough of its deferences and protocols: the Ballets des Champs-Élysées offered him the liberty he needed to establish ballet in some kind of live connection with the actualities of the modern world rather than offering an escape into either fairy tale, abstraction or symbolism.

He was not entirely alone in this endeavour: a desire for some degree of realism was in the *Zeitgeist*, picked up in the United States by Antony Tudor's *Pillar of Fire* (1942) and Jerome Robbins's *Fancy Free* (1944) and in Britain by Robert Helpmann's *Miracle in the Gorbals* (1944). But Petit would go further, pioneering in particular a more honest depiction of human sexuality than ballet had ever previously dared. The delicate kisses, ethereal lifts and courtly bows of the classics were replaced by entwined limbs, thrusting pelvises and pre- or post-coital Gauloises: *Les Amours de Jupiter* unambiguously showed repeated rape; *Carmen* removed all the picturesque pseudo-Hispanic wrappings around Bizet's music to expose the dynamics of an erotic infatuation, illustrated through an explicit physicality that the cinema wouldn't match for another decade (Richard Buckle described it to Lincoln Kirstein as 'a forty-minute fuck').[10] Its candour would be a hugely liberating influence on the style of a younger generation of choreographers, notably Kenneth MacMillan.

Petit could also cook up elegant fantasy – in *Les Demoiselles de la nuit*, he cast his girlfriend Margot Fonteyn as an alluring white cat – but as one of his dancers, Violette Verdy, put it, 'He wanted things to go through the mud a bit.'[11] He was 'full of punk, piss and vinegar, irreverent about anything classical or traditional', according to Leslie Caron, a sixteen-year-old he spotted in Preobrajenska's ballet school. She was signed up then and there. 'I was paid fifty francs a month, nothing at all, and lived off coffee and cigarettes,' she recalls. 'I suffered from boils and weak ankles, and sometimes I would faint. But I took to it like a duck to water and had fun in the pond from beginning to end. Roland didn't care much about your technique. He just wanted personality.'[12]

That quality emerged most piquantly in *Les Forains*, a melancholy comedy in which an endearingly hopeless band of strolling circus folk emerge from their booth and vainly try to entertain a gawping but unappreciative crowd, dressed in ordinary clothes, as though they had walked in off the street. From the simplest of means Bérard's designs conjured the most evocative of atmospheres: there were echoes of *Petrushka* and *Parade* here (as well as the *saltimbanques* of Picasso's rose period), but no concession was made to spectacle: the shabbiness of the sets and costumes was authentic, harvested by Bérard from flea markets and building sites. Even grittier were *Le Rendez-vous*, set in a mean-streets bistro with designs based on blown-up photographs of the Métro by Brassaï, and the Ballets des Champs-Élysées's most celebrated and durable work *Le Jeune Homme et la mort* (1946). This was a short sharp shocker, based on a scenario by Cocteau, with music (an ironically serene Bach passacaglia) added by Petit at the last moment of rehearsal as if it were merely an atmospheric film soundtrack. In a Parisian garret, a shirtless young painter in shabby dungarees is smoking and checking his watch nervously. The woman he desires appears, but she taunts him in a sadistic sex game and leaves him unsatisfied. He hangs himself in despair. The woman returns hierophantically robed and wearing the mask of death: she leads the young man's ghost out over the rooftops into a magically revealed cityscape of Paris in which the Eiffel Tower is illuminated with a flashing Citroën sign.

This miniature fable resonated in a France still running high on the emotional roller-coaster of *libération* and *épuration*. And at its heart was Jean Babilée, who created the role of the *jeune homme* and will always be identified with it. The half-Jewish son of a prominent surgeon, Babilée was a solitary and sickly child sent to ballet school as a means of controlling both his volcanic temper and his epilepsy. Even less suited to the rigours of the Opéra than his friend and coeval Petit, he was a natural born rebel and in the latter years of the war he escaped Paris and the round-ups to join the Resistance in the Touraine. Or so he rather vaguely claimed.

No male dancer between Nijinsky and Nureyev caught the public's imagination to the extent that Babilée did, and to French youth of the later 1940s, he embodied much of the same tormented, alienated, restless introversion that Marlon Brando and James Dean would bring to American cinema in the ensuing decade. He had superb technique, electric vitality, theatrical presence: barely five foot tall with a pronounced aquiline nose and a wayward untethered sexiness, he used his stockily muscular build to develop a cat-like spring and a phenomenally powerful style more virile than elegant but unfazed by the demands of feats of classical virtuosity (he could knock off a dazzling Blue Bird in *The Sleeping Beauty*). He wasn't easy to deal with, unsurprisingly, and when his career exasperated him, he would rev up his scarlet motorbike and travel across Asia or Africa, armed with a jack knife, to explore spiritualities of a Gurdjieffian nature. No wonder he was a pin-up and, in France, his legend remained potent until his death in 2014.[13]

After Bérard's heedlessly abused body succumbed to a cerebral embolism in 1949 when he was forty-seven, Kochno lost heart: their partnership had been seamless and he was left bereft. Petit had just broken away to establish his own company, Ballets de Paris, and the Ballets des Champs-Élysées soon ran out of steam. When Babilée decamped to New York (where, predictably, he fell out with everyone), it shut down, unable to compete against the Rockefeller-endowed efforts of the Marquis de Cuevas. Slender and darkly alluring in his youth, Kochno retreated, ending up as 'fat as Buddha' and eventually unable to walk without sticks. He continued to function – 'if there was something to do he did it'[14] – but alcohol hollowed him out, and he became a specimen of Dickensian eccentricity, retreating to a ramshackle house near Les Halles stuffed with his obsessively hoarded art collection and memorabilia. The two books about ballet that he published were half what they could have been.* Although he was in pole position to tell the inside story, discretion or indolence inhibited him and the chalice passed instead to an Englishman who had never set eyes on Diaghilev or seen any performance of the original Ballets Russes performances – Richard Buckle.

Critic, biographer, connoisseur, conspirator, gadfly and shameless show-off, Buckle was quite something, with a personal life that was even more of a mess than Kochno's or Bérard's. Prone to disastrous entanglements with seedy young men on the make and catastrophic collapses of his health and finances, he was the despair of his friends, with virtually all of whom he quarrelled cantankerously at some point or other. He struggled against alcoholism and sometimes surrendered to it. His wit and charm meant that he was

---

* *Le Ballet* and *Diaghilev and the Ballets Russes*: both are essentially pictorial, with commentary.

invariably forgiven, but he was a loose cannon, as feared for his scurrilous rudeness as he was respected for his no-shit honesty. Yet through all his wobbles, his balletomania remained steadfast, and his loud and doughty defence of the art served to counter the curse of twee gentility that stifled it during the post-war era.[15]

Born in 1916, the black sheep of a distinguished military family with aristocratic connections, Buckle claimed that he 'had never heard of ballet' until he was a sixteen-year-old schoolboy at Marlborough College and caught sight of the cover photograph of Romola's newly published biography of Nijinsky at a station bookstall. Intrigued, he was soon gobbling up Arnold Haskell's *Balletomania* and attending performances of de Basil's Ballets Russes. Having dropped out of his modern languages course at Balliol College, Oxford, he went to art school instead: 'Since I saw no other way of becoming Diaghilev's successor, which is what I should have loved to be, I aimed to become a ballet designer.'[16] But he lacked the technique and the discipline and after several rebuffs, he realised his talent might lie more with the written word.

In 1939, he began by publishing a new monthly magazine entitled simply *Ballet*. Its progress was soon halted by the outbreak of war, during which Buckle served with some distinction as a captain in the Scots Guards – mentioned in dispatches during the Italian campaign, during which he also camped it up at regimental dinners and befriended a seductively handsome and susceptible art student fighting with the partisans called Franco Zeffirelli.[17]

After the war, *Ballet* was resumed: undaunted by the paper shortage, it flouted the rigours of austerity by indulging in what Edwin Denby called 'a specifically English elegance', decorating its pages with drawings commissioned from the cream of young British artists. Its tone was unabashedly cosmopolitan. Buckle's flights of fancy and sly scattering of idle insults made the politesse of Arnold Haskell and Cyril Beaumont seem mealy-mouthed and the decent *Dancing Times* look stolidly insular. As Denby explained, *Ballet* 'seemed to promise that inside the covers one would be addressed not as a harried fellow-professional but – for once – as a guest at a pretty supper party. Pretty but not entirely safe.'[18] Fun, in other words, but not enough fun to keep Buckle's attention for long. Impatient for a more creative role, he attempted to contribute bright ideas to the leadership of Sadler's Wells Ballet, newly ensconced at Covent Garden. But Ninette de Valois rightly identified him as trouble and kept him at bay, forcing him to seek other outlets for his Diaghilev complex.

*Ballet* was always a maverick operation and nobody was surprised when it went bust in 1952. Buckle needed bread and butter, and found it in writing weekly columns for the *Observer* (between 1948 and 1955) and the *Sunday Times* (1959–75). From these promontories, like his theatrical contemporary Kenneth Tynan, he was a kingmaker, combining stylish insouciance with stiletto-sharp judgement (the single syllable 'No' was his verdict on the Bolshoi's *Carmen*) and flurries of ecstatic poetry (Fonteyn 'danced as simply as a stream flows . . . she has thought herself into beauty').[19] Erudite and eclectic, he always looked outwards: 'I went to operas, plays, concerts and art exhibitions and tried to relate ballet to the other arts. It was a grave danger that ballet should exist in a little hothouse of its own, unruffled by the breeze of new ideas.'[20]

Buckle reciprocated Denby's admiration, hailing his as 'the sharpest eye, keenest ear and most evocative pen' of all living writers on dance, but Buckle was blessed with an additional quality that the unworldly Denby lacked – wickedly subversive humour.[21] 'Most ballet critics', he wrote, 'are either Fairies or Witches, or both, and I'm a Jester.'[22] He giggled, he teased, he mocked, he provoked, he teetered on the edge of decency and occasionally went over the top, even though his praise could be generous and ready. It was a high-wire act that beguiled his readers but also one that left his employers anxiously attempting to moderate his excesses and slow him down.

A romantic at heart, Buckle worshipped at the feet of the three great ageing Diaghilev ballerinas who had settled in Britain. Karsavina was one, graciously receptive to his attentions; Lydia Lopokova another, until she sank into reclusive grumpiness. His closest relationship, however, was with Lydia Sokolova, born Hilda Munnings, an Essex girl whose life hadn't been easy. Her maverick father had been imprisoned for posing as a fraudulent medium, and she had nearly died in the terrible aftermath of the First World War. Her health never recovered, and after Diaghilev's demise, her stage career petered out early. After two disastrous affairs while she was in the Ballets Russes, she married a kindly bank clerk and did some teaching, before retiring to a two-up, two-down cottage in a village near Sevenoaks. She had no money or glamour, and despite ranking as Britain's greatest gift to the Ballets Russes, she was shamefully left without public honour.

But Buckle realised that she had a great story to tell and that she would utter it without fear or favour: after all, she had signed up with Diaghilev in 1913 and was still with him at the end, eyewitness to all the great events and personalities and what lay behind and between them. Buckle taped and edited her recollections and the result, published in 1960, was a sharp corrective to existing histories such as Romola Nijinsky's myth-making biography of her husband and Sergei Grigoriev's straight-faced record of his managerial perspective.

More was to come. In 1967 Buckle was summoned by Harry Salzman, co-producer of the James Bond franchise, to explore the possibility of a film based on Romola's biography to be directed by

Ken Russell with Rudolf Nureyev in the title role:* could Buckle act as consultant, might he even write the screenplay? In the way of the movie business, the project soon stalled and morphed[23] but Buckle came out of the discussion with a contract to write a balanced and researched replacement for Romola's book. All the salient survivors (including Romola herself, who took a cut of Buckle's royalties) contributed material and the substantial tome that emerged in 1971 enjoyed great success. It was followed in 1979 by a similar door-stopper focused on Diaghilev.

Both Buckle's biographies are what Henry James would have called 'large, loose, baggy monsters', and even after 70,000 words were cut from *Diaghilev*, it still seems too long and heavy on superfluous names, details and flourishes.[24] He can be criticised for bias, in particular towards unreliable Romola and Boris Kochno, who gave him access to many previously unseen documents; and his research suffered from the pre-*glasnost* inaccessibility of the Russian sources (the latter exhaustively examined by Sjeng Scheijen in his more balanced and meticulous biography of Diaghilev published some thirty years later). But Buckle's exuberant intelligence is irresistible, and his first-hand interviews with the survivors as well as his archival research in Paris and New York laid invaluable groundwork for all future studies not only of the personalities involved but also of their cultural epoch. Ninette de Valois – who became, as Buckle sensed, 'envious' of Diaghilev's legend – snorted, 'There's nothing left to say,' when he told her of his project.[25] He proved her scepticism unjustified.

Yet Buckle's deeper influence on this history was as the curator of the exhibition commissioned by the Edinburgh International Festival

---

* A decade later Nureyev would play Valentino, directed by Russell; in 1980 Salzman produced *Nijinsky*, directed by Herbert Ross.

to mark the twenty-fifth anniversary of Diaghilev's death in 1954. The moment was timely: the torch had passed to New York where Balanchine was at his peak, Jerome Robbins was the coming thing, and the 'modern dance' movement pioneered earlier in the century by the likes of Martha Graham, Doris Humphrey and Ruth St Denis was gathering momentum. Most of what passed on stage as deriving from the Ballets Russes now looked over-familiar, if not pallid and tatty. Public taste was ready to move on, but Buckle's touch restored some of their original glory and the shock of their splendour.

The inspiration was Diaghilev's own early exhibitions of Russian paintings, which had been stylishly enhanced with appropriately atmospheric decor. But Buckle went further. Transforming the stony halls of Edinburgh's neo-classical College of Art, he displayed designs, costumes, documents and relics in what today would be called 'an immersive environment'. Works by all the great visual artists associated with the Ballets Russes – Roerich, Benois and Bakst; Larionov and Goncharova; Picasso, Cocteau, Matisse and Derain – were included, but it was the piped music, the subtle lighting, the painted columns, the *trompe l'œil*, the gilded papier-mâché statuary dreamed up by Buckle in collaboration with Leonard Rosoman that transformed an art exhibition into a theatrical show.

Its enthusiastic reception led to a transfer to London and Forbes House, a disused mansion in Belgravia (now owned by a Qatari sheikh and said to be worth £300 million). Buckle and Rosoman mapped a route through its interior. After passing through an enfilade of fourteen upper rooms – one presenting a recreation of a Parisian street in 1910, another a 'haunted theatre' strewn with abandoned costumes and sprayed with Diaghilev's favourite scent, Mitsouko by Guerlain – visitors descended a marble staircase, at the foot of which was Rosoman's tableau of the 'Palace of the Sleeping Beauty', opening into a pavilion 'representing a tangled forest, with

sleeping huntsmen on horseback in the distance'.[26] With carpets of
different hues and ceilings swagged in gathered silk and hung with
borrowed chandeliers, the whiff of vulgarity proved a bit much for
the more fastidious. Ninette de Valois, for instance, felt that Diaghilev would have been 'irritated' by the 'Madame Tussaud's effect' and
in retrospect even Buckle himself admitted to a fairground 'tunnel of love' element. But the success it had enjoyed in Edinburgh
redoubled, and anyone who was anybody – Princess Margaret, Noel
Coward, Audrey Hepburn, Somerset Maugham – came to see it, as
did some 140,000 ordinary folk. To the elderly it brought back memories: 'The scattered impressions of the last fifty years fell into place,'
wrote E. M. Forster, who remembered Karsavina and Nijinsky in the
pre-war seasons, 'and I realised that I had assisted at an attempt of
the twentieth century to create civilised pleasure';[27] to the young, like
balletomane Adrian Brown, it was simply 'so beautiful it made me
ache';[28] Buckle was rightly but ruefully proud of its success.

> The Diaghilev exhibition came at a time when Britain, backwards in
> everything, was still slowly recovering from the mess and shortages
> of war, and it seemed to light up the lives of Londoners. People
> remembered long afterwards the impression it made on them, and
> although I later planned shows that were more carefully constructed
> and more numerously attended,* I was doomed for decades to find
> that the only spark of interest I aroused in strangers was when they
> were told I had arranged the Diaghilev exhibition.[29]

Liberating the possibilities for exhibition design as well as bringing
Diaghilev back in to fashionable conversation, this was only one of

---

* Among them an exhibition for Shakespeare's quatercentenary at
Stratford-on-Avon in 1964.

Buckle's more solid achievements. In the late 1960s and 1970s he also played a major role in establishing a Theatre Museum in London and making original Ballets Russes material central to its collection.

Although the bulk of designs and costumes had landed with Boris Kochno and Serge Lifar, all manner of people connected with the company had in the course of time acquired, come by or walked off with items. The Wadsworth Athenaeum in Hartford, Connecticut, was the first major beneficiary. To get himself out of a tight spot, Serge Lifar had sold this institution some of what he had inherited (by fair means or foul) for $10,000 (about $200,000 today). There would be no further large-scale change of ownership until 1967, when the octogenarian Sergei Grigoriev, in straitened circumstances, sold off what he had, including two of Nijinsky's costumes. Buckle wrote the introduction to Sotheby's catalogue. The prices went way beyond their estimates and the market became excited by a new collectible.

At this point a questionable Greek 'financier' living in Surrey called Tony Diamantidi got in touch with Buckle. A balletomane since the 1930s, he had acquired a hoard of sets and costumes from Colonel de Basil's widow. Now in his eighties, tired of paying the cost of storage, he wanted to sell up. He took Buckle to a warehouse in suburban Paris where 'hundreds of baskets, trunks and bundles', untouched for years, were pulled out. For Buckle, this was a moment of fairy-tale magic. 'The dirt was incredible. We were covered in dust and choked with it. Yet . . . I was as thrilled as Aladdin in his cave.' Among the booty was at least half of Bakst's costumes for *The Sleeping Princess*.[30]

Sotheby's agreed to take on the sale, and Buckle would devise a presentation modelled by Royal Ballet School students appropriately choreographed by Lydia Sokolova, in the Scala Theatre (now demolished) off Oxford Street. Most spectacular of all were the backcloths, including Picasso's front curtain for *Le Train bleu* – a scene painter's gigantically expanded version of Picasso's gouache of two women running across a beach that so impressed the artist that he gave it the mark of authenticity by signing it. Alas, when it was unfolded after a long period in storage, clouds of distemper flaked off the canvas and vast areas including Picasso's signature had to be quickly repainted. The cloth sold for £69,000 to a consortium of the great and the good who donated it to Buckle's proposed Theatre Museum: nobody had let on as to the degree to which it had been hurriedly patched up.[31]

This second sale was even more successful than the first. Attics were then raided as everyone rushed to cash in, and two further auctions were held in London in 1969 and 1973. The *Sgt Pepper*ish eclecticism of Swinging London meant that Ballets Russes costumes also found their way into vintage boutiques such as I Was Lord Kitchener's Valet in Carnaby Street. Chelsea had been the heart of the cult of the Ballets Russes in the 1920s; half a century later, it returned to the King's Road as part of a trendy hippie wardrobe.[32]

Of the many later sales, continuing into 2002 and some filled with detritus of dubious provenance and value, two were specially significant. The first was held in New York in 1984 when Lifar auctioned off more of his treasures – three Ballets Russes scrapbooks kept by Lady Ripon and her daughter Lady Juliet Duff inexplicably went for double their reserve at over $200,000, purchased by an anonymous benefactor who gave them to his alma mater Harvard; and a record-breaking $40,000 was paid for the original costume for the Chinese Conjuror in *Parade*, designed by Picasso. First worn by Massine in 1917, it subsequently passed to Leon Woizikowski, who danced the role in 1926. During the war, Woizikowski buried it in a wood in his native Poland to protect it from pillagers; how or why it came into Lifar's hands is unclear. In 1991 Sotheby's in Monaco sold the works of art in Kochno's collection; his letters and correspondence had previously been acquired by the Bibliothèque nationale. As he was a compulsive hoarder, this trove is of enormous value to historians.[33]

Buckle's heroically altruistic mission to salvage something of the Ballets Russes legacy for the British nation caused him much grief and anxiety: pledges went unfulfilled and, as is the way with patrons of the arts, Anthony Diamantidi proved both munificent and less than good as his word. Part of the problem, however, was Buckle's Diaghileffitis – not satisfied with being ballet's critic and chronicler, he longed to play the impresario who produced it too. In 1971 this quixotic ambition led him to disaster when he hired the London Coliseum in order to stage a gala extravaganza with the aim of raising money for the Theatre Museum and the acquisition of Titian's painting *The Death of Actaeon* for the National Gallery (having been sold by Lord Harewood, it was under offer to the Getty Museum in Los Angeles).

The original concept behind what Buckle – with tongue-in-cheek Barnum bravado – called *The Greatest Show on Earth* was a one-off performance of newly commissioned ballets from Buckle's friends Balanchine, Ashton and Robbins, 'to be followed by breakfast with the greatest dancers in the world and the most beautiful people in London, with tickets at astronomical prices'. This soon dwindled into something marginally more realistic – a '*répétition générale* or dress rehearsal for *The Greatest Show on Earth*' that ended up as a ragbag lasting a chaotic four hours.

'Poor Dicky,' lamented Buckle's neighbour in rural Wiltshire, Cecil Beaton. 'A meeting with A. Warhol sent him off his rocker. He at once thought he could command the same publicity as Andy and started to show off in a most atypical manner.' The producer

John Field had quit after 'a hysterical scene' and several big names fell by the wayside. One meagre afternoon of rehearsal meant that 'the drops were poorly lit. Dicky's own slides were in the wrong order, and the amplification wretched.'[34] Microphones kept cutting out. Yet the line-up remained dazzling, a reflection of Buckle's power to call in favours: participants included Margot Fonteyn and Rudolf Nureyev, Zizi Jeanmaire and Roland Petit, the Indian dancer Kama Dev and the flamenco firebrand Pilar Lopez. Patrick Procktor, Duncan Grant and Leonard Rosoman were among those who painted scenery, and for the happy few with memories stretching back half a century, there was a heart-rending finale in which Bakst's backcloth for the last act of 1921's *The Sleeping Princess* was revealed, with Diaghilev veterans Anton Dolin and Alexandra Danilova as the King and Queen graciously blessing the nuptials of Fonteyn and Nureyev as Aurora and her prince. Unfortunately it was past midnight when this transpired and most of the audience had fled to catch last trains.

On a Tuesday evening in June at prices drastically reduced from £100 to £10 (and at the last minute distributed for nothing), there were hundreds of empty seats and the takings fell far short of any putative financial target. Although nobody was paid a fee for their services, expenses weren't recouped and poor Buckle ended up in a terrible muddle of financial embarrassment. 'Dicky will never have anything but rocks and weeds surrounding his cottage,' Beaton continued, with a degree of barely repressed *Schadenfreude*. 'I'm sure the bills go as far as the bankruptcy court . . . No one takes him seriously.'[35] The press was largely snide – *The Times* review bewailed the 'amateurish' execution, 'exhausting' length and 'hopeless circumstances' of the enterprise;[36] the *Guardian* compared it to 'a sumptuously wrapped present', which, on being opened, 'proved to be a bit small'.[37]

One fiasco of farcical incompetence had exploded and exposed the pretensions of the entire Diaghilev enterprise, even if its heart was in the right place and its ambitions had been noble. The Titian was saved by other efforts, and in 1974 a Theatre Museum was established as a branch of the Victoria and Albert Museum: today the world's most comprehensive holdings of Ballets Russes material are lovingly preserved there. The costumes are so fragile that they can be displayed only in special circumstances – the dancers' salted sweat has made the fabrics friable and the garments cannot be dry-cleaned or treated. But the *Train bleu* drop curtain will be more permanently displayed when the museum opens new premises in Stratford East in 2023–4.

Buckle seems to have relished making enemies, and it is hardly surprising that he should show irritable disdain for a man eighteen years younger who shared his obsession with Diaghilev and was competing to present his own version of the story. In the mid-1960s John Drummond was an upcoming producer of music and arts programmes for BBC Television.[38] His knowledge was encyclopedic, his enthusiasm passionate, his ambition intense. Although a Cambridge graduate, he came from a lower social class than Buckle, and since both men were snobs, this registered and rankled. Buckle's correspondence and diaries barely mention a man he must have found presumptuous and irrelevant – a Johnny-Come-Lately to a field of which he had long claimed ownership – but Drummond painted a caustically score-settling picture of his rival in an account of his attempt to enlist Buckle's assistance with a filmed documentary history of the Ballets Russes:

> I . . . have to say that I was not much taken with Dickie as a
> person, and to tell the truth I don't think he cared much for me
> either. Somehow the chemistry was not right, and it never became

a comfortable relationship. I found that in spite of his observant eye and his flair for the telling phase, he lacked warmth . . . At one cool session at a very costly restaurant at my expense he referred to someone, and perhaps too quickly, I said, 'Yes, I know about her.' He said glacially, 'You know it all, don't you?'[39]

Buckle was well ahead of the game, but having offered a fee of £200 ('four times as much as almost everyone who featured in the programmes got'), Drummond gained access to his useful address book. Two hour-long films were the eventual outcome, broadcast on BBC1 in 1968. Shortly before they were aired, Drummond 'met Dickie on the stairs at Covent Garden, and said, "Hope you'll watch." "Watch?" he said. "What do you mean? I thought it was on the radio."'[40]

Narrated by Benois's great-nephew Peter Ustinov, the films have considerable archival value as the only substantial audio-visual record of the major figures of the Diaghilev era still living and compos mentis. Buckle's gaudy exhibition had reminded the drab mid-1950s of the Ballets Russes's lush sensuality; Drummond's more austere black-and-white films reminded the 'Swinging Sixties' of the stature of its makers and the seriousness of their endeavour. Drummond later consolidated his achievement with an excellent book including the unedited texts of all the interviews he conducted and wryly amusing reminiscences of his adventures stalking the likes of Karsavina, Sokolova, Lifar ('a silly person'[41]), and the seventy-year-old Massine, still compulsively active and globe-trotting even though his star had long waned, lording it over the tiny islands off the Amalfi coast that he had made his faintly sinister base.

A physically expansive and naturally domineering man of relentless energy and fearsome charm, Drummond was also very prickly, quick to flare up and take umbrage – one of his closest colleagues believes that his sensitivity can be ascribed to an outsider complex, the result of a residual feeling of social inferiority and intellectual shortfall combined with anxiety about exposing his homosexuality. But in matters of high culture he would brook no argument: many found his *ex-cathedra* decrees on matters of taste intimidating, and his passionate commitment to the art he genuinely loved could come across as arrogance. Buckle was right: Drummond did indeed know it all, and appeared to know them all too – his namedropping was legendary.

When Serge Lifar asked him how and why he had become interested in the saga of Diaghilev, Drummond replied, '*Par jalousie.*'[42] The émigré Russian seemed to have enjoyed the freedom to ignore the balance sheets and commission marvels; Drummond was a cog in the corporate machinery of the BBC. 'Diaghilev is for me almost an acronym for artistic authority,' he wrote. 'It has little to do with democracy and even less with accountability. It depends on the judicious exercise of limited tyranny.'[43] Impatient in the face of red tape, the small print and the pother of committees and hierarchies, though skilled at negotiating them, Drummond dreamed of a position from which he could act the untrammelled impresario.

So he left the BBC to become director of the Edinburgh International Festival, where he chose to focus his first programme in 1979 on honouring Diaghilev, his pretext being the almanac's marking of a half-century since his death: by some divine chance, the proceedings were scheduled to open on the precise day of the anniversary, 19 August. Two operas, three ballet evenings, six concerts, six lectures and an exhibition all had a Diaghilev 'motif'. But here too he would be frustrated, both by his own thin skin ('I never felt really welcome in the city,' he admitted in his memoirs[44]) and by the tight-fisted puritanism of the City Fathers on whose funding the festival depended. His assistant in Edinburgh, Richard Jarman, feels that 'dance, ironically, was the weakest element of his Festival programming'.[45] Drummond left after five years in the job and returned to the BBC as Controller of Music, charged with responsibility for Radio 3 and the Proms. Here he became progressively more enraged by a culture that prioritised bean-counting management over imaginative creativity, and his memoirs, published in 2000, conclude with a violent tirade:

> The lowest common denominator, accessibility-at-any-price,
> anti-intellectual laziness of so many of today's leaders not only
> in politics, but also in education and the arts, is for me a form of
> appeasement. Failing or refusing to differentiate between the good
> and the indifferent, while sheltering under a cloak of spurious
> democracy, is simply not good enough. It is a betrayal of all our
> civilisation has stood for.[46]

A heroic but doomed rearguard action this, its weakness being the arrogation of the authority to pontificate over what was 'good' and what was 'indifferent'. In recent years, Drummond's detractors have pretty much triumphed, and such a position can no longer be held, as the canon that imperially championed the work of white Western males has been forced to acknowledge more diverse demographic constituencies. If Diaghilev was ahead of his time, Drummond was behind his.

Complementing Drummond's 1968 film is *Ballets Russes*, a documentary released in 2005. Its source was a three-day conference in New Orleans organised in 1999 by a wealthy American arts administrator and balletomane called Douglas Blair Turnbaugh.[47] Toumanova had died in 1996, Danilova a year later, but several stars of the 1930s could still reminisce and radiate: Baronova and

Riabouchinska from de Basil's company, for example, and Markova and Franklin from Denham's. Members of Denham's company are still alive at the time of writing.[48]

Carved through the air, great dancing evanesces like perfume. It has a short uncertain life once its progenitors have passed on: very little choreography has the eternal force of poetry or painting. The camera can only flatten it into two dimensions: its external movement may be transmitted through video and notation, but not its soul. Tracing the subcutaneous filigree of gesture and implication relies on the choreographers themselves or those who worked with them, but as distance grows, memory reshapes the original, adding or subtracting or simply misremembering. Corners are cut to suit other bodies and sensibilities, nuances blur and edges blunt and movement evolves into something else, a living thing. We think differently from our forefathers and we move differently too. As Lydia Lopokova wrote in her obituary of Pavlova, 'a dancer can leave nothing behind her. Music will not help us see her again and to feel what she gave us, nor the best words.'[49] Likewise we can only imagine Nijinsky's art, and what we fantasise must bear scant relation to the reality. Styles change, as do human physiques and ideas about formative training and elegant technique. Would Petipa recognise much of what is now performed in his name? He would surely be amazed at the height and skinniness of the ballerinas; he might well be aghast at the extreme extension of their legs and the complex aerial manoeuvres of their male partners, not to mention the glare of electric stage lighting or the Lycra tights. Perhaps Karsavina's charm and Nijinsky's charisma would today look merely quaint.

And thus what remains of the Ballets Russes in the twenty-first century is the stuff of shadows and outlines, images frozen in books, memories of other people's memories. The delicately perfumed romanticism of Fokine's *Les Sylphides* has faded into the genteel and archaic; his *Scheherazade*, once so perversely erotic, looks like tawdry kitsch. The best that can be said of Millicent Hodson's and Kenneth Archer's efforts between 1987 and 1996 to reconstruct Nijinsky's *The Rite of Spring, Jeux* and *Till Eulenspiegel* from the flotsam of fragmentary memories, critical accounts and photographs is that they are speculative to the point of being hypothetical;[50] only the relatively static miniature *L'Après-midi d'un faune* survives in what can be presumed fairly 'authentic' form, thanks largely to the interpretation of Nijinsky's notes by Ann Hutchinson Guest in the 1980s. But its interest is now primarily academic. Massine's oeuvre, extolled as challengingly innovative in the pre-war years, had dated fatally by the 1960s as its grandly abstract visual statements about existence were exposed as portentously hollow and the hyperactive jerky jokiness of its marionettish comedies calcified. In 1959, using an open-air theatre in the resort of Nervi near Genoa, he made a last attempt to organise a ballet festival that revived the Diaghilev dream of fusing all the arts: money was thrown at it, big names were commissioned and youthful talents promoted, but the over-ambitious enterprise barely lasted two summers.[51]

What of Diaghilev's commissions still lives without artificial support, what retains its immediate artistic impact? Three works only: Balanchine's *Apollon musagète* (now known as simply *Apollo*) and *The Prodigal Son*, both of which he revived and refreshed several times from 1950 onwards for New York City Ballet; and Nijinska's *Les Noces*.

Of the careers of all the major choreographers, Nijinska's was the most itinerant, volatile, stop–start and miscellaneous, peppered with rows and walk-outs. Today this would doubtless be explained as the result of disadvantages and prejudice relative to her gender, but the evidence points the blame at her exasperating and exigent temperament. Capable of nurturing kindness if she liked or rated someone, she could be violently rude if she didn't (underling Adrian Brown remembers her 'punching me aggressively in the belly when I made a slight mistake in rehearsal'[52]). In 1966, at the age of seventy-five, fat, deaf and shouty, she came to London at the invitation of its director, Sir Frederick Ashton, to restage her greatest work for the Royal Ballet.* For the dancers, rehearsals were hellish as this growling arthritic old lady communicated, or failed to communicate, in a macaronic patois of Russian, French and English, abetted by a taciturn husband who sat in a corner disconcertingly scribbling everything into a little black notebook. Monica Mason recalled:

> She couldn't even count one to three in English, and the music for *Les Noces* is so tricky. She would sort of half demonstrate, but she even had difficulty getting us to understand kneeling or bending over with your arms in fifth position facing the front. So it was very slow, and it was exhausting, absolutely exhausting. She asked for total concentration and maximum physical effort a hundred per cent of the time she was in the room. There was no question that you ever marked anything, ever. She was, I think, the most demanding person I've ever worked for. And an eagle eye, she didn't miss a thing.[53]

But she got results. Four decades after its 1923 première, in Goncharova's austere designs, the power of *Les Noces*, drawing on a folk culture that resisted being prettily coloured or emotionally comforting, emerged undimmed. The *Observer* described it as 'the sacrament of a nation's soul';[54] the *Sunday Times* simply gasped,

---

* Two years earlier she had also revived *Les Biches* – a piece that required a theatre smaller than the Royal Opera House to make its full effect.

'There is nothing quite like it.'[55] And even now, at a further half-century of distance, it remains mesmerisingly strange and thrillingly unnerving, a challenge to the conventional canons of classicism, romanticism and modernism.

One last twist. Established in 1974 and itinerant worldwide ever since, Les Ballets Trockadero de Monte Carlo is an all-male drag company with a huge following that presents innocently camp parodies of the Petipa-to-Balanchine repertory. According to its website, 'The comedy is achieved by incorporating and exaggerating the foibles, accidents, and underlying incongruities of serious dance' in a spirit that 'enhances rather than mocks the spirit of dance as an art form'.[56]

With their silly pratfalls and pantomime Russian names – Ludmila Beaulemova, Nadia Doumiafeyva, Varvara Laptopova and so forth – the Trocks, as they are affectionately known, could be seen as representing the *coup de grâce* for the tradition this book has traced, emptying ballet of all its pretensions. Yet beneath the grotesque impersonations and the crude slapstick, there is something touchingly sincere about the way these creatures dance: in their waking dreams they are Karsavina or Baronova. Yes, they are true balletomanes all, making a reverent bow of sorts to Diaghilev's revolutionary endeavour – a phenomenon of rich progeny that enchanted and exalted millions and leaves its mark on history as one of the greater beauties created by the fraught and largely ugly twentieth century.

The basic sources for this chapter are Richard Buckle, *In the Wake of Diaghilev*, passim; Barbara Newman, *Striking a Balance*, passim; Julie Kavanagh, *Secret Muses: The Life of Frederick Ashton*, pp. 280–531; John Drummond, *Speaking of Diaghilev*, passim; Meredith Daneman, *Margot Fonteyn*, pp. 198–527: Robert Gottlieb (ed.), *Reading Dance*, passim; Jennifer Homans, *Apollo's Angels*, pp. 396–550; Jane Pritchard, *Diaghilev and the Golden Age of the Ballets Russes 1909–1929*, pp. 187–204.

# ACKNOWLEDGEMENTS

———

I owe special thanks to Jane Pritchard, the curator of the dance collection of the Victoria and Albert Museum, who read the manuscript with an eagle eye and saved me from many gaffes and omissions. What remains is, of course, my responsibility.

I am also grateful to many other friends and colleagues for their generous help and interest, as well as those who kindly answered queries – among them Adrian Brown; Leslie Caron; Harry Cocks; Eric Colleary; Peter Conrad; Sarah Crompton; Charles Duff; Virginia Fraser; Pamela, Lady Harlech; Nicky Haslam; Selina Hastings; Richard Jarman; Julie Kavanagh; Nancy Lassalle; Bob Lockyer; Alastair Macaulay; Andrew L. Phelan; John Phipps; Miranda Seymour; Nicola Shulman; Belinda Taylor; Ann Webb; Joy Williams.

Acknowledgement for permission to quote is due to Harper-Collins for Richard Buckle, *In the Wake of Diaghilev*; to Faber, for John Drummond, *Speaking of Diaghilev*; and to Suhrkamp Verlag for *The Diaries of Harry Kessler*. Dance Books and the Estate of Richard Buckle have been exceptionally generous in this regard. Every effort has been made to trace other copyright holders.

Libraries whose collections I have consulted are the London Library; British Library; the Victoria and Albert Museum; Trinity Laban; Royal Academy of Dance; Bibliothèque de l'Opéra, Paris; New York Public Library for the Performing Arts at Lincoln Center; Harry Ransom Center, University of Texas at Austin; Ballets

Russes Collection, University of Oklahoma at Norman. The coronavirus pandemic has made archival research much more difficult, but all these institutions have done a heroic job in cruelly difficult circumstances.

I want to pay equal tribute to my wonderful agent of forty years' standing Caroline Dawnay and her assistant Kat Aitken; to my peerless editors Belinda Matthews at Faber and Jeff Seroy at FSG; as well as to Kate Ward's magnificent team at Faber – Jill Burrows, Sam Matthews, Robert Davies and Robbie Porter.

My greatest debt is to my partner Ellis Woodman. No balletomane himself, he has borne manfully with the parturition of this book, as well as making many imaginative and illuminating contributions to my thinking and my prose.

# PICTURE CREDITS

─────

# NOTES

---

Publication details are given in the Bibliography.

## 1 BOUNDARIES

1 Arlene Croce, 'Dance in Film', in *After Images*, p. 439.
2 Lynda Nead, *The Tiger in the Smoke: Art and Culture in Post-War Britain*, p. 551.
3 Michael Powell, *A Life in Movies*, p. 653.
4 Adrienne McLean, '"The Red Shoes" Revisited', p. 77.
5 Croce, p. 439.
6 Steve Rose, *Guardian*, 14 May 2009.
7 Powell, p. 653.
8 Edwin Heathcote, *Financial Times*, 11 April 2020.
9 Quoted in Richard Buckle, *The Adventures of a Ballet Critic*, pp. 224–6; see also pp. 172–6.
10 Kenneth Tynan, *A View of the English Stage*, pp. 348–50.
11 A. H. Franks, *Ballet: A Decade of Endeavour*, p. 43.
12 Quoted in Rupert Christiansen, *The Visitors*, p. 165.
13 Ramsay Burt, *The Male Dancer*, and Peter Stoneley, *A Queer History of the Ballet*, passim.
14 John Drummond, *Speaking of Diaghilev*, pp. 49–50.
15 Richard Hough, *First Sea Lord*, p. 59.
16 See Victoria Philips, *Martha Graham's Cold War*, passim; Malcolm McCormick and Nancy Reynolds, *No Fixed Points: Dance in the Twentieth Century*, pp. 393–9; Susan Au, *Ballet and Modern Dance*; and Jack Anderson, *Ballet and Modern Dance*, passim.
17 See Julie Kavanagh, *Secret Muses: The Life of Frederick Ashton*, and David Vaughan, *Frederick Ashton and his Ballets*, passim.
18 See Robert Gottlieb, *Balanchine: The Ballet Maker*; Bernard Taper, *Balanchine*, and Robert Garis, *Following Balanchine*, passim.
19 Jennifer Homans, *Apollo's Angels*, pp. 547–9.

## 2 ROOTS

1 Prince Peter Lieven, *The Birth of the Ballets Russes*, p. 27.
2 Arnold Haskell, *Diaghileff*, p. 42.
3 Rupert Christiansen, *The Voice of Victorian Sex: Arthur H. Clough*, pp. 27–8.
4 See Ivor Guest, *Ballet in Leicester Square*, passim.
5 Alexandra Carter, *Dance and Dancers in the Victorian and Edwardian Music Hall Ballet*, p. 64.
6 Ivor Guest, *The Paris Opéra Ballet*, p. 66.
7 Rayner Heppenstall, in Lincoln Kirstein, *Ballet Alphabet*, p. 12.
8 Anatole Chujoy, 'Russian balletomania', p. 49.
9 Ibid., p. 52.
10 Ibid., p. 67.
11 See Marius Petipa, *Mémoires*; and Nadine Meisner, *Marius Petipa: The Emperor's Ballet Master*, passim.
12 'Tchaikovsky at the Russian ballet', souvenir programme for *The Sleeping Princess*, Alhambra Theatre, London, 1921, p. 8.
13 Quoted in Roland John Wiley, *Tchaikovsky's Ballets*, p. 275.
14 Quoted in Haskell, p. 42.
15 Alexandre Benois, *Memoirs*, vol. ii, pp. 18 and 79.
16 Quoted in Haskell, p. 42.
17 Benois, p. 76; quoted in Sieng Scheijen, *Diaghilev: A Life*, pp. 54–5.
18 Quoted in Scheijen, p. 15.
19 See Dan Healy, *Homosexual Desire in Revolutionary Russia*, pp. 25–30.
20 Quoted in Scheijen, p. 5.
21 Ibid., p. 80.
22 Quoted in Lieven, p. 32.
23 Cyril Beaumont, *The Diaghilev Ballet in London*, p. 232.
24 Quoted in Haskell, p. 76.
25 Quoted in Scheijen, p. 95.
26 Benois, pp. 216–17.
27 Quoted in Scheijen, p. 134.
28 Benois, p. 250.
29 Quoted in Richard Buckle, *Diaghilev*, p. 111.

## 3 BEGINNINGS

1 Michael Fokine, *Memoirs of a Ballet Master*, p. 69.

2  See Isadora Duncan, *My Life*, autobiographical but very unreliable, and Peter Kurth, *Isadora: A Sensational Life*, passim.

3  Nikolai Legat, *The Story of the Russian School*, p. 66.

4  See Keith Money, *Anna Pavlova: Her Life and Art*, and Jane Pritchard and Caroline Hamilton, *Anna Pavlova: Twentieth-Century Ballerina*, passim.

5  For a personal perspective, see Nesta Macdonald, *Tamara Karsavina*; for the years up to 1918, Andrew R. Foster, *Tamara Karsavina: Diaghilev's Ballerina*, passim; for her later years, Richard Buckle, *In the Wake of Diaghilev*, pp. 91–9; and Tamara Karsavina, *Tamara Karsavina: Beyond the Ballerina*, passim.

6  For critical assessment of his dancing style, see Edwin Denby, 'Notes on Nijinsky Photographs', and Lincoln Kirstein, *Nijinsky Dancing*, passim.

7  Richard Buckle Collection (as yet uncatalogued), Harry Ransom Center, University of Texas, Doc. Box 3.

8  Ibid., Doc. Box 24.

9  Igor Stravinsky, *Memories and Commentaries*, p. 35.

10  Richard Buckle Collection, Doc. Box 3.

11  *Dancing Times*, June 1938, pp. 268–9.

12  Marie Rambert, *Ballet*, May 1950, p. 22.

13  S. L. Grigoriev, *The Diaghilev Ballet 1909–1929*, pp. 4–5.

14  Prince Peter Lieven, *The Birth of the Ballets Russes*, p. 225.

15  Arnold Haskell, *Diaghileff*, p. 182.

16  Tamara Karsavina, *Theatre Street*, p. 229.

17  Quoted in Buckle, *In the Wake*, p. 200.

18  Lieven, p. 95.

19  Quoted in Haskell, p. 178.

20  Cyril Beaumont, *The Diaghilev Ballet in London*, p. 16.

21  Legat, pp. 75–6.

22  *Le Figaro*, 26 May 1909.

23  Arnold Bennett, *Paris Nights*, p. 69

24  See Michael de Cossart, *Ida Rubinstein: A Theatrical Life*, passim.

25  Lieven, p. 119.

26  Alexandre Benois, *Memoirs*, vol. II, p. 241.

27  Marcel Proust, *La Prisonnière*, chapter 42.

28  Harry Kessler, *Journey to the Abyss: The Diaries of Count Harry Kessler 1880–1918*, p. 494.

29  Alexandre Benois, *Reminiscences of the Russian Ballet*, pp. 299–300.

30 Lieven, p. 94.

31 Vaslav Nijinsky, *The Diary of Vaslav Nijinsky*, pp. 103–4.

32 Quoted in Scheijen, p. 191.

33 Fokine, p. 156.

34 Quoted in Charles Spencer, *Léon Bakst*, p. 70.

35 Benois, *Reminiscences of the Russian Ballet*, pp. 315–16.

36 Osbert Lancaster, *Homes, Sweet Homes*, p. 58. See also Mary E. Davis, *Ballets Russes Style*, passim.

37 Lieven, pp. 125–6.

38 Muriel Draper, *Music at Midnight*, p. 141.

39 Quoted in Lieven, p. 160.

40 V. Nijinsky, *The Diary of Vaslav Nijinsky*, p. xliv.

41 Benois, *Reminiscences of the Russian Ballet*, p. 334.

42 Georges Banks, 'Pétrouchka – The Russian Ballet', p. 58.

43 Stewart Headlam, *The Ballet*, passim; see also Rupert Christiansen, *The Visitors*, pp. 197–9.

44 Lydia Kyasht, *Romantic Recollections*, p. 171.

45 See Alexandra Carter, *Dance and Dancers in the Victorian and Edwardian Music Hall Ballet*, and Catherine Hindson, *Female Performance Practice on the fin-de-siècle Popular Stages of London and Paris*, passim.

46 Virginia Woolf, *Mr Bennett and Mrs Brown*, p. 3.

47 Ralph Furse, *Aucuparius*, p. 43.

48 Quoted in Susan Jones, 'Diaghilev and British Writing', p. 68.

49 *Daily News*, 22 June 1911.

## 4 TRIUMPHS

1 S. L. Grigoriev, *The Diaghilev Ballet 1910–1929*, p. 65.

2 Quoted in Sjeng Scheijen, *Diaghilev: A Life*, p. 253.

3 Letter to Richard Buckle from Duncan Grant, 23 March 1968, Richard Buckle Collection, Harry Ransom Center, Doc. Box 26.

4 Cyril Beaumont, *The Diaghilev Ballet in London*, p. 69. See also Kenneth Archer and Millicent Hodson, 'The Lost Pleasure Garden'.

5 Tamara Karsavina, *Theatre Street*, p. 285.

6 Quoted in Scheijen, p. 268.

7 Prince Peter Lieven, *The Birth of Ballets Russes*, p. 189.

8 Vaslav Nijinsky, *The Diary of Vaslav Nijinsky*, p. 207.

9 See Gillian Moore, *The Rite of Spring: The Music of Modernity*, pp. 63–124.

10 Igor Stravinsky, *Memories and Commentaries*, p. 34.

11 Marie Rambert, *Quicksilver*, passim.

12 Lydia Sokolova, *Dancing for Diaghilev*, p. 42.

13 Beaumont, p. 73.

14 Rambert, pp. 63–4.

15 Jean Cocteau, *A Call to Order*, p. 46; quoted from *L'Intransigeant* by Ton van Kalmthout and F. T. Marinetti, '"Batailles et ideés futuristes": 17 Letters from F. T. Marinetti, 1912–13', p. 140.

16 Harry Kessler, *Journey to the Abyss: The Diaries of Count Harry Kessler 1880–1918*, p. 619.

17 Jean Cocteau, *Cock and Harlequin: Notes Concerning Music*, p. 48.

18 Kessler, p. 619.

19 Quoted in Romola Nijinsky, *Nijinsky*, pp. 165–6.

20 Sokolova, p. 43.

21 Robert Craft and Igor Stravinsky, *Conversations with Igor Stravinsky*, p. 46.

22 Kessler, pp. 619–20.

23 Cocteau, *A Call to Order*, p. 52.

24 Quoted in Lucy Moore, *Nijinsky*, p. 134.

25 Kessler, pp. 619–20.

26 'Easter 1916', in W. B. Yeats, *The Poems*, p. 228.

27 Lucy Moore, p. 144.

28 Quoted in Nesta Macdonald, *Diaghilev Observed*, p. 97.

29 Quoted in Jonathan Croall, *Sybil Thorndike: A Star of Life*, p. 92.

30 Quoted in Rupert Christiansen, *The Visitors*, p. 233.

31 Richard Buckle Collection, Doc. Box 3.

32 Grigoriev, p. 92.

33 Quoted in Lucy Moore, p. 171.

34 Michel Fokine, *Memoirs of a Ballet Master*, p. 227.

35 Karsavina, pp. 295–6.

36 Beaumont, p. 99.

37 Charles Ricketts, *Self-Portrait Taken from the Letters and Journals of Charles Ricketts*, pp. 233–7.

38 See Leonide Massine, *My Life in Ballet*, pp. 11–43.

39 Quoted in John Richardson, *A Life of Picasso: The Triumphant Years 1917–1932*, pp. 7–8.

40 Richard Buckle Collection, Doc. Box 3.

41 Quoted in Scheijen, p. 296.
42 Richard Buckle, *Diaghilev*, p. 270.
43 Sokolova, p. 64.
44 Buckle, p. 274.


## 5 WAR

1 Leonide Massine, *My Life in Ballet*, p. 70.
2 Lydia Sokolova, *Dancing for Diaghilev*, p. 71.
3 Quoted in Vicente Garcia-Marquez, *Massine*, p. 48.
4 Ibid., pp. 49–54.
5 See Judith Mackrell, *Bloomsbury Ballerina*, passim, and Milo Keynes, *Lydia Lopokova*, passim.
6 Richard Buckle Collection, Harry Ransom Center, Doc. Box 6.
7 *Kansas City Star*, 5 March 1916.
8 S. L. Grigoriev, *The Diaghilev Ballet 1909–1929*, p. 111.
9 Sokolova, p. 77.
10 *New York Journal*, 7 April 1916.
11 Quoted in Richard Buckle, *Diaghilev*, p. 313.
12 Jean Cocteau, *Le Rappel à l'ordre*, pp. 54–8.
13 Sokolova, p. 87.
14 Robert Edmond Jones, 'Nijinsky and Til Eulenspiegel'.
15 Ibid., p. 4.
16 *New York Times*, 17 October 1916.
17 Richard Buckle Collection, Doc. Box 3.
18 Sokolova, p. 86.
19 Grigoriev, p. 115.
20 Quoted in Lucy Moore, *Nijinsky*, p. 188.
21 Grigoriev, p. 117.
22 Richard Buckle Collection, Banker's Box 11.
23 Lynn Garafola, 'The Ballets Russes in America', p. 73.
24 Grigoriev, p. 119.
25 Sjeng Scheijen, *Diaghilev: A Life*, p. 331.
26 Arthur Gold and Robert Fizdale, *Misia: The Life of Misia Sert*, p. 225.
27 See Kenneth E. Silver, *Esprit de Corps: The Art of the Parisian Avant-garde*, pp. 113–32.
28 Jean Cocteau, *Call to Order*, p. 238.

29 Grigoriev, p. 121.

30 Michel-Georges Michel, *Ballets Russes: Histoire anecdotique*, p. 30.

31 Quoted in Roger Nichols, *Poulenc*, p. 14.

32 Quoted in Buckle, p. 331.

33 Ibid., p. 98.

34 Jane Stevenson, *Baroque between the Wars*, pp. 282–3.

35 Ibid., p. 122.

36 See María Gabriela Estrada, *The Legacy of Félix Fernández García*, pp. 113–17.

37 Ibid., p. 122.

38 Vicente Garcia-Marquez, *Massine*, p. 111.

39 Quoted in Buckle, p. 342.

40 Ibid., p. 135.

41 Ibid., p. 125.

42 Quoted in Garcia-Marquez, p. 118.

43 Ibid., p. 128.

44 *Observer*, 11 September 1918.

45 Richard Buckle Collection, Doc. Box 3.

46 'Dancers of the Twenties', *Dancing Times*, February 1967, p. 252.

47 *Sunday Times*, 22 June 1919.

48 *The Nation*, 18 June 1919.

49 Garcia-Marquez, p. 129.

50 Buckle, p. 358.

51 Sokolova, p. 134.

52 Massine, pp. 141–2.

53 *Observer*, 27 July 1919.

54 Tamara Karsavina, *Theatre Street*, p. 300.

55 Harry Kessler, *The Diaries of a Cosmopolitan 1918–1937*, p. 269.

56 Romola Nijinsky, *Nijinsky*, p. 393.

57 Maurice Sandoz, *The Crystal Salt-cellar*, pp. 72–6.

58 Igor Stravinsky and Robert Craft, *Expositions and Developments*, p. 113.

59 Sokolova, p. 151.

60 Buckle, p. 362.

61 Igor Stravinsky and Robert Craft, *Memories and Commentaries*, p. 42.

62 Grigoriev, p. 159.

63 Sokolova, p. 166.

64 *The Times*, 28 June 1921.

65 Quoted in André Levinson, *Dance Writings from Paris in the Twenties*, p. 40.

66 Sokolova, p. 161.
67 Richard Buckle Collection, Banker's Box 11.
68 Sokolova, p. 161.
69 Ibid., p. 173.


## 6 NOVELTIES

1 S. L. Grigoriev, *The Diaghilev Ballet, 1909–1929*, p. 157.
2 Quoted in Sjeng Scheijen, *Diaghilev: A Life*, p. 349.
3 *Observer*, 27 July 1919.
4 André Levinson, 'A Crisis in the Ballets Russes', p. 787.
5 Cyril Beaumont, *The Diaghilev Ballet in London*, p. 227. See Richard Buckle, *In the Wake of Diaghilev* pp. 20–36 and 321–34. A full biography of this remarkable but evasive figure is wanting.
6 Quoted in Richard Buckle, *Diaghilev*, p. 377.
7 Ibid., p. 379.
8 Sotheby's, *Collection Boris Kochno* (auction catalogue), p. 188.
9 Ibid., p. 190.
10 Quoted in Boris Kochno, *Diaghilev and the Ballets Russes*, pp. 284–5.
11 Scheijen, p. 368.
12 Grigoriev, p. 170.
13 Quoted in Lynn Garafola, *Diaghilev's Ballets Russes*, p. 124.
14 Charles Spencer, *Léon Bakst*, p. 189.
15 Ibid.
16 Beaumont, p. 202.
17 *Daily Mail*, 3 November 1921.
18 *The Times*, 3 November 1921.
19 *Vogue*, December 1921.
20 Lytton Strachey, *Ballet – To Poland*, p. 17.
21 Quoted in Lynn Garafola, *Legacies of Twentieth-century Dance*, p. 66.
22 Quoted in Grigoriev, p. 174.
23 Quoted in Kochno, p. 172.
24 Ibid.
25 Osbert Lancaster, *With an Eye to the Future*, p. 17.
26 Richard Buckle, *The Diaghilev Exhibition*, p. 3.
27 See Mark Braude, *Making Monte Carlo: A History of Speculation and Spectacle*, passim.

28 Lancaster, p. 101.

29 Stephanie Jordan, programme for *Les Noces*, Royal Ballet (1954), p. 29.

30 Quoted in Scheijen, p. 384.

31 Lydia Sokolova, *Dancing for Diaghilev*, p. 207.

32 See Serge Lifar, *Ma Vie: from Kiev to Kiev: An Autobiography*, passim, and Jean-Pierre Pastori, *Serge Lifar: la beauté du diable*, passim.

33 Anton Dolin, *Last Words*, pp. 38–9.

34 Quoted in John Drummond, *Speaking of Diaghilev*, p. 46.

35 Beaumont, p. 246.

36 Garafola, *Diaghilev's Ballets Russes*, p. 130.

37 Roger Nichols, *Poulenc*, pp. 59–60.

38 Grigoriev, p. 195.

39 Dolin, p. 115.

40 See Alexandra Danilova, *Choura*, passim.

41 Vernon Duke, *Passport to Paris*, p. 137.

42 Sokolova, p. 233.

43 Igor Stravinsky and Robert Craft, *Memories and Commentaries*, p. 41.

44 Duke, pp. 124–5.

45 William McBrien, *Cole Porter*, pp. 96–9.

46 *Observer*, 11 January 1925.

47 *Vogue*, December 1925.

48 *Morning Post*, 4 June 1925.

49 Quoted in Nesta Macdonald, *Diaghilev Observed*, p. 323.

50 See Alicia Markova, *Markova Remembers*, passim.

51 Richard Buckle Collection, Harry Ransom Center, Doc. Box 3.

52 Sokolova, p. 233.

53 Polly Hill and Richard Keynes (eds), *Lydia and Maynard: Letters*, p. 266.

54 Bernard Taper, *Balanchine*, p. 90.

55 Ethel Mannin, *Young in the Twenties: A Chapter of Autobiography*, p. 114.

56 Danilova, p. 71.

57 Quoted in Garafola, p. 249.

58 Grigoriev, p. 220.

59 Ibid.

60 *The Diaghilev Ballet in England*, exhibition catalogue, p. 53.

61 Ibid., p. 55.

62 Lincoln Kirstein, *Mosaic*, p. 244.

63 Constant Lambert, *Music Ho!*, p. 86.

64 Lydia Lopokova, *Vogue*, 2 August 1926.
65 Alexandre Benois, *Reminiscences of the Russian Ballet*, pp. 376–7.
66 *The Times*, 29 June 1926.
67 Buckle, *Diaghilev*, p. 485.
68 Sokolova, p. 259.
69 Beaumont, p. 278.
70 Grigoriev, p. 242.
71 *Morning Post*, 10 July 1928.
72 Lifar, p. 68.
73 Harry Kessler, *The Diaries of a Cosmopolitan 1918–1937*, p. 355.
74 Tamara Karsavina, *Theatre Street*, p. 295.
75 Grigoriev, p. 242.
76 See Igor Markevitch, *Être et avoir été*, passim.
77 Ibid., p. 177.
78 Ibid., p. 192.
79 Quoted in Scheijen, p. 443.
80 Ibid., p. 442.
81 Scheijen, p. 444.

## 7 RIVALS

1 S.O., 'The Russians at Drury Lane', *English Review* (June 1914), p. 562.
2 Austen Harrison, letter in private collection.
3 Quoted in Rupert Christiansen, *The Visitors*, p. 234.
4 Michael Holroyd, *Lytton Strachey*, p. 291.
5 Anne Chisholm (ed.), *Carrington's Letters*, pp. 123, 113.
6 Quoted in Lucy Moore, *Nijinsky*, p. 115.
7 Ada Leverson, *Tenterhooks*, chapter 6.
8 Lynn Garafola, *Diaghilev's Ballets Russes*, p. 322.
9 D. H. Lawrence, *Women in Love*, chapter 8.
10 Cecil Beaton, *Ballet*, p. 19.
11 Ethel Mannin, *Young in the Twenties: A Chapter of Autobiography*, p. 114.
12 Quoted in John Drummond, *Speaking of Diaghilev*, p. 211.
13 Ethel Mannin, *Confessions and Impressions*, p. 262.
14 Quoted in Lisa Immordino Vreeland, *Love, Cecil*, p. 73.
15 Quoted in Martin Burgess Green, *Children of the Gods*, p. 86.
16 *Vogue*, 11 July 1928.

17  Quoted in Allison Abra, *Dancing in the English Style*, p. 92.

18  Mannin, *Young in the Twenties*, p. 31.

19  James Laver, *Between the Wars*, pp. 98–9.

20  *The Criterion*, 1/3 (1923), pp. 305–6.

21  See Karen Eliot, *Albion's Dance*, pp. 14–21, for biographical essays on
    Beaumont and Richardson.

22  See Lillian Browse, *The Duchess of Cork Street*, pp. 29–48, for a vivid
    account of ballet classes with Craske and others in the 1920s and 1930s.

23  Garafola, pp. 330–44, and *The Sitwells and the Arts of the 1920s and 1930s*,
    exhibition catalogue, passim.

24  See James Harding, *Cochran*, passim.

25  Leslie Norton, *Léonide Massine and the 20th Century Ballet*, p. 105.

26  Anton Dolin, *Autobiography*, pp. 40–41.

27  *Daily Mirror*, 23 September 1927.

28  Quoted in Kathrine Sorley Walker, 'The Camargo Society'.

29  Richard Buckle, *The Adventures of a Ballet Critic*, p. 46.

30  *Dancing Times*, January 1929, p. 856.

31  See Ninette de Valois, *Come Dance with Me: A Memoir, 1898–1956*, passim.

32  *Dancing Times*, February 1926, pp. 589–90.

33  Quoted in Kathrine Sorley Walker, *Ninette de Valois: Idealist Without
    Illusions*, p. 86.

34  See Marie Rambert, *Quicksilver*, pp. 125–61; and Julie Kavanagh, *Secret
    Muses: The Life of Frederick Ashton*, pp. 60–89.

35  Arnold Haskell, *Balletomania Then and Now*, p. 203, and *In His True Centre:
    An Interim Autobiography*, pp. 96–102.

36  See Alexander Bland, *The Royal Ballet: The First 50 Years*; Zoe Anderson,
    *The Royal Ballet: 75 Years*; Mary Clarke, *Dancers of Mercury: The Story of the
    Ballet Rambert*; and Clement Crisp, Anya Sainsbury and Peter Williams
    (eds), *Ballet Rambert: 50 Years and On*; all passim.

37  Roger Nichols, *The Harlequin Years*, p. 25.

38  See Louis Epstein, 'Impresario, Interrupted: Comte Étienne de Beaumont
    and the Soirées de Paris'.

39  Quoted in Richard Buckle, *Diaghilev*, p. 426.

40  Quoted in Boris Kochno, *Diaghilev and the Ballets Russes*, p. 256.

41  Polly Hill and Richard Keynes (eds), *Lydia and Maynard: Letters*, p. 190.

42  *Les Ballets Suédois: Une compagnie d'avant-garde 1920–1925*, p. 19. See
    also Erik Naslund, *Rolf de Maré: Art Collector – Ballet Director – Museum*

*Curator*, passim; George Dorris, 'Jean Börlin'; Lynn Garafola, 'Rivals
for the New: The Ballets Suédois and the Ballets Russes', in *Legacies of
Twentieth-century Dance*, pp. 107–24; and George Dorris, 'The Many
Worlds of Rolf de Maré'.

43 Quoted in Lynn Haney, *Naked at the Feast*, p. 104.
44 Ibid., p. 54.
45 Harry Kessler, *The Diaries of a Cosmopolitan 1918–1937*, p. 280.
46 Julie Kavanagh, *Secret Muses: The Life of Frederick Ashton*, pp. 100–101; Charles
   S. Mayer,'Ida Rubinstein: A Twentieth-Century Cleopatra', and Elaine
   Brody, 'The Legacy of Ida Rubinstein: Mata Hari of the Ballets Russes'.
47 Quoted in Sjeng Scheijen, *Diaghilev: A Life*, p. 427.
48 *The Times*, 13 July 1929.

## 8 SUCCESSORS

1 *The Times*, 20 August 1929.
2 *Daily Express*, 21 August 1929.
3 Quoted by 'The Sitter Out', *Dancing Times*, September 1929, p. 512.
4 Arnold Haskell, *Diaghileff*, p. 16.
5 Vicente Garcia-Marquez, *Massine*, p. 209.
6 Arnold Haskell, *Balletomania: The Story of an Obsession*, pp. 240–4.
7 Alexandra Danilova, *Choura*, pp. 16, 134.
8 Kathrine Sorley Walker, *De Basil's Ballets Russes*, p. 37.
9 Michael Meylac, *Behind the Scenes at the Ballets Russes*, p. 45.
10 Robert Gottlieb, *George Balanchine: The Ballet Maker*, p. 65.
11 *Dancing Times*, 10 August 1933, p. 457. See also *Les Ballets 33*, Brighton Art
   Gallery exhibition catalogue, passim.
12 See Lincoln Kirstein, *Mosaic*, passim.
13 Quoted in Gottlieb, *Balanchine*, p. 69.
14 Ibid.
15 See James Steichen, *Balanchine and Kirstein's American Enterprise*, passim.
16 Lesley Blanch, *Journey into the Mind's Eye*, p. 212.
17 Adrian Stokes, *Tonight the Ballet*, p. 125. For the legacy, Andrew Forge
   interview, Tape 36, Side B, British Library co466x.
18 Sorley Walker, p. 21.
19 Garcia-Marquez, *Massine*, p. 222.
20 Ibid., p. 229.

21 A. V. Coton, *A Prejudice for Ballet*, p. 80.

22 Ibid., p. 89.

23 Haskell, *Balletomania: The Story of an Obsession*, p. 250.

24 Edwin Denby, *Dance Writings*, pp. 39–40.

25 Lincoln Kirstein, *Blast at Ballet*, p. 11.

26 Vicente Garcia-Marquez, *The Ballets Russes: Colonel de Basil's Ballets Russes de Monte Carlo*, p. 136.

27 Arnold Haskell, *In his True Centre: An Interim Autobiography*, p. 134.

28 Quoted in Meylac, p. 48.

29 Quoted in Judith Chazin-Bennahum, *Rene Blum and the Ballets Russes*, p. 125.

30 Quoted in Meylac, p. 46.

31 Quoted in Victoria Tennant, *Irina Baronova and the Ballets Russes de Monte Carlo*, p. 77.

32 Quoted in Meylac, p. 24.

33 Ralph Furse, *Aucuparius*, p. 43.

34 Gottlieb, *Balanchine*, p. 65.

35 Sorley Walker, p. 65.

36 Quoted in Sorley Walker, p. 51; see also *Reminiscences of Ballets Russes Dancers*, p. 16.

37 Danilova, p. 120.

38 Tennant, p. 82.

39 See Haskell, *In his True Centre*, passim.

40 Arnold Haskell, *Balletomania Then and Now*, p. 185.

41 *Dancing Times*, November 1934, pp. 129–30.

42 Ibid., October 1936, p. 3.

43 Quoted in Leslie Baily, *Leslie Baily's BBC Scrapbooks*, p. 145.

44 *Dancing Times*, September 1938, p. 628.

45 Francis Toye, *Illustrated London News*, 30 July 1938.

46 Leslie Baily, *Leslie Baily's BBC Scrapbook: 1918–1939*.

47 Vernon Duke, *Passport to Paris*, pp. 328–9.

48 Stephen Williams, *Evening Standard*, 27 July 1938.

49 Caryl Brahms and S. J. Simon, *A Bullet in the Ballet*, chapter 5.

50 Haskell, *Balletomania: The Story of an Obsession*, p. 299. See also Ramsay Burt, *The Male Dancer*, passim.

51 See Arlene Croce, 'Dance in Film', in *Afterimages*, pp. 427–45; Adrienne McLean, 'The Image of the Ballet Artist in Popular Films', and *Dying Swans and Madmen: Ballet, the Body, and Narrative Cinema*, passim.

52  *Dancing Times*, October 1938, p. 22

53  John Culhane, *Walt Disney's Fantasia*, p. 170.

54  Janet Flanner, *The New Yorker*, 24 July 1937.

55  *New York Times*, 6 February 1938, p. 6.

56  Quoted in Leslie Norton, *Frederic Franklin*, p. 30.

57  Arnold Haskell, *Dancing Times*, July 1938, p. 393.

58  Haskell, *Balletomania Then and Now*, p. 187.

59  Cyril Beaumont, *Dancers under my Lens*, pp. 126–37.

60  *Dancing Times*, June 1939, p. 261.

61  Edwin Denby, *Looking at the Dance*, p. 195.

62  Garcia-Marquez, *Massine*, p. 272.

63  Sol Hurok, *Sol Hurok Presents: A Memoir of the Dance World*, p. 126.

64  Jack Anderson, *The One and Only: Ballet Russe de Monte Carlo*, p. 63.

65  Quoted in Robert Gottlieb, *Reading Dance*, p. 556.

66  Kirstein, p. 21.

67  See Dominick Dunne, 'The Rockefeller and the Ballet Boys'; Gérard Mannoni, *Le Marquis de Cuevas*, passim; Francisca Folch-Couyoumdjian, *The Marquis de Cuevas: Pushing the Boundaries of Self*, passim.

68  Press cuttings in Marquis de Cuevas Collection, Harry Ransom Center, University of Texas, undated.

69  See Julian Braunsweg, *Braunsweg's Ballet Scandals*, passim.

70  Ibid., p. 157.

71  Jennifer Homans, *Apollo's Angels*, p. 353. See also Jonathan Gray, 'Sixty Years of the Bolshoi', and Anne Searcy, *Ballet in the Cold War*, passim.

## 9 SURVIVORS

1  Nesta Macdonald, *Tamara Karsavina*, passim; Richard Buckle, *In the Wake of Diaghilev*, pp. 91–6, 304–8.

2  Buckle, *Wake*, p. 93.

3  Quoted in Meredith Daneman, *Margot Fonteyn*, p. 304.

4  Quoted in Barbara Newman, *Striking a Balance*, p. 252.

5  Romola Nijinsky, *Nijinsky*, pp. 341–3; also Peter Ostvald, *Vaslav Nijinsky: A Leap into Madness* (a detailed psychiatric case study), passim; and Lucy Moore, *Nijinsky*, pp. 218–34.

6  Buckle, *Wake*, p. 87.

7  Lincoln Kirstein, *Mosaic*, p. 212.

8 Muriel Draper, *Music at Midnight*, p. 188.

9 See Buckle, 'Les Quatre Saisons de Boris Kochno', pp. 7–11; Boris Kochno, *Christian Bérard*, passim; Marie-Françoise Christout and Fernande Bassan, 'Les Ballets des Champs-Elysées'.

10 Richard Buckle, *The Adventures of a Ballet Critic*, p. 171; see also Gérard Mannoni, *Roland Petit* and *Roland Petit: Rythme de vie*, passim.

11 Quoted in Daneman, p. 212.

12 Personal interview.

13 Ibid. See also Buckle, *Adventures*, p. 74, and Sarah Clair, *Jean Babilée*, passim.

14 Buckle, 'Les Quatre Saisons', p. 9.

15 See *The Most Upsetting Woman*, *The Adventures of a Ballet Critic* and *In the Wake of Diaghilev*. These three volumes of autobiography overlap considerably. See also *Buckle at the Ballet: Selected Criticism*, passim. Buckle's papers are deposited in the Harry Ransom Center, University of Texas at Austin.

16 Buckle, *Wake*, p. 39.

17 Buckle, *The Most Upsetting Woman*, p. 245.

18 Edwin Denby, *Dancers, Buildings and People in the Streets*, p. 221.

19 Buckle, *Buckle at the Ballet*, pp. 250, 255.

20 Buckle, *Wake*, p. 283.

21 Ibid., p. 67.

22 Ibid., p. 266.

23 Ibid., pp. 266–7.

24 Ibid., p. 334.

25 Ibid., p. 325.

26 Ibid., p. 164.

27 E. M. Forster, *Observer*, 25 December 1955.

28 Personal interview.

29 Buckle, *Wake*, p. 174, and *The Diaghilev Exhibition*, passim. See also Alexander Schouvaloff, 'The Diaghilev Legend' in John E. Bowlt et al., *A Feast of Wonders: Sergei Diaghilev and the Ballets Russes*, pp. 95–9.

30 Ibid., p. 223. On Diamantidi, see https://elhg.org.uk/discovery/lives/lives-anthony-diamantidi.

31 Alexander Schouvaloff, *The Art of the Ballets Russes*, p. 98.

32 *Sunday Times*, 25 February 1973, and Jane Pritchard, *Diaghilev and the Golden Age of the Ballets Russes*, pp. 166–7.

33 Lynn Garafola, *Legacies of Twentieth-century Dance*, pp. 377–400, and *The Times*, 10 May 1984.

34 George Dorris, 'Dicky's Greatest Show'.

35 Cecil Beaton, *The Unexpurgated Beaton*, pp. 213–14.

36 *The Times*, 23 June 1971.

37 *Guardian*, 23 June 1971.

38 John Drummond, *Tainted by Experience*, passim.

39 John Drummond, *Speaking of Diaghilev*, pp. 7–8.

40 Ibid., p. 8.

41 Ibid., p. 75.

42 Ibid., p. 73.

43 Ibid., p. ix.

44 Drummond, *Tainted by Experience*, p. 236.

45 Personal interview.

46 Drummond, *Tainted by Experience*, p. 459.

47 Leigh Windreich, 'Memory Lane'.

48 For example, Joy Williams, a member of the company 1945–8 and subsequently of Roland Petit's Ballets de Paris.

49 Quoted in Lucy Moore, p. 252.

50 Kenneth Archer and Millicent Hodson, 'The Lost Pleasure Garden', and Joan Acocella, 'The Lost Nijinsky'.

51 Vicente Garcia-Marquez, *Massine*, pp. 355–62.

52 Personal interview.

53 Quoted in Newman, pp. 308–9.

54 *Observer*, 27 March 1966.

55 *Sunday Times*, 27 March 1966.

56 https://trockadero.org.

# BIBLIOGRAPHY

Abra, Allison, *Dancing in the English Style* (Manchester, 2017)

Acocella, Joan, 'The Lost Nijinsky', *New Yorker*, 7 May 2001

Anderson, Jack, *The One and Only: Ballet Russe de Monte Carlo* (London, 1981)

—, *Ballet and Modern Dance* (Trenton, NJ, 2018)

Anderson, Zoe, *The Royal Ballet: 75 Years* (London, 2011)

Archer, Kenneth, and Millicent Hodson, 'The Lost Pleasure Garden', *Dance Now*, v/2 (summer 1996), pp. 19–23

Au, Susan, *Ballet and Modern Dance* (London, 2012)

Baily, Leslie, *Leslie Baily's BBC Scrapbook: 1918–1939* (London, 1966)

—, *Leslie Baily's BBC Scrapbooks* (London, 1968)

*Les Ballets 33*, Brighton Art Gallery exhibition catalogue (Brighton, 1987)

*Ballets Russes*, film directed by Danya Goldfine and Dan Geller, DVD (Revolver, 1920)

'The Ballets Russes 1932–1962: A Symposium', *Dance Chronicle*, xv/2 (1992), pp. 191–220

*Ballets Suédois, Les: Une compagnie d'avant-garde 1920–1925* (Paris, 2014)

Banks, Georges, 'Pétrouchka – The Russian Ballet', *Rhythm*, ii/6 (July 1912), pp. 57–60

Baronova, Irina, *Irina: Ballet, Life, Love* (Gainesville, FL, 2005)

Beaton, Cecil, *Ballet* (London, 1951)

—, *The Unexpurgated Beaton*, edited by Hugo Vickers (London, 2002)

Beaumont, Cyril, *The Diaghilev Ballet in London* (London, 1940)

—, *Dancers under my Lens* (London, 1949)

Bennett, Arnold, *Paris Nights* (London, 1913)

Benois, Alexandre, *Reminiscences of the Russian Ballet* (London, 1941)

—, *Memoirs*, vol. ii, trans. Maura Budberg (London, 1964)

Blanch, Lesley, *Journey into the Mind's Eye* (London, 1968)

Bland, Alexander, *The Royal Ballet: The First 50 Years* (London, 1981)

Bowlt, John E., *The Silver Age: Russian Art of the Early Twentieth Century and the World of Art Group* (Newtownville, MA, 1982)

Bowlt, John E., Zelfira Tregulova and Natalie Rosticher Giordano (eds), *A Feast of Wonders: Sergei Diaghilev and the Ballets Russes* (Milan, 2009)

Brahms, Caryl, and S. J. Simon, *A Bullet in the Ballet* (London, 1937)

Braude, Mark, *Making Monte Carlo: A History of Speculation and Spectacle* (London, 2016)

Braunsweg, Julian, *Braunsweg's Ballet Scandals* (London, 1973)

Bridgman, Elena, 'Mir iskusstva' in Nancy van Norman Baer (ed.), *The Art of Enchantment*

Brody, Elaine, 'The Legacy of Ida Rubinstein: Mata Hari of the Ballets Russes', *Journal of Musicology*, IV/4 (autumn 1985– autumn 1986), pp. 491–506

Browse, Lillian, *The Duchess of Cork Street* (London, 1999)

Buckle, Richard, *The Adventures of a Ballet Critic* (London, 1953)

—, *The Diaghilev Exhibition*, Forbes House exhibition catalogue (London, 1954)

—, *Diaghilev* (London, 1979)

—, *Buckle at the Ballet: Selected Criticism* (London, 1980)

—, *Nijinsky* (London, 1980)

—, *The Most Upsetting Woman* (London, 1981)

—, *In the Wake of Diaghilev* (London, 1982)

—, 'Les Quatre Saisons de Boris Kochno', in *Collection Boris Kochno*, Sotheby's auction catalogue (Monte Carlo, 1991), pp. 7–11

Burt, Ramsay, *The Male Dancer* [1995] (Abingdon, 2007)

Butler, Christopher, *Early Modernism* (Oxford, 1994)

Caddy, Davinia, *The Ballets Russes and Beyond* (Cambridge, 2012)

Cannon, Henry 'Chips', *The Diaries 1918–38*, edited by Simon Heffer (London, 2021)

Carter, Alexandra, *Dance and Dancers in the Victorian and Edwardian Music Hall Ballet* (London, 2005)

Cave, Richard Allen, and Libby Worth (eds), *Ninette de Valois: Adventurous Traditionalist* (Alton, 2012)

Chazin-Bennahum, Judith, *Rene Blum and the Ballets Russes* (New York, 2011)

Chisholm, Anne (ed.), *Carrington's Letters* (London, 2017)

Christiansen, Rupert, *The Visitors* (London, 2000)

—, *The Voice of Victorian Sex: Arthur H. Clough* (London, 2001)

Christout, Marie-Françoise, and Fernande Bassan, 'Les Ballets des

Champs-Elysées', *Dance Chronicle*, xxvii/2 (2004), pp. 157–98

Chujoy, Anatole, 'Russian balletomania', *Dance Index*, vii/3 (March 1948)

Clair, Sarah, *Jean Babilée* (Paris, 1995)

Clarke, Mary, *Dancers of Mercury: The Story of the Ballet Rambert* (London, 1962)

Cocteau, Jean, *Cock and Harlequin: Notes Concerning Music*, translated by Rollo H. Myers (London, 1921)

—, *Le Rappel à l'ordre* (Paris, 1926); *A Call to Order*, translated by Rollo H. Myers (London, 1926)

Connelly, Mark, *The Red Shoes*, Turner Classic Movie Guide (London and New York, 2005)

Cossart, Michael de, *Ida Rubinstein: A Theatrical Life* (Liverpool, 1987)

Coton, A. V., *A Prejudice for Ballet* (London, 1938)

Craft, Robert, and Igor Stravinsky, *Conversations with Igor Stravinsky* (London, 1959)

Craine, Debra, and Judith Mackrell, *The Oxford Dictionary of Dance* (Oxford and New York, 2000)

Crisp, Clement, Anya Sainsbury and Peter Williams (eds), *Ballet Rambert: 50 Years and On* (London, 1981)

Croall, Jonathan, *Sybil Thorndike: A Star of Life* (London, 2008)

Croce, Arlene, *Afterimages* (London and New York, 1978)

Crowson, Lydia, 'Cocteau and "Le Numéro Barbette"', *Modern Drama*, xix/1 (spring 1976), pp. 79–87

Culhane, John, *Walt Disney's Fantasia* (New York, 1987)

Daneman, Meredith, *Margot Fonteyn* (London, 2004)

Danilova, Alexandra, *Choura* (New York, 1986)

Davis, Mary E., *Ballets Russes Style* (London, 2010)

Denby, Edwin, *Dancers, Buildings and People in the Streets* (New York, 1965)

—, 'Notes on Nijinsky Photographs', *Looking at the Dance* (New York, 1968), pp. 240–47

—, *Dance Writings* (New York, 1986)

Dery, Mark, *Born to be Posthumous: the Eccentric Life and Mysterious Genius of Edward Gorey* (London, 2018)

*Diaghilev Ballet in England, The*, exhibition catalogue, Sainsbury Centre for Visual Arts (Norwich, 1979)

Dolin, Anton, *Autobiography* (London, 1960)

—, *Last Words: A Final Autobiography* (London, 1985)

Dorris, George, 'Jean Börlin', *Dance Chronicle*, xxvii/2 (1999), pp. 167–88

—, 'Dicky's Greatest Show', *Dance Now*, xi/2 (spring 2002), pp. 88–92

—, 'The Many Worlds of Rolf de Maré' (review of Erik Naslund, *Rolf de Maré: Art Collector – Ballet Director – Museum Curator*), *Dance Chronicle*, xxxiii/1 (2010), pp. 153–8

Draper, Muriel, *Music at Midnight* (New York, 1929)

Driberg, Tom, *Ruling Passions* (London, 1977)

Drummond, John, *Speaking of Diaghilev* (London, 1997)

—, *Tainted by Experience* (London, 2000)

Duberman, Martin B., *The Worlds of Lincoln Kirstein* (New York, 2007)

Duke, Vernon, *Passport to Paris* (Boston, MA, 1955)

Duncan, Isadora, *My Life* (London, 1928)

Dunne, Dominick, 'The Rockefeller and the Ballet Boys', *Vanity Fair*, February 1987

Eliot, Karen, *Dancing Lives* (Chicago, 2007)

—, *Albion's Dance* (Oxford, 2016)

Epstein, Louis, 'Impresario, Interrupted: Comte Étienne de Beaumont and the Soirées de Paris', *Revue de Musicologie*, cii/1 (2016), pp. 91–130

Estrada, María Gabriela, *The Legacy of Félix Fernández García* (Seville, 2012)

Fokine, Michel, *Memoirs of a Ballet Master* (London, 1961)

Folch-Couyoumdjian, Francisca, *The Marquis de Cuevas: Pushing the Boundaries of Self*, unpublished PhD thesis (University of Texas at Austin, 2014)

Foster, Andrew R., *Tamara Karsavina: Diaghilev's Ballerina* (London, 2010)

Franko, Mark, 'Serge Lifar et la collaboration', *Vingtième Siècle*, 132 (December 2016), pp. 27–41

Franks, A. H., *Ballet: A Decade of Endeavour* (London, 1956)

Furse, Ralph, *Aucuparius* (London, 1962)

Garafola, Lynn, 'The Ballets Russes in America' in Nancy van Norman Baer (ed.), *The Art of Enchantment*

—, *Diaghilev's Ballets Russes* (Oxford and New York, 1989)

—, *Legacies of Twentieth-century Dance* (Middletown, CT, 2005)

Garafola, Lynn, and Nancy van Norman Baer (eds), *The Ballets Russes and its World* (New Haven and London, 1999)

Garcia-Marquez, Vicente, *The Ballets Russes: Colonel de Basil's Ballets Russes de Monte Carlo* (New York, 1990)

—, *Massine* (London and New York, 1996)

Garis, Robert, *Following Balanchine* (New Haven and London, 1995)

Gibbon, Monk, *The Red Shoes Ballet: A Critical Study* (London, 1948)

Gold, Arthur, and Robert Fizdale, *Misia: The Life of Misia Sert* (London, 1980)

Gottlieb, Robert, *George Balanchine: The Ballet Maker* (New York, 2004)

— (ed.), *Reading Dance* (New York, 2008)

Gray, Jonathan, 'Sixty Years of the Bolshoi', *Dancing Times*, July 2016, pp. 17–19

Green, Martin Burgess, *Children of the Gods* (London, 1977)

Grigoriev, S. L., *The Diaghilev Ballet 1909–1929* (London, 1953)

Guest, Ivor, *Ballet in Leicester Square* (London, 1992)

—, *The Paris Opéra Ballet* (Alton, 2006)

Häger, Bengt, *Ballets Suédois* (London, 1990)

Haney, Lynn, *Naked at the Feast* (London, 1987)

Harding, James, *Cochran* (London, 1988)

Haskell, Arnold, *Balletomania: The Story of an Obsession* (London, 1934)

—, *Diaghileff* (London, 1947)

—, *In His True Centre: An Interim Autobiography* (London, 1951)

—, *Balletomania Then and Now* (London, 1977)

Headlam, Stewart, *The Ballet* (London, 1894)

Healy, Dan, *Homosexual Desire in Revolutionary Russia* (Chicago, 2001)

Hill, Polly, and Richard Keynes (eds), *Lydia and Maynard: Letters* (London, 1989)

Hindson, Catherine, *Female Performance Practice on the fin-de-siècle Popular Stages of London and Paris* (Manchester, 2007)

Holroyd, Michael, *Lytton Strachey* (London, 1994)

Homans, Jennifer, *Apollo's Angels* (London and New York, 2010)

Hook, Philip, *Art of the Extreme 1905–14* (London, 2021)

Hough, Richard, *First Sea Lord* (London, 1969)

Hurok, Sol, *Sol Hurok Presents: A Memoir of the Dance World* (New York, 1953)

Jones, Robert Edmond, 'Nijinsky and Til Eulenspiegel', *Dance Index*, iv/4 (April 1945), pp. 44–54

Jones, Susan, 'Diaghilev and British Writing', *Dance Research Journal*, xxvii/1 (summer 2008)

Jordan, Stephanie, programme for *Les Noces*, Royal Ballet, Royal Opera House (London, 1954)

Joseph, Charles M., 'Diaghilev and Stravinsky', in Garafola and van Norman Baer (eds), *The Ballets Russes and its World*

Kalmthout, Ton van, and F. T. Marinetti, '"Batailles et idées futuristes": 17 Letters from F. T. Marinetti, 1912–13', *Simiolus*, xxi/3 (1992), pp. 139–61

Karsavina, Tamara, *Theatre Street* [1930] (London, 1981)

—, *Tamara Karsavina: Beyond the Ballerina*, edited by Andrew L. Phelan (Norman, OK, 2018)

Kavanagh, Julie, *Secret Muses: The Life of Frederick Ashton* (London and New York, 1996)

Kessler, Harry, *The Diaries of a Cosmopolitan 1918–1937* (London, 1971)

—, *Journey to the Abyss: The Diaries of Count Harry Kessler 1880–1918*, edited by Laird M. Easton (New York, 2011)

Keynes, Milo, *Lydia Lopokova* (London, 1983)

Kirstein, Lincoln, *Blast at Ballet* (self-published, 1938)

—, *Ballet Alphabet* (New York, 1939)

—, *Nijinsky Dancing* (London, 1975)

—, *Mosaic* (New York, 1994)

Kochno, Boris, *Le Ballet* (Paris, 1954)

—, *Diaghilev and the Ballets Russes* (New York, 1970)

—, *Christian Bérard* (London, 1988)

Kurth, Peter, *Isadora: A Sensational Life* (London, 1992)

Kyasht, Lydia, *Romantic Recollections* (London, 1929)

Lambert, Constant, *Music Ho!* [1934] (London, 1985)

Lancaster, Osbert, *Homes, Sweet Homes* (London, 1939)

—, *With an Eye to the Future* (London, 1967)

Laver, James, *Between the Wars* (London, 1961)

Lawrence, D. H., *Women in Love* (New York, 1920)

Legat, Nikolai, *The Story of the Russian School* (London, 1932)

Leverson, Ada, *Tenterhooks* (London, 1912)

Levinson, André, 'A Crisis in the Ballets Russes', *Theatre Arts Monthly*, x/11 (November 1926), pp. 785–92

—, *Dance Writings from Paris in the Twenties*, edited by Joan Acocella and Lynn Garafola (Hanover, NH, 1991)

Lieven, Prince Peter, *The Birth of the Ballets Russes* (London, 1936)

Lifar, Serge, *Ma Vie: From Kiev to Kiev: An Autobiography* (London, 1970)

Lindsay, David, *The Crawford Papers: The Journal of David Lindsay, Twenty-seventh Earl of Crawford and Tenth Earl of Balcarres, 1871–1940, during the Years 1892 to 1940*, edited by John Vincent (Manchester, 1986)

McBrien, William, *Cole Porter* (London, 1998)

McCormick, Malcolm, and Nancy Reynolds, *No Fixed Points: Dance in the Twentieth Century* (New Haven, CT, and London, 2003)

Macdonald, Nesta, *Diaghilev Observed* (New York and London, 1975)

—, *Tamara Karsavina* (New York, 1979)

Mackrell, Judith, *Bloomsbury Ballerina* (London, 2008)

McLean, Adrienne, '"The Red Shoes" Revisited', *Dance Chronicle*, xi/1 (1988), pp. 31–83

—, 'The Image of the Ballet Artist in Popular Films', *Journal of Popular Culture*, xxv/1 (summer 1991), pp. 1–19

—, *Dying Swans and Madmen: Ballet, the Body, and Narrative Cinema* (New Brunswick, NJ, 2008)

Mannin, Ethel, *Confessions and Impressions* (London, 1930)

—, *Young in the Twenties: A Chapter of Autobiography* (London, 1971)

Mannoni, Gérard, *Roland Petit* (Paris, 1984)

—, *Roland Petit: Rythme de vie* (Lausanne, 2003)

—, *Le Marquis de Cuevas* (Paris, 2003)

Markevitch, Igor, *Être et avoir été* (Paris, 1980)

Markova, Alicia, *Markova Remembers* (London, 2004)

Massine, Leonide, *My Life in Ballet* (London and New York, 1968)

Mayer, Charles S., 'Ida Rubinstein: A Twentieth-Century Cleopatra', *Dance Research Journal*, xx/2 (winter 1988), pp. 33–51

Meisner, Nadine, *Marius Petipa: The Emperor's Ballet Master* (New York, 2019)

Meylac, Michael, *Behind the Scenes at the Ballets Russes* (London and New York, 2018)

Michel, Michel-Georges, *Ballets Russes: Histoire anecdotique* (Paris, 1923)

Money, Keith, *Anna Pavlova: Her Life and Art* (London, 1982)

Moore, Gillian, *The Rite of Spring: The Music of Modernity* (London, 2019)

Moore, Lucy, *Nijinsky* (London, 2013)

Naslund, Erik, *Rolf de Maré: Art Collector – Ballet Director – Museum Curator* (Alton, 2009)

Nead, Lynda, *The Tiger in the Smoke: Art and Culture in Post-War Britain* (New Haven and London, 2017)

Newman, Barbara, *Striking a Balance* (London, 1982)

Nichols, Roger, *The Harlequin Years* (London, 2002)

—, *Poulenc* (London, 2020)

Nijinska, Bronislava, *Early Memories* (New York, 1981)

Nijinsky, Romola, *Nijinsky* [1933] (London, 1970)

Nijinsky, Vaslav, *The Diary of Vaslav Nijinsky*, edited by Joan Acocella (London and New York, 1999)

Norman Baer, Nancy van (ed.) *The Art of Enchantment* (San Francisco, CA, 1988)

Norton, Leslie, *Léonide Massine and the 20th Century Ballet* (Jefferson, NC, and London, 2004)

—, *Frederic Franklin* (Jefferson, NC, 2007)

Ostvald, Peter, *Vaslav Nijinsky: A Leap into Madness* (London, 1991)

Pastori, Jean-Pierre, *Serge Lifar: la beauté du diable* (Paris, 2009)

Petipa, Marius, *Mémoires* (Arles, 1990)

Philips, Victoria, *Martha Graham's Cold War* (Oxford, 2019)

Powell, Michael, *A Life in Movies* (London, 1986)

Pritchard, Jane, *Diaghilev and the Golden Age of the Ballets Russes 1909–1929*, Victoria and Albert Museum exhibition catalogue (London, 2010)

Pritchard, Jane, and Caroline Hamilton, *Anna Pavlova: Twentieth-Century Ballerina* (London, 2012)

Rambert, Marie, *Quicksilver* (London, 1972)

Reminiscences of Ballets Russes Dancers (New Orleans, 2000)

Richardson, John, *A Life of Picasso: The Triumphant Years 1917–1932* (London, 2007)

Ricketts, Charles, *Self-Portrait Taken from the Letters and Journals of Charles Ricketts*, collected and compiled by T. Sturge Moore, edited by Cecil Lewis (London, 1939)

Roslaveva, Natalia, *Era of the Russian Ballet* (London, 1966)

Sandoz, Maurice, *The Crystal Salt-cellar* (Guildford, 1954)

Scheijen, Sjeng, *Diaghilev: A Life* (London, 2009)

Scholl, Tim, *From Petipa to Balanchine* (London, 1994)

Schouvaloff, Alexander, *The Art of the Ballets Russes*, Wadsworth Athenaeum exhibition catalogue (Hartford, CT, 1997)

—, 'The Diaghilev Legend', in John E. Bowlt et al. (eds), *A Feast of Wonders*

Searcy, Anne, *Ballet in the Cold War* (New York, 2020)

Shattuck, Roger, *The Banquet Years* (London, 1968)

Silver, Kenneth E., *Esprit de Corps: The Art of the Parisian Avant-garde* (Princeton, NJ, 1992)

*Sitwells and the Arts of the 1920s and 1930s, The*, exhibition catalogue, National Portrait Gallery (London, 1995)

Sokolova, Lydia, *Dancing for Diaghilev*, edited by Richard Buckle (London, 1960)

Sorley Walker, Kathrine, *De Basil's Ballets Russes* (London, 1982)

—, *Ninette de Valois: Idealist Without Illusions* (London, 1987)

—, 'The Camargo Society', *Dance Chronicle*, xviii/1 (1995), pp. 2–7

# BIBLIOGRAPHY

Sotheby's, *Collection Boris Kochno* (auction catalogue) (Monte Carlo, 1991)

Spencer, Charles, *Léon Bakst* (London, 1973)

Steichen, James, *Balanchine and Kirstein's American Enterprise* (New York, 2018)

Stevenson, Jane, *Baroque between the Wars* (Oxford, 2018)

Stokes, Adrian, *Tonight the Ballet* (London, 1934)

Stoneley, Peter, *A Queer History of the Ballet* (Abingdon, 2007)

Strachey, Lytton, *Ballet – To Poland*, edited by Arnold Haskell (London, 1940)

Stravinsky, Igor, and Robert Craft, *Memories and Commentaries* (London, 1960)

—, *Expositions and Developments* (London, 1962)

Taper, Bernard, *Balanchine* (London and New York, 1974)

Tennant, Victoria, *Irina Baronova and the Ballets Russes de Monte Carlo* (Chicago, IL, 2014)

Tynan, Kenneth, *A View of the English Stage* (St Albans, 1975)

Valois, Ninette de, *Come Dance with Me: A Memoir, 1898–1956* (London, 1957)

Vaughan, David, *Frederick Ashton and his Ballets* (London, 1977)

Vreeland, Lisa Immordino, *Love, Cecil* (New York, 2017)

Wiley, Roland John, *Tchaikovsky's Ballets* (Oxford, 1985)

—, *A Century of Russian Ballet* (Oxford, 1990)

Windreich, Leigh, 'Memory Lane' *Dance Now* ix/3 (autumn 2000), p. 747

Woolf, Virginia, *Mr Bennett and Mrs Brown* (London, 1924)

Yeats, W. B., *The Poems*, edited by Daniel Albright (London, 1992)

# INDEX

Numbers in **bold** refer to pages with illustrations.